Maigret's World

Maigret's World

A Reader's Companion
to Simenon's Famous Detective

MURIELLE WENGER *and*
STEPHEN TRUSSEL

McFarland & Company, Inc., Publishers
Jefferson, North Carolina

ISBN (print) 978-1-4766-6977-9
ISBN (ebook) 978-1-4766-2925-4

LIBRARY OF CONGRESS CATALOGUING DATA ARE AVAILABLE

BRITISH LIBRARY CATALOGUING DATA ARE AVAILABLE

Front cover image of a detective © 2017 bobmadbob/iStock

Printed in the United States of America

*McFarland & Company, Inc., Publishers
Box 611, Jefferson, North Carolina 28640
www.mcfarlandpub.com*

Table of Contents

A Note from John Simenon

By offering this original panoramic view, while highlighting the smallest details of *Maigret's World*, Murielle and Steve have first of all given me great joy in rediscovering, from a different angle, this universe that I love so much. And moreover, this work has quickly become a working tool, an indispensable reference for me and all those who, like me, work with this prodigious saga.

I thank the authors from the bottom of my heart, and wish all their readers the same pleasure.

John Simenon is the son of Denyse Ouimet and Georges Simenon. He is a film producer and founder of the official George Simenon website, Simenon.com. In addition, he manages and holds the rights to the works of his father.

Abbreviations

Throughout this book, titles of the *Maigrets* are often followed by a 3-letter code, and sometimes by a number. These codes uniquely identify the titles, allowing lookup of the various English titles, as listed below. The numbers following the 3-letter codes in the text are the chapters in which the citation appears. In this list, codes in lower case represent short stories, those in upper case are the novels. Immediately following the codes are the original French titles, as used throughout the text.

AMI *Mon ami Maigret*, My friend Maigret, The methods of Maigret

amo *L'amoureux de Madame Maigret*, The stronger vessel, Madame Maigret's admirer

AMU *Maigret s'amuse*, Maigret's little joke, None of Maigret's business

arr *Jeumont, 51 minutes d'arrêt!*, Jeumont, 51 minutes wait!, Inspector Maigret deduces, Jeumont, 51 minutes stop

ASS *Maigret aux assises*, Maigret in court

BAN *Maigret et l'homme du banc*, Maigret and the man on the boulevard, Maigret and the man on the bench, The man on the boulevard

bay *La vieille dame de Bayeux*, The old lady of Bayeux, The Bayeux murder

bea *L'affaire du boulevard Beaumarchais*, The affair of the Boulevard Beaumarchais, The mysterious affair in the Boulevard Beaumarchais

ber *Mademoiselle Berthe et son amant*, Maigret and the frightened dressmaker, Mademoiselle Berthe and her lover

BRA *Maigret et les braves gens*, Maigret and the black sheep

CAD *L'inspecteur Cadavre*, Maigret's rival, Inspector Cadaver

CEC *Cécile est morte*, Maigret and the spinster, Cécile is dead

ceu *Ceux du Grand Café*, The group at the Grand-Café

CHA *Maigret et Monsieur Charles*, Maigret and Monsieur Charles

CHE *Maigret chez le coroner*, Maigret at the coroner's, Maigret and the coroner

cho *Le témoignage de l'enfant de chœur*, Elusive witness, According to the altar boy, Crime in the Rue Sainte-Catherine, The evidence of the altar-boy

CLI *Maigret et le client du samedi*, Maigret and the Saturday caller

CLO *Maigret et le clochard*, Maigret and the dosser, Maigret and the bum
COL *La colère de Maigret*, Maigret loses his temper
CON *Une confidence de Maigret*, Maigret has doubts
COR *Maigret et le corps sans tête*, Maigret and the headless corpse
DAM *Maigret et la vieille dame*, Maigret and the old lady
DEF *Maigret se défend*, Maigret on the defensive
ECH *Un échec de Maigret*, Maigret's failure
ECL *L'écluse n° 1*, The lock at Charenton, Maigret sits it out, Lock N° 1
ECO *Maigret à l'école*, Maigret goes to school
ENF *L'ami d'enfance de Maigret*, Maigret's boyhood friend
err *Une erreur de Maigret*, Maigret's mistake
eto *L'Étoile du Nord*, At the Étoile du Nord
FAC *Maigret se fâche*, Maigret in retirement, Maigret gets angry
FAN *Maigret et le fantôme*, Maigret and the ghost, Maigret and the apparition
FEL *Félicie est là*, Maigret and the toy village, Félicie
fen *La fenêtre ouverte*, The open window, Inspector Maigret smokes his pipe
FIA *L'affaire Saint-Fiacre*, Maigret and the Countess, The Saint-Fiacre affair, Maigret goes home, Maigret on home ground
FLA *Chez les Flamands*, The Flemish shop, Maigret and the Flemish shop, The Flemish house
FOL *La folle de Maigret*, Maigret and the madwoman

FOU *Le fou de Bergerac*, The madman of Bergerac
GAI *La danseuse du Gai-Moulin*, At the "Gai Moulin," Maigret at the "Gai Moulin," The dancer at the Gai-Moulin
GAL *Monsieur Gallet, décédé*, The death of Monsieur Gallet, Maigret stonewalled, The late Monsieur Gallet
GRA *Maigret et la Grande Perche*, Inspector Maigret and the burglar's wife, Maigret and the burglar's wife, Maigret and the tall woman
GUI *La guinguette à deux sous*, Guinguette by the Seine, Maigret and the tavern by the Seine, Maigret to the rescue, A spot by the Seine, The bar on the Seine, The Twopenny Bar
HES *Maigret hésite*, Maigret hesitates
HOL *Un crime en Hollande*, A crime in Holland, Maigret in Holland
hom *L'homme dans la rue*, The man on the run, Inspector Maigret pursues, The man in the street
IND *Maigret et l'indicateur*, Maigret and the flea, Maigret and the informer
JAU *Le chien jaune*, A face for a clue, Maigret and the Concarneau murders, Maigret and the yellow dog, The yellow dog
JEU *Maigret et la jeune morte*, Inspector Maigret and the dead girl, Maigret and the young girl
JUG *La maison du juge*, Maigret in exile, The Judge's house
lar *Les larmes de bougie*, Journey into time, Journey backward into time, Death of a woodlander
LET *Pietr le Letton*, The strange case

of Peter the Lett, The case of Peter the Lett, Maigret and the enigmatic Lett, Pietr the Latvian

LIB *Liberty Bar*, Liberty Bar, Maigret on the Riviera

LOG *Maigret, Lognon et les gangsters*, Inspector Maigret and the killers, Maigret and the gangsters, Maigret, Lognon and the gangsters

lun *Monsieur Lundi*, Mr. Monday, Inspector Maigret hesitates

MAI *Maigret*, Maigret returns, Maigret

MAJ *Les caves du Majestic*, Maigret and the Hotel Majestic, The Hotel Majestic, The cellars of the Majestic

mal *Maigret et l'inspecteur Malgracieux*, Maigret and the surly Inspector

man *Tempête sur la Manche*, Storm in the Channel, Storm over the Channel

MEM *Les mémoires de Maigret*, Maigret's memoirs

men *Menaces de mort*, Death threats

MEU *Maigret en meublé*, Maigret takes a room, Maigret rents a room

MIN *Maigret chez le ministre*, Maigret and the Minister, Maigret and the Calame report

MME *L'amie de Madame Maigret*, Madame Maigret's own case, Madame Maigret's friend, The friend of Madame Maigret

MOR *Maigret et son mort*, Maigret's dead man, Maigret's special murder, Maigret and his dead man

NAH *Maigret et l'affaire Nahour*, Maigret and the Nahour case

NEW *Maigret à New York*, Maigret in New York, Inspector Maigret in New York's underworld, Maigret in New York's underworld

noe *Un Noël de Maigret*, Maigret's Christmas

not *Le notaire du Châteauneuf*, Inspector Maigret and the missing miniatures, The three daughters of the lawyer

noy *L'auberge aux noyés*, The Inn of the Drowned, The Drowned Men's Inn

NUI *La nuit du carrefour*, The crossroad murders, Maigret at the crossroads, The night at the crossroads, Night at the crossroads

obs *Le client le plus obstiné du monde*, The most obstinate man in Paris, The most obstinate customer in the world, The most obstinate man in the world

OMB *L'ombre chinoise*, The shadow in the courtyard, Maigret mystified, The shadow puppet

owe *L'improbable Monsieur Owen*, The unlikely Monsieur Owen

PAR *Maigret et le voleur paresseux*, Maigret and the lazy burglar, Maigret and the idle burglar

PAT *La patience de Maigret*, The patience of Maigret, Maigret bides his time

pau *On ne tue pas les pauvres types*, Death of a nobody, Not the sort to get murdered

pei *Peine de mort*, Inspector Maigret's war of nerves, Death penalty

pen *La péniche aux deux pendus*, The barge with two hanging bodies, Inspector Maigret thinks, Dead man's barge, Two bodies on a barge

PEU *Maigret a peur*, Maigret afraid, Maigret is afraid

PHO *Le pendu de Saint-Pholien*, The Crime of Inspector Maigret,

Maigret and the hundred gibbets, The hanged man of Saint-Pholien

PIC *Maigret au Picratt's,* Maigret and the strangled stripper, Maigret in Montmartre, Inspector Maigret and the strangled stripper, Maigret at Picratt's

pig *Rue Pigalle,* Rue Pigalle, Inspector Maigret investigates, In the Rue Pigalle

pip *La pipe de Maigret,* Maigret's pipe

POR *Le port des brumes,* Death of a harbo(u)r master, Maigret and the death of a harbor master, The misty harbor

PRE *La première enquête de Maigret, 1913,* Maigret's first case, Maigret's first case

PRO *Le charretier de La Providence,* The crime at Lock 14, Maigret meets a Milord, Lock 14, The carter of *La Providence*

REN *Au rendez-vous des Terre-Neuvas,* The Sailors' Rendezvous, Maigret answers a plea, The Grand Banks Café

REV *Le revolver de Maigret,* Maigret's revolver

SCR *Les scrupules de Maigret,* Maigret has scruples

SEU *Maigret et l'homme tout seul,* Maigret and the loner

SIG *Signé Picpus,* To any lengths,

Maigret and the fortuneteller, Signed Picpus

sta *Stan le Tueur,* Stan the killer

TEM *Maigret et les témoins récalcitrants,* Maigret and the reluctant witnesses

TEN *Maigret tend un piège,* Maigret sets a trap

TET *La tête d'un homme,* A battle of nerves, Maigret's war of nerves, The patience of Maigret, A man's head

TRO *Maigret se trompe,* Maigret's mistake

TUE *Maigret et le tueur,* Maigret and the killer

VAC *Les vacances de Maigret,* A summer holiday, No vacation for Maigret, Maigret on holiday, Maigret's holiday

ven *Vente à la bougie,* Under the hammer, Inspector Maigret directs, Sale by auction

VIC *Maigret à Vichy,* Maigret takes the waters, Maigret in Vichy

VIE *Maigret et les vieillards,* Maigret in society

VIN *Maigret et le marchand de vin,* Maigret and the wine merchant

VOL *Le voleur de Maigret,* Maigret's pickpocket, Maigret and the pickpocket

VOY *Maigret voyage,* Maigret and the millionaires

Introduction

Chief Inspector Maigret of the Paris Metropolitan Police, was the creation of the Belgian author Georges Simenon in the early 1930s, and the novels and stories recounting his investigations, translated into over 50 languages, and transformed into numerous cinema and television adaptations, have made him one of the world's most popular literary heroes.

With Maigret, Simenon blazed a new trail for the detective story. Up until then, heroes of the genre were expected to be brilliant detectives, unselfconsciously eccentric, or superhero-like adventurers, all of them sharing a display of superiority to the police, whose representatives were often portrayed as incompetent or ridiculous. Simenon had the genius to recognize the need for a new type of character, whose physical appearance, social status, and methods of investigation, would be the polar opposite of those most readers were familiar with.

Simenon's editor at that time, Arthème Fayard, when presented with the first Maigret manuscript, was unconvinced. While the idea of renewing the genre and presenting truly French detective novels—to counter the English literary "invasion"—was seductive, Simenon's new character was a veritable revolution! Maigret was a solid civil servant, with middle-class origins and habits, practicing his métier with a sense of duty, without brilliant actions, and with no great fanfare. The novels presenting his investigations contained no romantic love stories, no happy endings, and neither villains nor innocent maidens, and even worse, there was no real mystery to be solved! Fayard might well have had some doubts about the potential success of such works.

On the other hand, the character did have something unique—Maigret's particular "method" of investigation, putting himself into another's place, whether victim or perpetrator, to search for a reason that could have led to murder. In this sense, the detective story as Simenon practiced it opened new perspectives, moving definitively away from the "whodunit." The goal was

1

no longer the elegant resolution of a mystery ("who killed and how")—sufficiently tangled so that only a brilliant detective could unravel the threads—but rather it became the policeman's obstinate search for the truth, the understanding of the "why," the motives which could propel someone to the point of murder. And it was this that gave a new psychological dimension to these novels. The culprit was not simply the person tracked through the story to be eventually unmasked, but another human being, driven by circumstances, having crossed a line to a point of no return.

Simenon's further stroke of genius was to endow his character with an extraordinary humanity, not only in his apprehension of those around him, but also by a mass of little descriptive traits, in brief, but tremendously effective sketches, giving Maigret a singular presence, reinforced by the accumulation of small details which increased with the number of novels Simenon wrote. Indeed, this character accompanied his creator through the writing of 75 novels and 28 short stories, spanning over 40 years. Over time, the relationship between them grew closer and closer, the novelist giving to his character, in parallel with his own advancing age, his own questions, his own way of sensing the world, and the novels featuring the Chief Inspector moved closer and closer to the other side of Simenon's work, his "*romans durs,*" the "hard" novels, where the psychology of the characters takes over the plot.

We have been able to extract the essence of a character from within a collection of texts—a collection which merits, in our opinion, the term "saga," as we have called it—which in addition to the undeniable quality of Simenon's production, has only been possible because of the significant *quantity* of amassed details, accumulated little by little, to develop the world surrounding the hero. He doesn't evolve from an empty canvas, but on the contrary, in one filled with characters, places, and settings, which are a part of the intrigue. Maigret has a wife, friends, collaborators, an apartment, an office at the *Police Judiciaire*, and he evolves in his city of Paris. Needless to say, the Chief Inspector has a personality as well, his particular habits and way of life that the novelist has described in a multitude of details strewn throughout the texts. And it's by bringing these scattered clues together that we have produced *Maigret's World* for the reader.

This book is not a "scholarly" analysis of the Maigret character, and certainly not a detailed study of the novels themselves (yes, we're working on one!), but rather a "synthesis" of the details we have extracted from throughout the texts, a composite picture of the Chief Inspector within his environment, in his world. Indeed, each novel reveals disparate information about Maigret, and we have put it all together to create a portrait, which, if perhaps not complete, should prove sufficiently precise to provide an understanding of this marvelous character, and instill in the reader the desire to read further. All the details mentioned—whether his clothing, his office, his country house in Meung-sur-Loire, his culinary preferences, etc.—are authentic and are all to be found in the texts.

While studies on Simenon and his work are quite numerous, most are in French, the language in which Simenon wrote. There are biographies of the novelist, varied and diverse essays on his work, and indeed some works discussing the Maigrets (see the bibliography). But the few English texts which concern the Chief Inspector are generally works dealing with Simenon's opus as a whole. What we present here is a book exclusively dedicated to Maigret, unlike any other. Rather than an impressionistic description of "what he's like," we offer an amazing analysis of Maigret "as he really is," based on detailed tabulations of "the data"—the texts of the saga—which will serve as the definitive description the character and his world, and will allow the reader to better understand the novels and stories, and, of course, Maigret himself.

We have arranged this book into three parts, each covering a component of Maigret's world. The first treats the character himself, presented under various aspects: physical, psychological, daily life, and relationships with those close to him. The second presents the policeman at work, in which setting he evolves, and his collaborators. The third section treats more specifically the saga itself, focusing on investigations, characters and novels. At the end of the text are a number of bibliographic lists, providing reference to other works which may prove interesting to Maigret readers, as well as a catalogue of all the novels and stories of the saga. The list of Abbreviations of the titles at the front of the book includes the titles of the English translations.

You can read this book in variety of ways, as you prefer ... straight through from start to finish, or dipping in wherever you like, selecting from the table of contents the themes you want to pursue. Whichever path you choose, we hope you'll share our passion for the world of Maigret and Simenon, and that you'll enjoy the journey as much as we've enjoyed ours in preparing it just.

1

Life Overview

Maigret's First Name

Ask a passerby on a Paris street, "What's Maigret's first name?," and he'll surely answer that the first name of the most famous Chief Inspector in the *Police Judiciaire* is Jules. Well, that's true of course, but it needs a little clarification...

The earliest mention of a first name for the Chief Inspector is in *L'écluse n° 1* (ECL: 5), when Ducrau asks Maigret to work for him, and he dictates to a secretary the words of a contract:

> "Between the undersigned Emile Ducrau and Maigret.... First name? ... and Maigret (Joseph), an agreement has been reached as follows. From March 18, M. Joseph Maigret will enter into the service of..."

And so it seems that at first, Maigret was called Joseph...

OFFICIAL VERSION

We find, however, in one of the first novels to appear from Presses de la Cité, an "official" version of Maigret's first name; it's in *La première enquête de Maigret* (PRE: 7) when Maigret imagines the police report written when he was the victim of an attack, *"...a person lying on the sidewalk, giving his name as Maigret, Jules, Amédée, François...."*

It's this official version that's used by Simenon in March 1966, in the foreword to Rencontre's edition of his *Complete Works*, which begins...

> Why Jules-Amédée-François Maigret, Divisional Chief Inspector of the Police Judiciaire, Chief of the Crime Squad, Quai des Orfèvres in Paris, one hundred percent French, was born in the harbor of Delfzijl, in the most northern part of the Netherlands, very close to the Ems, is what I would like to try to explain...

Mᴹᴱ MAIGRET

In the first dialogue (from the point of view of the chronology of the writing, and not that of the internal biography of the Chief Inspector) between Maigret and his wife, she calls him by his family name, "*'Tell me, Maigret…'* *she said when she came back*" (*Pietr le Letton*, LET: 19).

In the very great majority of cases, Mᵐᵉ Maigret uses his family name to address her husband. For several reasons:

> "*First of all, for many years, no one had called him Jules, to the extent that he had almost forgotten his first name. His wife herself had the habit, which made him smile, of calling him Maigret*" [*Maigret se fâche*, FAC: 1].
>
> "*She called him Maigret under certain circumstances, when she recognized that he was the man, the master, the power and intelligence of the household!*" [*Le fou de Bergerac*, FOU: 6].
>
> "*For the longest time, maybe because once they'd done so and laughed about it, they'd called each other Maigret and Mᵐᵉ Maigret, and they'd almost gotten to where they'd forgotten they had first names like everyone else*" [*Le témoignage de l'enfant de chœur*, cho: 2].

In fact, this way of calling each other had become a game, but also a kind of complicity, a tenderness at the heart of the couple…

> "*He didn't call her by her first name, nor she by his. She didn't call him dear, nor did he her. What for, since they felt in a way that they were the same person?*" [*Maigret et le fantôme*, FAN: 6].

Even on the phone,

> "*'Is that you, Maigret?' His wife. For his wife had never gotten used to calling him other than by his family name*" [*Maigret à New York*, NEW: 1].

She'd called him "Jules" at first, when they'd met, and at the beginning of their marriage…

> "*What are you thinking about, Jules? She didn't call him Maigret yet, at that time, but she already had for him that sort of respect he was due*" [*La première enquête de Maigret*, PRE: 2].

But Mᵐᵉ Maigret had quickly understood that her husband had little affinity for his first name, which he didn't seem to particularly like. So it's not surprising that she prefers to call him by his family name, and we note that already in *La première enquête de Maigret*, while she calls him Jules throughout the novel, she slips in "*Tell me, Maigret!*" in Ch. 5.

The cases where she still calls him Jules are rarities. We find *Maigret et l'affaire Nahour* (NAH: 1), which opens with a phone call awakening Maigret in the middle of the night. Since he has a hard time extracting himself from the unpleasant dream in which he is immersed, his wife has to call him. And she calls him by his first name, "*Jules! … Telephone!…*"

And, in *Maigret et le corps sans tête* (COR: 7):

"*Is there something on the tip of my nose?*" *he ended up grumbling.*
"*No.*"
"*So why are you laughing at me?*"
"*I'm not laughing. I'm smiling.*"
"*Like you're making fun of me. Is there something funny about me?*"
"*There's nothing funny about you, Jules.*"
It was rare for her to call him that, and it was only when she was feeling tender.

VOICES FROM THE PAST

It's at the beginning of the Presses de la Cité period that we find another mention of his given name. Indeed, in *Maigret se fâche* (FAC: 1) the Chief Inspector is called—to his great displeasure—*Jules*, by an old schoolmate from *lycée*, Ernest Malik:

"*Jules! For goodness' sake! What are you doing here?*" "*I'm sorry…*" *First of all, for many years, no one had called him Jules…*

Not only did Maigret dislike being called by his first name, but further, he had a "*horror of those people emerging from your past, who give you a friendly tap on the shoulder and address you with 'tu'*" (*Maigret se fâche*, FAC: 2). And among these "*people emerging from your past,*" there are those former classmates, most of whom are presented less than sympathetically in the saga. And so he hastens to refuse Fumal's familiarity (*Un échec de Maigret*, ECH: 1),

"*What's it like seeing me again? As for me, I knew you'd become a cop, since I've seen your picture in the papers. You know, we used to be on pretty familiar terms.*" "*Not any more,*" *the Chief Inspector commented, emptying his pipe.*

And for Florentin in *L'ami d'enfance de Maigret* (ENF: 1), Maigret is relieved that while Florentin insists on using "*tu*,"

"*At least he didn't call him Jules, because at school they'd had the habit of calling each other by their family names!*"

In *Maigret a peur* (PEU: 1), we find a mention of *Jules*, when the mother of another old classmate of Maigret's, Julien Chabot, greets him with, "*It's you, Jules!*" *How many years had it been since anyone had greeted him like that?*

FAMILIARITY MADE IN USA

It's the Americans, with their habit of using first names, who "force" the Chief Inspector to—reluctantly—admit to his own (*Maigret chez le coroner*, CHE: 1),

"What's your first name?"
He couldn't very well tell them he didn't have one, and so he was forced to admit that his name was Jules. His questioner thought for a moment.
"Oh! yes.... Julius!"
They pronounced it Julius, which didn't seem as bad to him.

And we encounter this American familiarity again in two other novels, *Maigret, Lognon et les gangsters* (LOG: 2), where the Chief Inspector is called *Jules* by his American colleague MacDonald, and in *Le revolver de Maigret* (REV: 1), where, on the revolver he received from the USA, was engraved the inscription, *To J.-J. Maigret, from his FBI friends.*

Why J.-J. Maigret? ... The Americans, who have the habit of using two first names, were informed of his. The two first, happily, Jules-Joseph. [Joseph again!] But in fact, he had a third name as well, Anthelme.

AND THE UNDERWORLD...

In *La première enquête de Maigret* (PRE: 6), Maigret is called *Jules* by Dédé the crook.

"By the way, what do they call you?" "Jules." "I like that, Jules. Sounds good. So, old Jules, what do they say?"

And that wasn't the last of the Chief Inspector's tribulations with regard to his name. In *Les mémoires de Maigret* (MEM: 5), he tells how, as a young inspector, he was teased about his name by prostitutes:

"I wouldn't have chosen Jules if they'd asked my opinion. But it no longer embarrasses me.... One day.... I was walking by one of the old girls installed in the doorway of a seedy hotel, when I heard through those rotten teeth, a laughing,
'Bonsoir, Jules!'
I thought she had picked a name at random, but a little further along, I was welcomed by the same words...
"So, Jules?"
...the famous Jules was integrated into a song which they proceeded to sing loudly whenever I appeared."

Oh well, unfortunately for him, Maigret had not chosen his own name, and it's his creator's fault that here he is obliged, in *Maigret aux assises* (ASS: 1), to declare his identity as a witness in court.

"Your name, given name, age and position...
Maigret, Jules, 53, Divisional Chief Inspector, Judicial Police, Paris."

What Year Was Maigret Born?

Simenon, in his novels, isn't overly concerned with chronological accuracy. Once he's established the idea that Maigret, in most of the novels, is about 45 to 55, his author allows himself to wander in time without too much concern about following a definite line.

There are but three novels in which a year is specifically indicated. In *Monsieur Gallet, décédé*, we find at the beginning of the first chapter, "June 27, 1930." In the first chapter of *La première enquête de Maigret*, there is the date "April 15, 1913." And lastly, in the first chapter of *Maigret et l'homme tout seul*, the year is shown as "1965."

These three novels can be seen to serve as "milestones" in the publishing chronology of the saga. *Monsieur Gallet, décédé* was the third novel written, but the first to be published, along with *Le pendu de Saint-Pholien*. *La première enquête de Maigret* is a novel from the beginning of the Presses de la Cité period, the one following the first novel in which Maigret was "reinstated" at the Quai des Orfèvres (*see Publication chronology* in *Part III. The Saga*). *Maigret et l'homme tout seul* is the next to the last novel of all in the saga. And perhaps we can also see Simenon's desire, more or less conscious, to present some sort of chronological "markers" in his character's life. Maigret's youth and his beginnings in the police in the years 1915–1920, his work as Chief Inspector in the 1930s, and finally, the end of his career in the 1960s.

It's clear that if we stop at these dates, they represent for Maigret quite a long active life, but we mustn't forget that the character lived a life parallel to that of his novelist, which is why Simenon was "obliged" to adapt the dates as a function of his time of writing, to maintain a certain "contemporaneity" between himself and his hero. Maigret lived, if not at the same rhythm, at least at the same time as he did, and Maigret more and more, with the passing of the years, had the same reactions and feelings about life as Simenon, (or perhaps it was the other way around...).

That having been said, the temptation still looms large, for Maigret fans, to attempt to anchor the Chief Inspector at a historic moment, and particularly to fix his date of birth, even while it remains but a research game, the results of which are only relative.

To establish a date of birth for the Chief Inspector, his biographers have relied primarily on three clues. One is that given in the first "official" novel of the saga, *Pietr le Letton*, written in 1929–1930. His author says there that Maigret is 45. Assuming a "contemporaneity" between the writing of the novel and the biography of the Chief Inspector, he would have been born in

1884. This is the track followed by Gilles Henry in "*La véritable histoire du commissaire Maigret.*" Another clue, taken into account by most other biographers (Jean Forest in "*Les archives Maigret,*" and again by Bernard Alavoine in "*Les enquêtes de Maigret*"), is the one given more explicitly by Simenon himself in *La première enquête de Maigret.* We know that the author places this investigation in 1913, and states therein that Maigret is 26. This establishes the year of his birth as 1887. Finally, Jacques Baudou, in "*Les nombreuses vies de Maigret,*" prefers the year indicated by Simenon in *Monsieur Gallet, décédé.* In this novel, which takes place in June 1930, Maigret is described as 45 years old. In other words, Maigret would have been born in 1885.

Now nothing stops us from using other clues as a point of departure to establish this birth year. We can mention specifically the first novel where Simenon evokes Maigret's origins in some detail, *L'affaire Saint-Fiacre.* In this novel, written in 1932, Maigret is 42, and this would mean he'd been born in 1890.

Maigret's Career

Maigret began his medical studies at Nantes, but the death of his father prevented him from continuing, and he left for Paris, to attempt to gain a living, seeking work in an office. One day, he made the acquaintance of his next-door neighbor, who told him about his work; … he was an inspector in the police. Maigret, immediately enthusiastic, decided to follow that career himself. He would begin as a uniformed policeman, charged with delivering mail, by bicycle, to all the different official offices of the police.

Following that, he was appointed secretary in a police station, before eventually arriving, at age 26, at the Quai des Orfèvres, as an inspector in the brigade of Chief Inspector Barodet. To learn the "criminal geography" of Paris, he worked in various divisions, public roads, morals, hotels, and stations. At age 30, he entered the Homicide Squad, under the command of Chief Inspector Guillaume.

Later, nearing his 40s, he himself would be appointed Chief Inspector of this squad, and that's the age that we can imagine him for most of the investigations in the saga. Indeed, when Simenon "created" Maigret in *Pietr le Letton,* he endowed him with certain physical characteristics, and he also assigned him a precise age; the Chief Inspector was, at that time, 45. From the outset, he imagined a character with a certain maturity, experience, permitting him some hindsight on the things of life, and this distance also gives him all his moral force. Certainly, it's evident that Maigret has also been active since he was 20 or 30, but it is the image of the Chief Inspector in his 40s, or young 50s, which remains the point of reference for the reader.

In the Fayard novels, Maigret's age is indicated, besides in *Pietr le Letton*, in *Monsieur Gallet, décédé* and *La tête d'un homme*, two novels where the Chief Inspector is 45, and, in *L'affaire Saint-Fiacre*, where he is 42. We can thus estimate that at the time of the Fayard investigations, from *Pietr le Letton* to *Liberty Bar*, Maigret is around 45. And we can probably also consider that this age of 45 is about that for the Gallimard novels as well.

We can estimate that in the novels of the first part of the Presses de la Cité period Maigret is between 45 and 50. Indeed, for the novels in the last part of the saga, the Chief Inspector's age is often indicated as a function of the perspective of his retirement, and there Maigret is a little more than 50, generally 52 or 53. Since the fact is also mentioned that Maigret will retire in two or three years, we can assume that this will be when he's 55. Which, in conclusion, gives Maigret a career of more than 30 years of experience in the police.

Maigret's Family and Childhood Memories

A significant element characterizing the Chief Inspector as both complex and captivating, is that his author endowed him with a past, and not only do elements of his past arise at various moments in the texts of the saga, but they also occupy an important position in Maigret's mental processes during an investigation.

Simenon first describes Maigret's childhood in *L'affaire Saint-Fiacre*, a novel of his 'return to his roots,' in which the Chief Inspector finds himself forced to confront his boyhood memories with the reality of his present adult life. Augmented here and there in the novels which follow, it is not until *Les mémoires de Maigret* that the author once more focuses on his character's biography. Following that, the Chief Inspector's childhood memories reappear from time to time, always by allusion, yet small as they may be, they are no less significant.

EVARISTE MAIGRET, HIS FATHER

An almost mythical character, whose portrait borrows from, among others, Simenon's own father. What do we learn of him? After having studied at a school of agriculture, for thirty years he was the steward of the château de Saint-Fiacre (*see* below), "*a property of 3,000 hectares, on which there were no fewer than 26 farms*" (*Les mémoires de Maigret*, MEM: 3). Very tall, very thin, with a long, reddish-blond moustache, he was conscientious, with a *"very strong sense of duty"* (MEM: 3). His premature death from pleurisy at 44, cut short his son's medical studies. He was buried in the small cemetery behind the church of Saint-Fiacre. Maigret, full of respect for the memory of the man who was his father, never really knew him well, and the image he retains of him is somewhat idealized, to the extent of seeking "substitute figures" like Xavier Guichard, his first chief at the Quai des Orfèvres.

His Mother

It's a rather faded image that Maigret retains of his mother, for she died in childbirth when he was eight. The few memories that he has are more like sensations, marked with sweet nostalgia ... a box where she put her buttons, a lithograph she liked, of a young woman at the edge of a lake, the perfume she wore on Sundays, the blue of her apron. He especially remembered her during the times he'd been ill, no doubt because she'd spent more time with him then. And so he remembered when he'd had the measles just before she died (his *"warmest, most comforting memory of her,"* *Maigret à Vichy,* VIC: 1), and the caramel cream she'd made for him when he'd had the flu. To his joy, Mme Maigret could make one just as well, taking on the role of a mother figure!

The Family

We know very little about the rest of Maigret's family, only a few clues here and there in the texts. We learn in *Les mémoires de Maigret* (MEM: 3), that on his father's side, Maigret's grandfather was a tenant farmer on the Saint-Fiacre lands that the Maigret family had worked for at least three generations. Grandfather Maigret had had seven or eight children, almost all of whom had died during a typhus epidemic, the only survivors the Chief Inspector's father and a sister who'd married a baker and settled in Nantes. When Maigret was 12, he'd been enrolled at the *lycée* in Moulins. But as he hadn't liked it there, his father had decided to send him to Nantes, to stay with his sister, who was childless. Maigret had stayed there eight years, the time he'd started at medical school. As for his mother's side of the family, the clues are even fewer; in *L'ombre chinoise* (OMB: 4), we learn that Maigret had an aunt who spent most of her time bemoaning her fate, and who, each time she came to visit his parents, began her complaints with, *"My poor Hermance! Let me tell you...."* This is the only place in the saga where we learn Maigret's mother's name; it's never mentioned elsewhere. In *Maigret à l'école* (ECO: 5), Maigret has a memory of one of his aunts who wore a blue checked apron and had her hair in a bun. And in *Maigret et les vieillards* (VIE: 5), it's a religious one he remembers.

EVOCATIONS OF THE PAST

Maigret's childhood memories, as evoked in the saga, except for a few nostalgic notes about lights, colors or odors, are almost never positive. Simenon frequently confronts his character with "backstage" images, which "dirty," in a way, Maigret's memories of his earliest years. The revered Countess, more an icon than a real figure, Maigret continues to see her through the eyes of a youth or adolescent, an image Maigret admired from afar in the park of the château, *"tall, thin, melancholic"* (*L'affaire Saint-Fiacre*, FIA: 1), she personified *"all femininity, all grace, all nobility"* (FIA: 1). In later years he sometimes dreamed of her still, as in *Maigret et les vieillards*. But now, she's no more than an old woman who keeps gigolos (*L'affaire Saint-Fiacre*); the aristocratic château has been bought by a vulgar butcher (*Un échec de Maigret*); and the friends of his childhood and youth, almost without exception, have become despicable characters: Fumal in *Un échec de Maigret*, Malik in *Maigret se fâche*, or Florentin in *L'ami d'enfance de Maigret*; none of them deserving Maigret's consideration. Chabot, in *Maigret a peur* and *Maigret chez le ministre*, is slightly better off, but he too has aged badly. Jorissen, in *Au rendez-vous des Terre-Neuvas*, is colorless, and Bouchardon, in *L'affaire Saint-Fiacre*, is a ceremonious fool, without even the merit of recognizing Maigret! And it's furthermore significant to note that not a single one of his classmates from *lycée* are mentioned in *Les mémoires de Maigret*. It's as if the Chief Inspector, in the end, was the only one to have "succeeded" in his life.

Maigret, in fact, seems to spend his time trying to escape from his childhood memories, or at least from the people he associated with at the time, only maintaining the somewhat faded image of his father, and a few colorful spots, warm and tender, of a mother gone too soon. And even his image of his father is not immune to attack. The Chief Inspector has hardly had time to visit his grave (*L'affaire Saint-Fiacre*) before the spineless Florentin (*L'ami d'enfance de Maigret*) is allowed to sully the memory of his revered father. After the death of the Countess and Fumal's purchase of the château (*Un échec de Maigret*), Florentin's comments about Maigret's father (ENF: 6), as well as the somewhat uncomfortable memory of the young girl of the Moulins pastry shop, constitute, in *L'ami d'enfance de Maigret*, the "final attack on Saint-Fiacre." In the last novels of the saga, allusions to Maigret's childhood will be only nostalgic, if agreeable, flashes, as if the Chief Inspector—and his creator—have definitively, in the soothing serenity of the coming age, settled their accounts with his youth.

THE ALTAR BOY

One of the only "positive" memories which surface in the reminiscences of Maigret's childhood, is that of his memories of being an altar boy, which are mixed, in reality, with Simenon's own memories. Maigret recalls on several occasions his past as an altar boy, and how it affected him, in a few small facts, always the same ... his progress on the route hardened by the frosty mornings, which numbed his fingertips, and the contrast with the soft warmth and the lights of the church... *"And Maigret recovered the sensations of yesteryear ... the cold, his eyes tingling, his icy fingertips, an aftertaste of coffee. Then, entering the church, a puff of heat, of soft light ... the smell of the candles, of incense..."* (*L'affaire Saint-Fiacre*, FIA: 1); *"He brought himself back to when he was a small boy, a young Maigret who, in his Allier village, walked on tiptoes and held his breath when day had hardly broken, his hands chapped, his nose red, entering the sacristy to don his altar boy's outfit"* (*Les vacances de Maigret*, VAC: 1); *"it hadn't been so long ago that he'd been wearing short pants and that he'd crossed the village square on chilly mornings, his fingertips numb, to go and serve the Mass in the little church lit only by candlelight"* (*Mon ami Maigret*, AMI: 8); *"However, he'd served the same Mass in the springtime, in summer, in the fall. Why was the memory he retained and which automatically returned, that of darkness, frost, numb fingers, his shoes cracking a film of ice on the road?"* (*Maigret et le voleur paresseux*, PAR: 1).

SAINT-FIACRE

Saint-Fiacre is a village organized around three poles, the church, the château, and the inn. At its center is a sloping main square, bordered on one side by the church erected on the embankment, and on the other by the Notre-Dame pond. Behind the church is the small cemetery, accessed via a gate. After the main square, planted with poplars, on the right is the mansard-roofed inn run by Marie Tatin, and on the left, a gravel drive bordered with oaks, leading to the château.

The Château

The vast château comprises two corner towers, and two wings. Access to the interior of the residence is via a set of white stairs leading to an entrance porch. The kitchens are in the basement, and in the attics are the servants' quarters. On the ground floor, a large paved corridor with doors opening off from it, the first leading to the dining room, the next to the lounge, the third to a smoking room, and the last to the library. In the lounge can be seen a portrait of the former Count de Saint-Fiacre. The walls of the dining room are covered with sculpted paneling, the panels illuminated by lamps in the form of candles. A round table, on which rests a seven-branched candelabra, is surrounded by Gothic chairs. At the beginning of the corridor is the staircase leading to the second floor, where the bedrooms are situated, including that of the Countess, just above the library. The Countess's bedroom has a heavy oaken door, and a four-poster bed.

In the courtyard, the outbuildings and the two-story steward's house where Maigret was born, with its red roof and pink brick walls. In the dining room, with its waxed parquet floor, an oak table, the corners decorated with carved lions, holding in their mouths copper rings. On the wall of Maigret's parents' bedroom was a lithograph of a young woman on the banks of a lake.

The Church

The little church of Saint-Fiacre is entered via an entrance porch, and we find there, among the puffs of warmth and soft light, in the scent of candles and incense, Marie Tatin's black chair with red velvet armrests, the rope of the church bell at the back of the church, the confessionals with their little green curtains. In the choir, a row of hard stalls, of old polished wood. On the floor, blue tiles. To the right of the altar, the door leading to the sacristy, with a vaulted window and an oil lamp lighting the room. Behind the sacristy, the presbytery garden, separated from the road by a small gate, and of course, the presbytery itself, residence of the curé.

The Village

The houses of the village are white, low, single story. On the main street, opposite the inn, a grocery, kept by the sacristan, with a public phone, and where, during Maigret's childhood, they sold tasteless biscuits. There was a wash house, and the house of the old notary, with a gate of golden arrows. When Maigret was a child, the village had a blacksmith, a baker and a butcher, whose shop had a door chime made of light metal tubes. There were arguments among the postmistress, the school teacher and the policeman. There was a town assistant who drank, card players, a postman who thought himself important, and an innkeeper who knew everyone's secrets. And there were two old maids who kept a boutique, and lilacs in the schoolyard.

2

Appearance

A Physical Presence...

"Were his shoulders really quite broad enough for the role he was about to play? In the language of the cinema, they'd call it 'presence'" (Maigret s'amuse, AMU: 7). It was Maigret who asked this question about Janvier, about to lead the final interrogation of Dr. Jave. This question raised by Maigret—and Simenon—is an essential one which must be asked by a director who has to choose an actor to incarnate the role of the Chief Inspector. This "presence," if it's also psychological, is no less embodied by his physical presence. Maigret's psychological "weight" would not be what it is without the physical weight of the Chief Inspector—the heaviness, the broad shoulders, the massive silhouette, are integral—and essential—parts of his character. We can't imagine a slender Maigret, small or skinny. The Chief Inspector, in the novels, more than once uses his physical presence to drive a culprit to confession, or to impose his placid mass on a recalcitrant suspect.

While the author has not provided a detailed physical portrait of his character, he has, however, strewn his novels with little descriptive phrases which sketch the silhouette of the Chief Inspector, and which allow, if not a complete image, at least an idea. It's the mark of Simenon's genius to have left of his character a silhouette rather than a detailed portrait, giving the freedom to each reader to "make his own movie," for each of us to design our own Maigret.

A BROAD AND HEAVY MASS

From the first novel of the saga, Simenon describes his character in terms which draw a silhouette in broad outline, but these terms are well enough chosen to give a well-rendered description, such that the physical aspect of the character is fixed in the memory of the reader. And further let's not forget that Maigret first appeared to the author as a characteristic silhouette (at least that's what he claims in the foreword to the Editions Rencontre volume: "*I began to see drawing itself the powerful and impassive mass of a gentleman who, it seemed me, would make an acceptable Chief Inspector*"). Thus, at the beginning of Ch. 1 of *Pietr le Letton* (LET), "*Maigret planted himself, broad and heavy, his two hands in his pockets, pipe in the corner of his mouth.*"

"Planted himself," "broad," "heavy," "hands in his pockets," these are terms which will reappear throughout the length of the saga to describe Maigret's way of standing, as he does before a window (*Maigret et l'homme du banc* (BAN: 8) "*For a good moment, Maigret stayed planted before the window, regarding the rain drawing rivulets on the panes*"), in front of his stove, back to the fire, or in front of a suspect (*Signé Picpus* (SIG: 8), "*He smokes his pipe, slowly, planted before Mme Le Cloaguen, terribly massive*"), we can imagine him easily "planting himself," which gives an idea of solidity and placidity. In *Pietr le Letton* (LET: 2), we find this sentence, "*Above all he had a way of planting himself somewhere which did not bring pleasure to many of his colleagues themselves.*" Physical solidity, but also psychological, which he "imposed" on others, and which permitted Maigret to give "*an impression of tranquil power*" (*Monsieur Gallet, décédé, GAL: 11*).

The "girth" of the Chief Inspector is given him by his "*plebeian build*" (*Pietr le Letton*, LET: 2), he is "*huge and bony*" (LET: 2), but his corpulence is all muscle ("*hard muscles*" LET: 2), and does not stop him from being agile, having "*a large man's dexterity*" (*Maigret à New York*, NEW: 4) and "*an unexpected lightness*" (*Maigret et son mort*, MOR: 9). Along with these terms "*broad*" and "*heavy*," the author employs other vocabulary to describe the appearance of his character, "massive," "weighty," "*large and broad, broad especially, thick, solid*" (*Le pendu de Saint-Pholien*, PHO: 7), "*powerful and broad like a Les Halles strongman*" (*La tête d'un homme*, TET: 2), "*much broader and thicker than the average*" (*Le port des brumes*, POR: 10), "*large and strong, solid in appearance like a rock*" (*Cécile est morte*, CEC: part 1: 2), Maigret is "*thick*" (*Mon ami Maigret*, AMI: 3), has "*a big belly*" (*Maigret se fâche*, FAC: 1), and when he's standing, he appears "*enormous.*" In short, he's "*broad and thick like a clothes cabinet*" (*Tempête sur la Manche*, man: 3)!

The description can go almost as far as caricature, as where "*he resembled certain characters in a child's nightmare, those monstrously fat expressionless characters who advance on the sleeper as if to crush him. Something implacable, inhuman, evoking an elephant heading for a goal from which nothing will deter him.*" (*Le pendu de Saint-Pholien*, PHO: 7). We note however, that with time, Simenon will diminish some of this "*elephantine*" aspect of Maigret, especially in the Presses de la Cité period, where the author hardly describes the physical aspect of his character, no doubt because he has sketched out the essential points in the first period, with Fayard, and also because, as Gilles Henry has written in *"La véritable histoire du commissaire Maigret" [The True History of Chief Inspector Maigret]*, *"Afterwards, Simenon will slim him down considerably, conserving his size, suppressing the heaviness, the weight and the 'bovine' side of his beginnings. Maigret will become more of an outline, much more internalized."*

Weights and Measures

To attain this high and weighty mass, it's evident that Maigret's measurements should be, quite possibly, 5'11" tall, and weighing 200 lbs. His weight makes mere chairs creak beneath him, as well as armchairs, and steps of stairs, and gives him a *"weighty walk"* (*La maison du juge*, JUG: 4). It's not just his walk which is weighty, and the adverb *"heavily"* is often used by Simenon to describe Maigret's gestures: he climbs or descends the stairs "heavily," sits "heavily," gets up "heavily," turns "heavily" in his bed, and falls asleep "heavily"! Once more, let's not forget, as said above, that this heaviness becomes more and more an internal and psychological heaviness as the novels progress through time.

Silhouette

But the Chief Inspector doesn't have only girth, we must also think in terms of build, that is to say that he is not only stout, but his broad shoulders, his "broad back," also give him his characteristic silhouette; we recall that it was as a silhouette that Simenon first saw him: see *Les mémoires de Maigret* (MEM: 2): *"The public must get used to you, to your silhouette, your walk. I'll eventually find the words, no doubt. For the moment, you're still but a silhouette, a back, a pipe, a way of walking, of grumbling."* This silhouette, which is qualified with *heavy, comfortable, thick, tall, enormous, massive, imposing*, is often of his back, or like a great shadow, *"a somber silhouette"* (*Pietr le Letton*, LET: 2): *"He remained there, enormous, with his impressive shoulders creating a great shadow"* (LET: 1), particularly when Maigret is back-lit before a window: *"his silhouette against the luminous rectangle was enormous"* (*Monsieur Gallet, décédé*, GAL: 5).

Shoulders, Hands and Face

And also contributing to the silhouette of Maigret are his *broad shoulders*. We recall that that was how he appeared in *La danseuse du Gai-Moulin* (GAI)—until Ch. 6, he's only designated by the words *"the man with the broad shoulders."*

From his shoulders let's move to his hands: like all the rest, they are *big, broad, fat, thick, rough*; they are *heavy paws, big paws, broad paws*, with *big fingers*, which sometimes closed into *big fists* in a burst of anger. Maigret's hands form part of two characteristic poses: he plants himself, and walks, *hands in his pockets*, or *thrust* into his overcoat, his jacket or his pants. Sometimes, but more rarely, he plants himself or walks with *his hands behind his back*.

Finally, let's speak of his face. It's *fleshy, heavy, thick*, it's *a thick face, broad*, even *coarse*. Maigret's hair is *thick, of a dark chestnut brown, in which you can hardly make out a few white strands around the temples* (*Pietr le Letton*, LET: 1), and his *large thick eyebrows* surmounting his *large eyes* with *heavy lids*. The color of his eyes must be light, of a *greenish gray, after a sleepless night* (*Liberty Bar*, LIB: 11).

If Maigret had a reddish or reddish brown moustache in his youth, whose tapered ends he straightened with a hot iron, it *"was reduced to little more than toothbrush length before disappearing completely."* (*Les mémoires de Maigret*, MEM: 5). Maigret had quickly decided to shave it off. From the time of *Pietr le Letton* (LET: 1), we learn that he shaves every morning, even on Sunday, even on vacation, and that if he can't do it at home, he'll sometimes shave in his office, at a hotel, on a train, or even have himself shaved at a barber's. We know that he has a heavy beard, that he uses shaving soap, a shaving brush, and a razor, which he sometimes has occasion to buy when he hasn't one at hand, unless he borrows one from an unfortunate victim (see *Maigret et son mort*, MOR: 4)!

ANIMAL METAPHORS

At the beginning of *L'homme dans la rue* (hom), Maigret is described as *"grumpy-looking, turning his head like a bear."* This isn't the only time that Simenon describes his character using animal metaphors. He frequently compares his hero to an animal, particularly in novels in the first part of saga, for, after that, at the same time as Maigret lost his "monstrous," "monolithic" aspect, he became more refined, both literally and figuratively, and the animalistic comparisons become rarer.

Like a bear...

Many times in the saga, Maigret's hands are described as *"big paws,"* which also evoke the idea of an animal. An animal that we find in *Le chien jaune*: *"he thought he could make out a dark mass, thickset, like an enormous animal lying in wait."* (JAU: 7)

In *Signé Picpus*, while the Director read to the Chief Inspector the letter written by M. Blaise, Maigret *"gave out the menacing sigh of an exasperated bear"* (SIG: 5). In *Félicie est là*, *"The patron of the Anneau-d'Or had brought him an old bicycle, on which Maigret brought to mind a trained bear"* (FEL: 3). In *Mon ami Maigret*, *"Maigret paced around the room like a bear"* (AMI: 9). This comparison with a bear is a fairly good one, considering the number of times the author describes his character as "grunting" or "growling."

Like an elephant...

We've already mentioned the citation in *Le pendu de Saint-Pholien*, evoking an "elephantine" Chief Inspector. We find this elephantine comparison again in two novels of the Gallimard period: In *Les caves du Majestic*, Maigret, prowling behind the scenes in the hotel, is addressed by the Director, who attempts in vain to soothe him. *"In those moments, the Chief Inspector had the inertia of an elephant"* (MAJ: 9); and in *L'inspecteur Cadavre*, the comparison is made by Clémentine Bréjon: *"'Do you know, Louise, who served as elephant driver for the Chief Inspector?'"* (CAD: 5).

And in *Maigret se fâche*, we find a description of Maigret in his garden, wearing *"blue canvas pants which slid down his hips, looking like the rear end of an elephant."* (FAC: 1). As mentioned above, the animal comparisons in the Presses de la Cité period will become very rare, then non-existent, and we can keep in mind this elephantine description of the Chief Inspector in his garden, evoking less the nightmarish pachyderm than a kind of nice big beast, like his author keeping the memory in later years. Indeed, in one of his *Dictées*, Simenon recalls a dream he'd had:

> *"I had a strange dream.... I regarded with curiosity a man I could only see from the back. He was bigger than me, with broader shoulders, heavier. Though seeing only his back, I felt in him a placidity that I envied. He was wearing blue canvas pants, a gardener's apron, and wore a battered straw hat. He was in a garden.... It took me a little while, in my semi-sleep, to realize that he wasn't a real person, but a character of my imagination. It was Maigret, in his garden at Meung-sur-Loire.... Those images will fade. I have them in my mind, and then that will be, for me, Maigret's retirement"* [in *Un homme comme un autre*, 1973].

Like a ram or a bull...

Bear or elephant or bull, it's evident that the heavy silhouette of the Chief Inspector can only be compared to a heavy and powerful animal. Thus, in *La patience de Maigret* (PAT: 8): *"He had lost his air of a menacing bull...*; or, in *L'ombre chinoise* (OMB: 8), Maigret clears a path in the crowd gathered in front of the hotel where Roger Couchet has just committed suicide, *"He charged through like a ram,"* again, an impression of blind force.

Like a dog...

But we also find evocation of a smaller animal, where the comparison is less physical than psychological, alluding to the Chief Inspector's tenacity. In *Au rendez-vous des Terre-Neuvas*, Maigret comes "to hang out" near the trawler around which the drama centers, *"Like dogs come to camp, sullen, obstinate, before a terrier where they scent something."* (REN: 9). Or in *Maigret se fâche*, when Ernest Malik leads Maigret to his home, *"they gave the impression of one pulling the other on a leash, and that this one, grumpy and clumsy like a big, long-haired dog, lets himself be dragged"* (FAC: 2).

In Maigret's Clothes Closet

The description of the clothing worn by Maigret constitutes an important part of his character. While positioning him in a specific epoch, it also renders him timeless, for his clothing, described in small strokes, gives us his familiar silhouette, an image traversing epochs and fashions.

When we form a mental picture of Maigret, what's the first image that comes to mind? No doubt an overcoat, a hat, and a pipe. Consider Simenon's famous text, *La naissance de Maigret*, the preface to Volume I of the *Complete Works* in the Rencontre edition:

> *Did I drink one, two, or maybe even three small gins tinged with a few drops of bitters? Still, after an hour, a little drowsy, I began to see drawing itself, the powerful and impassive mass of a gentleman who, it seemed me, would make an acceptable Chief Inspector. During the remainder of the day, I added a few accessories to this character ... a pipe, a bowler hat, a thick overcoat with a velvet collar. And, since it was cold and humid in my abandoned barge, I granted him, for his office, an old cast iron stove.*

Let's take a look into Maigret's clothes closet...

HIS OVERCOAT

Maigret's famous overcoat tends to render the silhouette of the Chief Inspector even more massive, as Simenon describes for us in *Pietr le Letton* (LET: 2), *"With his large black overcoat with the velvet collar, it was impossible not to spot him immediately."* And we'll find this sketch of his appearance again in other novels. *"And we could only see his broad back, his black overcoat with the velvet collar, fading into the distance"* (*Le pendu de Saint-Pholien*, PHO: 11); *"He smoked constantly, wrapped warmly in the enormous overcoat that was famous at the Quai des Orfèvres"* (*La tête d'un homme*, TET: 7); *"And an enormous shape emerged from the shadows, Chief Inspector Maigret, encased in his heavy overcoat with the velvet collar, his hands in his pockets"* (*L'ombre chinoise*, OMB: 10); *"his great overcoat made him appear to be carved in stone."* (*Chez les Flamands*, FLA: 1).

We know other details about this garment. Besides the velvet collar, which Maigret often raises to protect himself from the cold, the coat has buttons, and pockets, very practical for thrusting in your hands, as Maigret does innumerable times, as well as other objects, even if it means deforming these pockets—the plans for Popinga's house in *Un crime en Hollande* (HOL), the Countess's missal in *L'affaire Saint-Fiacre* (FIA), the hammer that killed Germaine in *Chez les Flamands* (FLA), a knife, billy and a suspect's revolver in *Rue Pigalle* (pig).

This black overcoat, thick and heavy, is naturally a garment which Maigret wears when it's cold or rainy. Enveloping the Chief Inspector, his overcoat has known many torrential rains, which made it even heavier … *"he put on his overcoat, which the rain had rendered twice as heavy"* (*Chez les Flamands*, FLA: 7), *"He sighed while taking off his heavy overcoat, which the fog had made even heavier"* (*L'inspecteur Cadavre*, CAD: 7) and it made him smell like a *"wet dog"*; Maigret more than once had to dry it in his office heated by the cast iron stove. *"His sodden overcoat hanging, completely stiff on the coat rack, kept the shape of his shoulders."* (*Pietr le Letton*, LET: 6).

This overcoat is also a little like a shield, a "fortress" where Maigret feels protected: *"And Maigret drew himself more deeply into his heavy overcoat, as if to shelter himself from all contact"* (*Cécile est morte*, CEC, 1st part: 4), a sort of warm and comfortable "cocoon." *"Maigret was warm, quite happily warm … he could pass, wrapped in his overcoat … for the incarnation of beatitude."* (CEC, 2nd part: 3).

We note that Maigret didn't wear only the black overcoat with the velvet collar, for he had others, as he made a point of explaining himself, in *Les mémoires de Maigret*: *"As for the famous overcoat with the velvet collar…. I had one, I admit. In fact I had many, like any man of my generation. Maybe it happened, around 1927, one very cold day, or during a heavy rain, that I wore one of those old ones"* (MEM: 2). In *La première enquête de Maigret*, we learn that he'd worn his black overcoat since his debut with the police. *"At that time, he had two overcoats, a large black one, with a velvet collar, which he'd worn for three years, and a light brown one, very short, which he'd bought recently, a kind he'd wanted since his adolescence"* (PRE: 8).

And note that if we consider the chronology of the saga, the velvet-collared overcoat appears during the period from Fayard through Gallimard, and the beginning of the Presses de la Cité period, up to Maigret's "correction" in *Les mémoires de Maigret*. After that, it will simply be mentioned as Maigret's "*overcoat*," which may still be "*heavy*" or "*large*," "*heavy with rain*," to the point of weighing "*200 pounds*"! (*Maigret a peur*, PEU: 2), or "black." *He wore his heavy black overcoat*" (*Maigret et le marchand de vin*, VIN: 1), but there's no longer any mention of a velvet collar.

The heavy overcoat, with or without its velvet collar, is reserved for investigations that take place in the fall or winter, but it is abandoned by the Chief Inspector in spring and summer for another coat. During these "fine seasons," Mme Maigret stores it away in mothballs, whose odor it still retains at the beginning of the following fall. From the arrival of the first fine days, Maigret starts to leave it in the office in the afternoon, before changing to a lighter one, a "mid-season coat," which he also often leaves in his office, wearing only his jacket for the warm spring afternoons.

HIS HAT

The "first style," Fayard-period Maigret, wears, as his headgear, a bowler, a derby. That's how he's introduced in *Pietr le Letton*: "*He took down his jacket and put it on, then his heavy black overcoat, and he put his bowler on his head.*" (LET: 1). The hat is furthermore representative of his function as Chief Inspector, which is why, for example, Maigret wears it when, already retired, he goes to Paris to help his nephew: "*We see Maigret come downstairs wearing his overcoat with the velvet collar and his bowler hat*" (*Maigret*, MAI: 1) or when he begins his investigation of the death of the butcher in *Ceux du Grand Café*: "*Maigret looked for his hat, and since he couldn't immediately find his old felt one that he used in the country, he wore his bowler, which was somehow symbolic.*" (ceu: 1). In the Gallimard period, Maigret always wore his bowler, an indispensible accessory. "*His hands in the pockets of his great overcoat with the velvet collar, famous at the Quai des Orfèvres, and which still smelled slightly of mothballs, his bowler hat pulled down tightly on his head, Maigret made his way on foot towards the Police Judiciaire*" (*Cécile est morte*, CEC, 1st part: 1).

This hat has certainly known its tribulations! The rain which transforms it into a "*reservoir of water suddenly emptying itself at the least movement*" (*L'auberge aux noyés*, noy: 1). The wind, which obliges Maigret to hold it on with his hand, blowing it off even into the sea. The cold... "*It was even colder than yesterday. Maigret, his overcoat collar raised, his hat pulled down to his eyes*" (*L'affaire Saint-Fiacre*, FIA: 5). We find it in all sorts of conditions: knocked askew during a search... "*He got out of the car, his pipe out, hat askew, a bloodstain on his cuff"* (*Pietr le Letton*, LET: 1), fallen on Mme Martin's bed when Maigret tries to take a paper from her (*L'ombre chinoise*, OMB: 10), used to protect him from a draft on the train (*Le fou de Bergerac*, FOU: 1), to hide a telephone with the receiver off the hook (*Maigret*, MAI: 9), and lost in a "brawl" at the Majestic (*Les caves du Majestic*, MAJ: 7).

Before putting his hat on his head, the Chief Inspector often checks its condition. *"Standing, he put on his heavy overcoat, brushed his bowler hat with his sleeve"* (*Le chien jaune*, JAU: 5). As a gesture of politeness, Maigret removes it when he speaks to women (sometimes awkwardly when he's uncomfortable, as with Aline in *L'écluse n° 1*, ECL: 3), but there are times when he keeps it on his head, as in protest. For example, in *La nuit du carrefour*, the difference in his attitude between his first visit with Else... *"Maigret was sitting in an easy chair, having placed his bowler hat on the rug"* (NUI: 4), and his second, after he had discovered that she had left her room. *"Maigret had kept his pipe in his mouth, his hat on his head."* (NUI: 5). When he sits somewhere, he can place his hat on the rug, on his knees, or on a chair.

And sometimes Maigret strikes a pose which the movies have made classic (You've no doubt seen one of these mysteries from the '50s with the hero in this typical look.).

"Maigret was there, plump, cordial, his pipe in his teeth, his hat pushed all the way back..." (*Le port des brumes*, POR: 10); *"He'd made himself at home, his elbows on the table, pipe in his teeth, his bowler hat shoved all the way back."* (*Liberty Bar*, LIB: 6); *"He sniffed, looked all around, his hands always in his pockets, his hat pushed back a little, in a familiar pose"* (*La fenêtre ouverte*, fen).

Maigret also uses his hat as a kind of salute: *"Maigret raised his hand to his bowler hat in greeting"* (*Rue Pigalle*, pig); *"Maigret allowed himself the pleasure ... of pushing open the door, touching the brim of his hat.... Salut, Pozzo"* (*Maigret, Lognon et les gangsters*, LOG: 4): *"Maigret ... framed in the doorway, larger than life, pipe in his mouth, touched the brim of his hat, murmuring, 'Bonsoir messieurs...'"* (*La pipe de Maigret*, pip: 4).

We note that Maigret had worn his bowler hat, like his overcoat with the velvet collar, since his beginnings with the police. In the Presses de la Cité period, Simenon no longer uses the term "bowler," probably for two reasons. Firstly, fashions had changed, and bowlers weren't worn after 1945 (and Maigret lives in a certain contemporaneity with his creator). Secondly, for the reason clarified so well in *Les Mémoires de Maigret* (MEM: 2)...

When young Sim entered the Quai des Orfèvres for the first time, I still had a bowler hat in my closet, but I only wore it on rare occasions ... for funerals or official ceremonies. Now it so happened that in my office was a photograph on the wall taken several years earlier, for I don't know what meeting somewhere, in which I appeared wearing this dratted hat. With the result that even today, when I'm introduced to someone I've never met, I hear, "Oh, you've changed your hat!"

Once he's taken to wearing the soft hat (described as *felt* in *Maigret et les témoins récalcitrants*, TEM), sometimes qualified with "black," or "lined," Maigret can expand his array of gestures. *"He raised the collar of his jacket, lowered the brim of his hat and crossed the street, hunching his shoulders"* (*Maigret en meublé*, MEU: 5); *"He moved slowly to one of the high stools, sat down, and unbuttoned his overcoat, pushing his hat back on his head"* (*Maigret et la jeune morte*, JEU: 8).

The soft hat also has its adventures ... pierced by a bullet in *Maigret, Lognon et les gangsters* (LOG), dripping cold water in *Maigret et l'homme du banc* (BAN), almost forgotten in a library as "unseemly," in *Maigret se trompe* (TRO), blown off by the wind and recaptured by the guard at the PJ in *Un échec de Maigret* (ECH), tossed down the stairs by the maid, old Catherine, in *Maigret et les témoins récalcitrants* (TEM), getting snowed on in *Maigret et le voleur paresseux* (PAR).

But Maigret has also worn other hats, of which the most typical is perhaps his straw hat, symbol of leisure time, the country, his retirement at Meung-sur-Loire. The idea of having a straw hat for his retirement may have come to him when he tried on the one which had belonged to Jules Lapie, in *Félicie est là... "He reached over and put on his head the broad-brimmed straw hat.... Well! Old Peg-leg had a head even bigger than his own, and he must have had to visit a number of hat shops to find one that fit. It set the Chief Inspector to daydreaming."* And later, *"Maigret couldn't help but thinking that one day he would be retired, and he too would have a little house in the country, a garden, a big straw hat..."* (FEL: 2). His dream realized, *"Pipe in his teeth, an old straw hat on his head, he floundered about blissfully in a plot of tomatoes..."* (*Le notaire de Châteauneuf*, not: 1).

He also wore a straw hat, probably a kind of Panama, when he took the cure in Vichy:

He hesitated to take his straw hat.
"You think you'll be laughed at?"
If so, too bad! He was on vacation, after all, and he set it gallantly on his head [Maigret à Vichy, VIC: 2].

And further, he'd already worn a straw hat, a boater, in his early years as a policeman, as he'd just remembered in *Maigret à Vichy* (VIC: 3).

His Suit

And beneath his overcoat, what does the Chief Inspector wear? A black or dark suit seems to be fairly standard, "normal" for Paris, but which "sticks out" a little when his investigation takes him to the south. This outfit is "a durable black serge suit" (*Maigret*, MAI: 2). After this, in the Presses de la Cité period, we can imagine a suit of another color, dark, but not necessarily black. We see, for example, in *La patience de Maigret*, Mme Maigret telling her husband, "*Wear your pepper-and-salt gray suit, it's lighter than the other.*" (PAT: 5). And in *Maigret et Monsieur Charles* (CHA), when Maigret asks his wife to prepare for him "*his best dark suit*," because the Chief Inspector is going to a night club. So we can imagine that Maigret only wears his dark or black suit on special occasions, and that he normally wears one of another color, perhaps gray or brown.

If his three-piece suit seems to indicate a certain propensity to stylishness, ("*His clothes were rather fine wool, well cut*," *Pietr le Letton*, LET: 2), the general appearance of the Chief Inspector is hardly that of a dandy! We see in *Le pendu de Saint-Pholien* that "*his careless attire emphasized the plebian in his build.*" (PHO: 7)

This suit has a jacket, slacks, and a vest. Maigret often removes the jacket when he's in his office, but he puts it back on when he has a visitor. When he goes out and it's a warm day, he carries it over his arm. When he's not wearing an overcoat, he puts his hands in his jacket pockets, where he puts other objects—bicycle pedals in *Le charretier de La Providence* (PRO), a bouquet of violets in *Le client le plus obstiné du monde* (obs). He sometimes turns up the collar of his jacket like that of his overcoat. Maigret wore another kind of jacket when he was taking the cure in Vichy, "*a light-weight jacket, almost white, of mohair*" (*Maigret à Vichy*, VIC: 1).

Maigret sometimes put his hands in his pants pockets, where other things are found as well… "*For years and years, you might say always, each of his pockets had been a clear destination, well defined. In his left pants pocket, his tobacco pouch and handkerchief—so that there were always shreds of tobacco in his handkerchiefs. The right-hand pocket, his two pipes and small change. His left hip pocket, his wallet, which, always filled with useless papers, gave him one buttock larger than the other…. He carried almost nothing in his jacket, just a box of matches in the right-hand pocket. That's why when he had newspapers to carry, or letters to mail, he slipped them into his left pocket*" (*Les vacances de Maigret*, VAC: 1). His slacks were made in France (by his "*little Jewish tailor on the Rue de Turenne*," *Les mémoires de Maigret*, MEM: 2) and he wore them well above his waist, which obliged him to wear suspenders.

We find numerous scenes in the novels where we see the Chief Inspector with his suspenders hanging, as when he's about to wash up or shave: "*Maigret was trying vainly to grasp his suspenders, which hung on his thighs*" (*Le charretier de La Providence*, PRO: 3); "*Maigret, his face lathered with shaving cream, suspenders hanging to his thighs...*" (*L'amoureux de Madame Maigret*, amo: 2). Note this fine scene, filled with Simenon's subtle humor: "*Maigret, after having filled his pipe, removed his jacket, displaying the mauve suspenders which his wife had bought him the week before. The local superintendant smiled at the sight of those suspenders, which, on top of everything else, were of silk, and Maigret made a face*" (*Signé Picpus*, SIG: 1). And occasionally the Chief Inspector wore other types of slacks; on vacation on the Côte d'Azur, he wore white flannel slacks (*L'improbable Monsieur Owen*, owe: 1), and in America, light slacks with a leather belt and a large silver buckle—a cowboy belt! (*Maigret chez le coroner*, CHE: 1).

As for his vest, Maigret sometimes unbuttoned it, or, like his jacket, removed it in his office. "*It was four o'clock in the morning when he pushed open the door of his office at the Quai des Orfèvres. He removed his overcoat with a sigh.... From time to time Maigret got up to poke the stove, then returned to his place, while abandoning one by one his jacket, false collar, and his vest.*" (*La tête d'un homme*, TET: 1).

With a suit, Maigret must obviously wear a shirt, which can hardly be other than white ("*in the sun, the sleeves of his shirt made two bright spots*" in *L'amoureux de Madame Maigret*, amo: 3). We see him often, in fact each time he removes his jacket, in shirt sleeves. In Maigret's early years, his shirts had a button-on false collar, as was the fashion of the time. It was detachable, celluloid, separate from the shirt, which is why we often see Maigret unbutton and remove it to make himself more comfortable: "*Maigret had already taken off his jacket, tie, and false collar*" (*Les caves du Majestic*, MAJ: 5). At the beginning of the Presses de la Cité period, the fashion contemporary with the time of writing, changed, the false collar being little by little replaced by shirts with integral collars. That's why, from this point, we see Maigret open his shirt collar when he's too warm. "*When he returned to his office, he took off his jacket and tie, opened the collar of his shirt...*" (*Maigret tend un piège*, TEN: 3). Since we're already looking at his collar, let's move to the accessory that accompanies it, his tie, an indispensable element of the masculine wardrobe of Maigret's time! What do we know about Maigret's ties? That he has a hard time tying the knot: "*he adjusted, as well as he could, his tie, which he'd never been able to knot correctly*" (*Pietr le Letton*, LET: 1); that his tie bothers him as often as his collar: "*And Maigret, in shirtsleeves, pipe in his teeth, false collar unbuttoned, tie undone...*" (*Monsieur Gallet, décédé*,

GAL: 5), "*Maigret ... took off his overcoat, and then, after a brief hesitation, his tie, which was too tight.*" (*Maigret et son mort*, MOR: 2). That tie was no doubt black in the early days, when Maigret wore a black suit. Later, he could wear ties with some color, subdued, certainly, as befit a Chief Inspector of the Police! On vacation, he permits himself more whimsy. "*Maigret searched for a tie to his taste among the six new ones his wife had given him for the trip*," "*Something else made him smile, picturing himself ... wearing a striped tie he had chosen, sporting the colors of an English university.*" (*L'improbable Monsieur Owen*, owe: 1)

OTHER OUTFITS

For going to bed, Maigret wears, in theory, a nightshirt, as Simenon says to him:

> "*For instance, up till now, you've had no family life, whereas Boulevard Richard-Lenoir and Mme Maigret actually take up a good half of your existence. You've thus far only telephoned your home, but you're going to be seen there.*"
> "*In my bathrobe and slippers?*"
> "*And even in bed.*"
> "*I wear nightshirts,*" I said ironically.
> "*I know. That completes the picture. Even if you were used to pajamas, I'd have made you wear a nightshirt*" [*Les mémoires de Maigret*, MEM: 2].

But Maigret has sometimes "cheated" Simenon, and worn, instead of his nightshirt, pajamas. Out of his bed, Maigret wears "*a dressing gown over his nightshirt with a collar decorated with little red crosses.*" (*Maigret et son mort*, MOR: 8).

Outside of his normal attire, Maigret sometimes has occasion to wear special outfits, according to the situation in which he's plunged during an investigation. Thus, in *Les caves du Majestic* (MAJ: 3), Maigret wears a tuxedo, complete with a dazzling white false shirt, decorated with two pearls, and complemented by shiny patent leather shoes which squeak. And further it was in evening dress that Maigret had made the acquaintance—and conquest—of Louise. It was, in fact, his father's wedding suit that the young Maigret had had tailored to his size. He wore a wing collar, tails, white tie, and patent shoes. (*Les mémoires de Maigret*, MEM: 4). Maigret also had a morning coat (the tails rounded from the button to the back), which he had had to wear for a royal visit (*La première enquête de Maigret*, PRE: 1). He'd even been photographed in frock coat and top hat when he was secretary to the Police Station! (*Les caves du Majestic*, MAJ: 8)

In spite of the fact that he doesn't know how to swim, Maigret has a bathing suit and a red robe, which he only uses to stretch himself out on the sand of the beach and watch the bathers! (*L'improbable Monsieur Owen,* owe: 1)

And lastly let's look at the *"old clothes"* that Maigret wears when he gardens at Meung-sur-Loire, *"a pair of blue canvas pants which slid off his hips, making him look like an elephant from the rear, a peasant shirt with complicated little designs"* (*Maigret se fâche,* FAC: 1).

Shoes, Gloves, and Other Accessories

Maigret wears lace-up shoes, which have done more than their share in accompanying the Chief Inspector in the exercise of his duties. *"When I was in the Public Roads Squad, I paced, during each day..., mile after mile of sidewalk, in every kind of weather ... the soles of my shoes, become porous, drank up the water of the gutters"* (*Les mémoires de Maigret,* MEM: 5). And in numerous other novels, we see Maigret with his shoes soaked with rain. *"Now his shoes spluttered dirty water with every step, his hat was shapeless, his overcoat and jacket soaked through and through"* (*Pietr le Letton,* LET: 5). Each year, by tradition, he bought a pair of shoes, at the first fine days, and when he first put them on, his feet hurt, so that he couldn't run after his thief (*Le voleur de Maigret,* VOL: 1). When he was young, he had once bought some light brown "goose-dung" shoes, which Mme Maigret had returned to the store, because she didn't want to see him wear them. This memory would connect Maigret to Louis Thouret (*Maigret et l'homme du banc,* BAN: 3). On vacation he allowed himself to wear *"red and white shoes with a most happy effect"* (*L'improbable Monsieur Owen,* owe: 2). When he went fishing, he wore Wellingtons. He also wore wooden shoes, varnished and yellow, which Mme Maigret had bought him in Alsace (*La guinguette à deux sous,* GUI: 11) and which he slipped on his bare feet in his retirement, to work in his garden.

Once dressed, shod, and wearing his raincoat, Maigret could still protect himself from the cold. If, over the years, he was satisfied to raise the collar of his overcoat and keep his hands in his pockets, with age, he took to wearing gloves and a scarf. Mme Maigret told him many times to wear his scarf, but the first time he agreed, it was a concession, not without melancholy, to the fact that he was getting older:

> *"You'd better wear your scarf."* His wife ran to get it, without suspecting that that little sentence would stick in his mind for a good while, and bring on a feeling of melancholy.... Because of this scarf ... a heavy muffler that his wife had knit, he felt old" [*Maigret et les témoins récalcitrants,* TEM: 1].

It was a woolen scarf, thick, navy blue, almost too warm, even stifling!

Since we're considering those accessories serving to protect him from inclement weather, we should note that beginning with the Presses de la Cité period, Maigret uses an umbrella. It's the most frequently voiced concern of Mme Maigret that her husband carry this object. To make her happy, he takes it with him on leaving the house, which doesn't stop him from leaving it later at the Quai des Orfèvres if he has to go out again! So, in *Maigret et l'inspecteur Malgracieux*, "*He walked down the Rue Lamarck, the collar of his jacket raised, since in spite of Mme Maigret's maternal advice, he had left his umbrella at the Quai des Orfèvres...*" (mal: 2).

3

Facing the World

Maigret's Pipe

It has often been noted—and it's a fact—that Simenon doesn't describe the way Maigret thinks. But we can discover it through the Chief Inspector's actions, particularly with regard to his pipe. In his way of filling it, lighting it, smoking, and then emptying it, we discover Maigret's path through an investigation, his relationship to others, and his way of understanding the world.

THE ATTITUDES OF A PIPE SMOKER

At the beginning of *Pietr le Letton* (LET: 1), we find this image of a characteristic position of Maigret, a pose we will see again and again... "*Maigret planted himself, broad and heavy, hands in his pockets, his pipe in the corner of his mouth.*" The phrases "*his pipe in his teeth*" and "*his pipe in his mouth*" appear innumerable times from the author's pen like a formula, serving to summarize his hero in a few words. Sometimes Maigret's pipe can be "*glued to his jaw,*" or "*clamped between his teeth.*" This manner of holding his pipe in his mouth gives him a certain power, "*Was it because he had his pipe once more between his teeth? ... It was always at this moment that he was more solid than ever. He was twice as much Maigret, you might say.*" (*Pietr le Letton*, LET: 12).

But it can also be his emotions which are revealed in his fashion of holding the pipe in his mouth. Very often, he "*clenches*" the stem of his pipe between his teeth, sometimes "*with force,*" or "*furiously.*" He may also "*chew on it,*" or "*munch on it*": "*He walked the halls of the PJ, heavy, menacing-looking, chewing on the stem of his pipe, his thoughts furious*" (*Cécile est morte*, CEC: 2nd part: 1). And sometimes, there's a certain gaiety which permeates his attitude, "*with a funny, short little laugh around the stem of his pipe*" (*La pipe de Maigret*, pip: 2).

31

These attitudes add up to an authentic "pipe smoker," as he recognized himself, "*Me, I'm an old pipe smoker*" (*La fenêtre ouverte*, fen), or as others define him as well, in *Le charretier de La Providence* (PRO: 4), it's Willy Marco who says to Maigret, "*It's true that you're a pipe smoker…*"; in *La maison du juge* (JUG: 5), it's Forlacroix, "*You only smoke a pipe, I believe?*"; in *Les scrupules de Maigret* (SCR: 1), an American criminologist, "*you're a pipe fanatic*"; in *Maigret hésite* (HES: 1), Parendon, "*You're not smoking? … I thought you always had your pipe in your mouth.*"; in *Maigret et le tueur* (TUE: 3) Monique Batille, "*I forgot that you smoke your pipe all day!*" It's also to preserve this identity, this image of himself, that he refuses other forms of tobacco; offered a cigar or cigarette, he responds, "*thanks, nothing but a pipe*," "*only the pipe*," "*always the pipe*," "*thanks, I prefer my pipe*," or "*thanks, I only smoke a pipe.*"

Pipe Play

We must recognize right off that Maigret does not smoke only a single pipe. While he may not have the more than 300 of his creator, he still has many. There are always two or three in his pockets (in theory, in his right-hand pants pocket, but sometimes also in those of his overcoat), which permits him to have "*a spare pipe.*" At the Quai des Orfèvres, we may find up to seven spread on his desk, which Simenon would have appreciated. "*There were, as usual, a good half dozen of them spread out, and he examined them with a connoisseur's eye*" (*Les mémoires de Maigret*, MEM: 1). That enables him to always have several filled at the same time, and to smoke them one after another "*It was a lazy afternoon in his overheated office, which he passed with the six or seven pipes spread out on his desk*" (*Maigret et l'affaire Nahour*, NAH: 4), going from a (too) hot pipe to a fresh one, one pipe following another, at a sometimes almost frantic pace!

So that must be part of the pleasure of smoking, to be able to take the time to compare them, to decide among them, and finally to choose the one you want to smoke. "*Maigret remained alone with his pipes, and chose one, the oldest, which he filled slowly, watching the rain flow down the windowpane*" (*Maigret et les témoins récalcitrants*, TEM: 4); "*He sat down heavily at his desk, selected the largest of his pipes, and filled it*" (*Maigret et les braves gens*, BRA: 3); "*he unconsciously arranged his pipes in size order, choosing one, the longest, which he filled with care*" (*Le voleur de Maigret*, VOL: 9); "*He sat in his chair, chose a curved pipe which he smoked less often than the others*" (*Maigret et le tueur*, TUE: 6); "*He chose one of the pipes lined up on his desk, the lightest one, and filled it slowly*" (*Maigret et le marchand de vin*, VIN: 3); "*each* time he filled one, he had carefully selected it according to his mood" (*Maigret et Monsieur Charles*, CHA: 1). If, as a rule, Maigret smokes a briar, he nonetheless also has a meerschaum. But Maigret's favorite pipe, "*the one to which he most readily returned, which he always carried with him … is a large briar pipe, slightly curved, that his wife had given him some ten years earlier as a birthday present, the one he called his 'good old pipe'*" (*La pipe de Maigret*, pip: 1). The size of the pipe is a symbolic reminder of Maigret's physical aspect: "*this pipe was on the same scale as his broad face: it could hold almost a quarter of a package of gray tobacco*" (*Le port des brumes*, POR: 2). The Chief Inspector has still other pipes at home, so that he leaves some in his office when he's on vacation. At home, he keeps his pipes in a pipe rack, which is kept in the dining room.

And it's also a bit of a compulsion, arranging them in size order, "*in Indian file like tin soldiers*" (*Maigret et les vieillards*, VIE: 7), putting them in order, as if ordering his thoughts. But it's also a game. "*Maigret played…. He didn't play with blocks, as when he was a child, but with some pipes…. Mechanically, with the greatest seriousness, he arranged the pipes on his blotter in a way of making more or less geometrical shapes, or suggesting some animal…. He played, his mind empty. The pipes, in their last arrangement, looked like a stork*" (*Maigret et Monsieur Charles*, CHA: 1).

All five senses enter into the game, and through them Maigret is "put in contact" with his pipe; the vision of the smoke emanating from Maigret's pipe, whose *thin blue stream rising in a spiral* enveloped his thoughts, giving its characteristic halo in the air, formed *a moving layer of fog at the level of the lamp* or Maigret's forehead, while his head was haloed with the smoke of his pipe. Maigret's silences, punctuated by the crackling of the tobacco in his pipe: "*The silence was not broken, but rather emphasized by the crackling of his pipe*" (*Pietr le Letton*, LET: 15); the heat of the tobacco burning in his pipe, that Maigret tamped with a finger, with little taps of his thumb or index finger; the material of the pipe… "*He emptied his pipe while taking another from his pocket, which he filled slowly, as if caressing the briar*" (*Une confidence de Maigret*, CON: 1), and the need to fiddle with them when he's lost in reflection. The taste and savor of the pipe, depending both on external circumstances and his mood: "*His large pipe itself had a flavor of spring.*" (*Félicie est là*, FEL: 1). "*Drawing on the pipe he'd just lit, and which, for the first time this year, had a taste of autumn*" (*Maigret et les braves gens*, BRA: 6). "*Maigret sat in a taxi, savoring both his pipe and the familiar bustle of the street*" (*Le pendu de Saint-Pholien*, PHO: 2). "*He had an uncomfortable feeling in his chest, and his pipe started to taste bad*" (*Maigret a peur*, PEU: 6). "*Didn't the tobacco seem to have a taste of a cold coming on?*" (*Maigret et le marchand de vin,* VIN: 1). The special odor of Maigret's office: "*He reentered his office, where the odor of tobacco always lingered*" (*La pipe de Maigret,* pip: 1); the pipe odor which had become a sort of "professional" hallmark of Maigret: "*Even the tobacco smell was a professional smell ... that of a pipe, extinguished the night before, relit in the middle of the night on being awakened for an emergency*" (*Maigret et les braves gens,* BRA: 1).

The events which befall Maigret's pipe are tied to the development of the investigation, which they change the course of or depend on. If Maigret knows well to hide his nervousness, it is however betrayed by the force with which he clamps down on the stem of his pipe, which cracks between his teeth and sometimes splits. And when the emotion is truly too strong, he chomps down on his pipe so strongly that it breaks: "*There was a dry little sound. It was the stem of Maigret's pipe which burst under the pressure of his jaw*" (after the discovery of the body of Antoinette Vague in *Maigret hésite,* HES: 5). It's very rare, almost exceptional, that Maigret forgets his pipe, but it happens in the saga in a single case, in *La tête d'un homme* (TET: 2), when Maigret assists in Heurtin's flight to the Citanguette café, where he's so caught up in the events that he forgets to pick up his fallen pipe. But Maigret can also pretend to forget a pipe, an excellent pretext to get into a place where he's unwelcome, as in *Le port des brumes* (POR: 6), when Maigret pretends to have forgotten his pipe in Grandmaison's office, and in *Maigret et l'homme du banc* (BAN: 5), where Maigret claims to have forgotten his pipe in Thouret's room at Mariette Gibon's, permitting him to send Lapointe to put a tap on the telephone.

Tobacco and Smoke

The Chief Inspector smokes "gray" tobacco (according to the *Petit Robert dictionary,* "ordinary tobacco in a gray paper package"), fairly strong, brown, sold in France, and which he prefers over other tobacco, like Belgian, "*blond and too light, which took away his desire to smoke*" (*Le pendu de Saint-Pholien,* PHO: 2). It sometimes happens, however, that he's tempted to be "unfaithful" to French tobacco, and to buy other sorts of tobacco, like Swiss in *Maigret voyage* (perhaps not so bad, after all; maybe Simenon, who lived in Switzerland, had recommended it to him?!).

When Maigret is out of tobacco, and doesn't have time to stop at a tobacconist, as he can't do without, he has someone buy it for him, unless he can "borrow" some from one of his pipe-smoking collaborators, like Torrence or Lucas, or someone else (Delvigne in *La danseuse du Gai-Moulin,* Ducrau in *L'écluse n° 1,* Point in *Maigret chez le ministre*). But we must recognize that he himself also offers his own tobacco, with a gesture of offering his pouch, since, while Maigret often has his package of "gray" simply slipped into a pocket, he has, nevertheless, a well-worn tobacco pouch, kept in his left pants pocket.

To light his tobacco, Maigret obviously needs some matches, contained in a matchbox, with a side for striking them (a gesture mentioned in many novels) and which often get wet during the adventures of his investigations. He sometimes borrows matches, but he also sometimes offers his own. His box of matches is found in the right-hand pocket of his jacket.

Maigret, in his manner of smoking, employs a sequence of actions, which are often in rapport with the progress of an investigation. The first step is the filling of the pipe; it's Maigret's first action when he takes his pipe from his pocket, and it's also, chronologically in the saga, Maigret's first gesture with his pipe. At the beginning of Chapter 1 of *Pietr le Letton* we find this phrase we will reread numerous times, "*he filled a pipe*." The inaugural act, the initial phase of an almost immutable ritual, in the relationship between Maigret and his pipe. This is the first sequence, the preparation, setting the scene, the *introit* of the ceremony.

Maigret fills his pipe to "get started" on an interrogation, or to gain the strength to continue it; to gain the patience to wait for something to happen, or to "return to reality" after an interrogation, to "recover" from a painful or violent scene; to give himself time to think or to regain his composure. Sometimes it's to avoid an embarrassing question, or more prosaically, to finish off a meal. Not to mention all the other times, when he "simply" wants to smoke for pleasure, or out of need—for this is often the case. To maintain and sustain his thoughts, Maigret needs to smoke his pipe, and as this rumination will last a certain amount of time, the Chief Inspector can't be satisfied with but a single one, which is why his pipes follow one after another, he smokes "*pipe after pipe.*" "*He didn't want to show his nervousness, but his pipes followed one after another with an unusual rapidity*" (*Maigret se fâche*, FAC: 6). The pipe itself becomes the symbol of the need to smoke, which is why he sometimes "*mechanically raises his empty pipe to his mouth*" (*Monsieur Gallet, décédé*, GAL: 7).

We note also that this gesture has truly become a necessary ritual, a required step in the course of an investigation, when Maigret arrives at stuffing his pipe "automatically," without particularly thinking of wanting to light it immediately to smoke it—"*Then, without realizing it, he slowly filled a pipe which he forgot to light*" (*La tête d'un homme*, TET: 8).

We soon realize how much this gesture resembles the beginning of a ceremony, how much solemnity it involves, when we study Maigret's manner of filling his pipe. Simenon describes it many times, in so ritualistic a sentence that it could be an immutable phrase from a Mass. "He/Maigret slowly fills/filled his/a pipe." The word *slowly* can be extended or replaced by another, like *quietly, calmly, carefully, meticulously, dreamily, voluptuously, thoroughly, methodically.*

Maigret uses no other instrument to fill his pipe but his fingers! If he sometimes uses his thumb, in general it's his index finger. "*Maigret stuffed his pipe with exaggerated slowness, tamping each pinch of tobacco with a dozen little taps of his index finger*" (*Monsieur Gallet, décédé*, GAL: 9).

Slowness, attention to detail, and pleasure (*voluptuously*) seem well to be the keywords for this gesture, which confirms Maigret in his ponderousness, his "quiet force," aids him to concentrate his energy against the difficulties of an investigation. How many times, had he not paused to stuff and light his pipe before confronting an unpleasant reality, would he have blown up at a reluctant witness, made too rapid a judgment about a suspect, or missed the solution by not letting his imagination run free, aided and sustained by the wisps of the smoke of his pipe.

Once the pipe is filled, it has to be lit. The second gesture of the ritual, the "firing" of the tobacco, whose combustion will allow Maigret to make those smoke rings he requires for his ruminations. Here too, Maigret lights his pipe for the same reasons as he filled it, since it's the logical continuation. To regain a footing in reality, "*he lit a pipe, as if to put himself in balance*" (*Les caves du Majestic*, MAJ: 5), to start or continue an interrogation, maintain his calm… "*Maigret relit his pipe, forcing himself to be patient*" (*L'ami d'enfance de Maigret*, ENF: 1), before reading a file, etc.

In the same way, this gesture can have the same solemn slowness as the filling; he can light his pipe *slowly, with a voluptuous slowness, placidly, with care…* "*Maigret is silent. He fills his pipe, lights it, contemplating the match which had burned itself up.*" (*Signé Picpus*, SIG: 7). In the absence of matches, he sometimes uses a folded piece of paper, a lighter for the gas, a piece of newspaper, or a paper torch.

The third step is the smoking of the pipe. Now we are at the heart of the Mass; Maigret's way of smoking is like the act of "communion" with his thoughts and reflections. The density of the smoke parallels the density of the pondering, almost like a machine, smoking or thinking. This act of smoking should prolong itself, like Maigret's reflections… "*He didn't stop smoking, regarding his companion with an amused look*" (*L'ombre chinoise*, OMB: 10). Maigret's most familiar way of smoking is to draw "*small puffs*" from his pipe. These puffs can also be, according to the Chief Inspector's mood, *abrupt, short, very spaced out, rapid, dense, thick, long, fat, nervous, reflective, gour-*

mand, *voluptuous, slow, lazy, angry, savage* or *regular*. Maigret smokes *slowly, tranquilly, gravely, blissfully, dreamily, peacefully, with an easy-going air, with a dreamy air,* or he draws on his pipe *softly*. But he also sometimes smokes *nervously, savagely, with a sullen air,* or even *joyously*: "*Maigret smoked his first pipe with an unadulterated joy*" (*Maigret*, MAI: 9). But it can also happen that, in the midst of a "tornado" of events, the Chief Inspector can even forget to smoke (believe it or not!).

We will soon come to the end of the ceremony; the tobacco is consumed, the ritual will be consummated. Often, the pipe goes out by itself, for Maigret has allowed the ritual to be accomplished without any action on his part. Or, caught up by an event, by his ruminations, he *lets his pipe go out*. But since, in fact, the ritual *should* be accomplished, Maigret is free to relight his cold pipe, to lead his investigation to its conclusion. "*Then, for the first time, we see the Chief Inspector embarrassed. He stuffed a pipe, lit it, let it go out.... He relit his pipe, to give himself time to reflect*" (*Un crime en Hollande*, HOL: 11).

Final step: The Mass is said, the nave is empty; Maigret empties his pipe, but he doesn't hesitate to fill another, because the ceremony is without end, infinitely repeatable (as we often read in the texts, "*he filled a new pipe*"). Maigret empties his pipe almost anywhere; in the coal scuttle in Judge Coméliau's office in *Pietr le Letton*; in the fireplace (at the Mayor's in *Le chien jaune*, at Grandmaison's in *Le port des brumes*, and Mlle Decaux's in *Maigret se trompe*); in an ashtray (at Ducrau's in *L'écluse n° 1*, Little John's in *Maigret à New York*, Mme Boursicault's in *Maigret en meublé*, the doctor's office in *Maigret et le clochard*, at the Nahour's in *Maigret et l'affaire Nahour*, Parendon's in *Maigret hésite*, and in his house at Meung [we can well imagine that Mme Maigret wouldn't permit her husband to empty his pipe on the floor!], and— even so!—in his own office, though at the PJ, he sometimes prefers the sawdust of the spittoons and above all, the coal bucket). To empty his pipe, Maigret most often taps the bowl against his heel, without worrying about the ashes falling on the rug (at Popinga's in *Un crime en Hollande*, Dandurand's in *Cécile est morte*, Forlacroix's in *La maison du juge*, the Le Cloaguens' in *Signé Picpus*, and at the hotel in *Maigret et la vieille dame*) or on the floor (in Big Louis's boat in *Le port des brumes*, in the Peeters's store in *Chez les Flamands*, at Laget's in *La fenêtre ouverte*, in the inspectors' office in *Les caves du Majestic* and *Maigret chez le ministre*, in Moers's laboratory in *Maigret et son mort* and *Maigret et la jeune morte*, and in Saint-Hilaire's office in *Maigret et les vieillards*). Sometimes, he taps his pipe against the window sill, as in his office or that of the Director of the PJ... "*And Maigret emptied his pipe with little taps against the window sill, so that the ashes fell somewhere on the quay, perhaps on some passerby's hat."* (*Stan le Tueur,* sta: 2).

PIPES IN RELATIONSHIPS

Maigret's relationships with others are often set under the sign of the pipe, which becomes a kind of symbol of these exchanges. Maigret smokes— or doesn't—in someone's presence, depending on his mood, the person before him, and his feelings for them; he *"hesitated to light his pipe"* before certain women (Mme Gallet in *Monsieur Gallet décédé,* Arlette in *Maigret et la vieille dame,* Mme Lognon in *Maigret, Lognon et les gangsters,* Mme Cuendet in *Maigret et le voleur paresseux,* Aline Bauche in *La patience de Maigret*), sometimes awaits, or requests, permission to smoke. Keeping his pipe in his mouth or not, taking it out, can be synonymous with a change of attitude towards a person. Thus, in *La nuit du carrefour,* at the time of his first visit to Else, *"Somewhat clumsily, he put his pipe back in his pocket, although it wasn't empty,"* while on his second visit, *"Maigret hadn't removed his pipe from his mouth."* In *Le port des brumes,* when Mme Grandmaison insists on offering cake to Maigret, *"Twice! That was too much! And Maigret almost, in protest, took his large pipe from his pocket,"* while later, at the time of their last meeting, after the death of her husband, *"He ... almost took his pipe from his pocket, shrugged his shoulders. A strange feeling of respect, of sympathy was born in him for this woman."* Not smoking his pipe can be a way of showing a sort of respect for someone. Thus, in *Chez les Flamands,* at the time of his last discussion with Anna: *"Finally the Chief Inspector put his pipe, still lit, in his pocket ... entered and reclosed the door behind him,"* and in *L'écluse n° 1,* when Maigret finds himself before Aline, who is nursing her infant, *"the Chief Inspector shoved his pipe ... his still-hot pipe, into his pocket."* In *Maigret se fâche,* with Mme Amorelle at the end of the investigation, *"as was fairly rare for him, he emptied his pipe and put it in his pocket before knocking on the door.... The gesture was simple, and yet it was like an homage to Bernadette Amorelle."*

We should give particular mention to Judge Coméliau, whose relationship with Maigret finds an original illustration in the manner in which the Chief Inspector smokes in his presence: *"Coméliau ... stared at Maigret's pipe, which he had never gotten used to. The Chief Inspector was actually the only one permitted to smoke in his office, and the judge felt a sort of defiance to it"* (*Maigret tend un piège,* TEN: 1). And in *Maigret et le corps sans tête* (COR: 4), the famous scene where Maigret is trying to explain the Calas affair to the judge is punctuated by Maigret's play with his pipe: *"Maigret had hesitated to take his pipe from his pocket, something that happened in fairly few places, and when he'd done so, he took on the innocent air of someone whose fingers are unconsciously operating while he's talking."* Further, *"Without seeming to, Maigret had his tobacco pouch in his left hand just awaiting the slightest inattention of the speaker to fill his pipe."* And finally, *"The trick was accomplished. A match had emitted a brief glow and Maigret's pipe was lit. Coméliau, who hated tobacco, stared at it, as each time Maigret had the nerve to smoke in his chambers, but the Chief Inspector had already decided to maintain his innocent air."* A similar scene takes place in the office of the Prefect in *Maigret se défend* (DEF: 1)—the confrontation between Maigret and the Prefect is punctuated by the Chief Inspector's use of his pipe. *"Maigret was at his grouchiest, and played with an empty pipe without daring to fill it."* Further, *"This time Maigret decided, and, teeth clenched, filled his pipe."* Still further, *"The match cracked and surprised the young man."* And finally, *"his fingers turned white with his grip on his extinguished pipe."*

Maigret's decision to smoke or not in a certain place depends a lot on his mood, his relationship with the place, and the stage of his investigation… *"Maigret was used to smoking anywhere, but not in the château! That was a place apart, which, throughout his youth, had represented what was the most inaccessible!"* (*L'affaire Saint-Fiacre*, FIA: 2). We find in *La vieille dame de Bayeux* numerous very characteristic examples: Maigret at the Deligeards', *"It was what he called a 'pipeless affair,' an investigation which took place in areas where the Chief Inspector couldn't decently keep his throat-burner in his mouth. That was why he was still smoking a little, before going in… 'This ought to be fun!' he sighed, tapping the bowl of his pipe against his heel;"* Maigret in conversation with Deligeard, who is telling of Cécile's lover, *"Either Maigret's indignation was real, or it was acted perfectly. It's true that he profited by taking his pipe from his pocket with a perfectly innocent air, as if he had forgotten the luxurious surroundings in which he found himself."* Further on, *"Maigret was at the Public Prosecutor's, a Maigret calm and ironic who played with his pipe in his pocket, since the Caen prosecutor wasn't the sort to let him smoke in his office."* Maigret learns that Deligeard is already in the prosecutor's office… *"A funny smile crossed Maigret's lips, and he didn't hesitate to fill his pipe."* Then he enters the prosecutor's office… *"Maigret shoved his lit pipe into his pocket."* In the prosecutor's office, where Maigret has shown him Deligeard's culpability, *"Maigret, as if unconsciously, but perhaps with some malicious pleasure, set himself to filling his pipe while pacing the office."*

Finally, we recall that the entire short story *La pipe de Maigret* revolves around the theft of his pipe by a young man who wants to emulate him. *"Maigret's pipe, well! And, you know, Maigret said these words with the certain satisfaction of a man whose pride was somehow agreeably tickled. Someone had stolen his pipe, like they might have swiped a famous writer's pencil"* (pip: 5).

As for Mme Maigret, she understood well her husband's need to smoke his pipe. And if she grumbled a little because she wished he'd smoke a little less, she knew well that she couldn't stop him, and, out of need, it's she who fills his pipe or holds his matches, particularly when he's bedridden: "*She scurried around the apartment, content ... asking from time to time, 'A pipe?'*" (*Pietr le Letton*, LET: 19). In *Le fou de Bergerac* (FOU), Mme Maigret is at the bedside of her wounded husband. She says to the doctor, "*There is one thing you must forbid him—his pipe! ... like the beer!*" Maigret, to his wife, "*Now, if you would be so kind, please fill me a pipe*" and further along, "*And, in a tender voice, he mumbled, his eyes half closed, 'Give me a pipe anyway!'*" And later, "*Mme Maigret ... came to sit next to the bed, mechanically picked up his empty pipe which she set herself to filling.*" And again, "*She had to fill his pipes for him, because he was unable to use his left arm, so she took advantage of it to make him cut back!*" We find the same sort of scenario in *Le témoignage de l'enfant de chœur*, where, this time, Maigret is in bed with the flu, and tries various ways to "swindle some pipes." "*Mme Maigret kept watch over him fiercely to prevent him from smoking his pipe,*" "'*Don't you think I could smoke just a couple of puffs on my pipe?' 'Are you crazy?,'*" "'*I know that at first you'll refuse, but it's indispensable.... Pass me my pipe and tobacco.... Just a few puffs.... She went to get his pipe on the mantle and gave it to him, resigned, with a sigh, 'I knew you'd find a good reason....'*'" The scenario becomes so familiar that Mme Maigret and her husband repeat it over time. Here, in *La première enquête de Maigret*, when Maigret is in bed following a blow he received to his head: "'*Will you give me a pipe?' 'You think you should?' 'Did the doctor say I can't smoke?' 'He didn't mention it.' 'Well, then...' she sets herself to filling a pipe, offers it to him, along with a match.*"

Maigret is a pipe smoker, as is Simenon as well, and that explains at once their meeting, their close relationship, and their more and more similar attitudes towards life. As proof, these few extracts from *Les mémoires de Maigret* (MEM): Simenon to Maigret, "*I see you too are a pipe smoker. I like pipe smokers.*" "*He [Simenon] smoked his pipe gravely, as if to add ten years to his age, to put himself on equal footing with the middle-aged man that I was then.*" Maigret to Simenon, "*Do you know that as the years go by your way of walking, of smoking your pipe, even of speaking are like 'your' Maigret?*"

Maigret's World of Sensations

In leading an investigation, Maigret supports his intuitions and his technique of immersing himself in an atmosphere, with an apprehension of the world via his senses; the Chief Inspector functions in a world of colors, sounds, odors and tastes, and various tactile impressions as well—the heat of the sun on his skin, the wet of the rain…

CHARACTERS IN COLOR

Colors have their importance in the setting of the action, helping to render an atmosphere, to illuminate sensations and impressions. Sometimes the color of a landscape is also a reflection of the "psychological atmosphere" of the moment: "*The sky, in unison with their consciences and moods, was a neutral gray, almost the same gray as the pavement* " (*Les scrupules de Maigret*, SCR: 1).

And colors also play an important role in Maigret's reactions to the characters he meets; how these inherent physical characteristics (color of hair, eyes, skin) "speak" to the Chief Inspector, who gleans from them a psychological aspect. We find that blondness can reveal a certain fragility, as that of Aline Gassin in *L'écluse n° 1*, Alain Lagrange in *Le revolver de Maigret*, Pierrot in *Maigret se trompe*, Jacques Pétillon in *Félicie est là*, or Justin Minard in *La première enquête de Maigret*. Similarly, blue eyes often indicate a certain spirit of innocence (those of Justin Minard in *La première enquête de Maigret*, of Dieudonné Pape, whose eyes reflect "*gentleness and timidity*" (*Maigret et le corps sans tête*), Judge Ancelin in *La patience de Maigret*, with his "*ingenuous blue eyes*"). Redheads with blue eyes are often psychologically fragile characters who attract Maigret's sympathy, as Prosper Donge (*Les caves du Majestic*) with his carrot red hair, Meurant (*Maigret aux assises*), Dr. Mélan (*Maigret se défend*), and Frans Steuvels (*L'amie de Madame Maigret*).

The "social" aspect of characters may be suggested by their clothing color, permitting us to assign them a likely social status. Consider the sad and dull gray, allowing a character to blend into the environment, the all-purpose gray, the gray of the humble and poorly-paid, the gray of the colorless, like the "*dark gray*" of Emile Gallet's coat (*Monsieur Gallet, décédé*) or the "*mouse gray*" of Lognon's suits (*Maigret et la jeune morte*). Red can be a color of seduction and temptation, the young girls and young women with "little red hats." "*Her red hat made her as sparkling as the spring*" (*Mademoiselle Berthe et son amant*, ber: 1). And we note a strange or unusual green, as we find in *Pietr le Letton's* coat, "*a green plaid traveling coat, of which the cut and the color were clearly Nordic*," in the "*ridiculous scarf of a much-too-bright green*" of Inspector Méjat (*La maison du juge*), in the "*spinach green*" dress of the concierge (*L'ami d'enfance de Maigret*). We find mauve in the clothing worn by middle-aged women, and those who use it to display their dignity, concealing at the same time a certain moral severity. Consider Mme Gallet, *"already armed with a mauve silk dress"* (*Monsieur Gallet, décédé*) or Mme Leroy, *"What color was her dress? Black, with mauve trim. One of those dresses worn by older women seeking distinction"* (*La pipe de Maigret*).

A POLICEMAN LISTENING

Maigret uses sounds in his own way, absorbing them as he imbibes atmospheres, and it's the hidden sides of things, what the sounds say about the beings he crosses and the places in which he immerses himself, which interest him. While it often seems as if he's not listening at all, in reality he's soaking it all in, merging with an atmosphere. More than what's said, it's the tone of voice he's sensitive to, more than the words, it's their meanings that interest him, and he only reacts to the sounds of a setting that tell him something about those who people it. Which is why we may find him installed in a café, listening to the conversations going on around him, imbibing the atmosphere of the place to understand its essence. In that, he's probably a reflection of his creator, also one to soak up the places he frequented, to extract their spirit in his writings. Here, for example, is Maigret in Ouistreham (*Le port des brumes*, POR: 13): *"A Maigret well-seated on a straw chair, pipe in his mouth, a glass of beer in his hand, listening to stories told around him by men in rubber boots and sailor's hats."* In *Le pendu de Saint-Pholien* (PHO: 7), the scene in which Maigret goes into the café to find the former "Companions of the Apocalypse," and observes their reactions; attentive to those around him, he literally feels them live: *"From time to time, Maurice Belloir swallowed, and Maigret had no need to look at him to be certain. He could hear him live, breathe, tense, cautiously move his feet."*

Maigret is very attentive to tone of voice, giving him clues about feelings and moods, how people react to their contact with him. Thus the *"drawling, hoarse, vulgar, but self-confident"* voice of the garage owner Oscar (*La nuit du carrefour*), the *"low, beautiful voice, deep and warm, made even sweeter by a slight Flemish accent"* of Mme Peeters (*Chez les Flamands*), Judge Forlacroix's *"dull little voice"* (*La maison du juge*), or the *"dry, cold, intentionally impersonal"* voice of Judge Coméliau (*Maigret et son mort*).

Maigret tracks, in the silence of locations and characters, the unsaid, the feelings, the significance of which will help him advance his investigation. But silence is also a weapon used by the Chief Inspector, when he becomes heavy, impermeable, opposing a mass of silence against the agitation of a witness or an accused. In *La maison du juge* (JUG: 9), silence punctuates the *"third degree"* that Maigret is giving Albert Forlacroix. The silences of Albert, marking his refusal to "sit down at the table," are countered by the actions and attitudes of Maigret: "*Silence. A heavy look from Maigret.... More silence. The town hall had, as usual, prepared bottles of wine on the table and Maigret poured himself a drink.... Silence. A new pipe. Some more coal in the stove.*" Here, the final scene of the interrogation in *L'inspecteur Cadavre* (CAD: 8), is characteristic of the "methods" of Maigret: "*Only at this point, and for the first time since he'd become involved in this case, did he 'play Maigret,' as was said at the Police Judiciaire.... Pipe in his teeth, hands in his pockets, back to the fire, he talked, growled, poked at the logs with the end of the tongs, and moved with a bear-like gait from one suspect to the other, either firing questions or suddenly breaking off and leaving a disturbing silence.*"

THE ODORS OF THE WORLD

Someone once wrote that Simenon was a "nose-novelist," referring to his ability to absorb the odors of things and weather, and through his descriptions, to make them perceptible to the reader. We might say as well that Maigret is a "nose-Chief Inspector," for he too is very sensitive to odors, not to mention that his working "method" is to *sniff, to absorb the scent*, the atmosphere of a location. His creator himself compared him to a bloodhound on the trail of the truth: "*Like a hunting dog, he needed to nose around in person, scratching, sniffing the odors*" (*Mon ami Maigret*, AMI: 6). Maigret is particularly sensitive to the odors of the locations he investigates; when he arrives on the scene, he begins to "sniff," literally and figuratively, the atmosphere of his surroundings. The smells of a place lead him to imagine the people who have been there, their behavior and their actions. Maigret is very sensitive to the odors of houses, and he has said, "*the primary characteristic of a home is its smell*" (*L'ombre chinoise*, OMB: 4), that "*each house has its smell*" (*Liberty Bar*, LIB: 1). The odor of a house tells much about those who live there; the smells of the "*old bachelor, the stale pipe smoke, the soiled underwear,*" which "*blended with a sickly, loathsome smell*" at Dandurand's (*Cécile est morte*, CEC: 1st part: 3, 4).

Often an odor acts like a reminiscence, like that of country houses, like those of the house at Meung-sur-Loire, which brought together all of Maigret's memories. "*It was cool in the house, where there was a good odor of polish, of cut hay, of fruits ripening and food simmering. That smell was that of his childhood, of his parents' house, and it had taken Maigret fifty years to rediscover it*" (*Maigret se fâche*, FAC: 1).

Among the memories of his apprenticeship in the hotels division, and those of young Sim arriving in Paris, it's the smell of dirt, of poverty, of questionable things, which dominate Maigret's visits to hotels. It is, for example, the odor of the *Hôtel Beauséjour*, Boulevard des Batignolles, where Jean-Luc Bodard lived (*L'ami d'enfance de Maigret*, ENF: 5), whose description suggests a curious collapsing of the memories of Maigret and his creator... *"From the dimly lit hallway, Maigret recognized the odor, for at the time of his arrival in Paris, he'd lived in the same kind of hotel in Montparnasse, the Hôtel de la Reine Morte.... It was a smell of warm sheets, of lives crammed together...."*

Another place Maigret loves to frequent for its smells is the market, where he also likes the colors, all of it evoking for him culinary memories... *"He'd always loved markets, the smell of the vegetables and fruits, the sight of quarters of beef, the fish, the lobsters still alive..."* (*Maigret à Vichy*, VIC: 1). The odors of bistros, cafés and restaurants are among those Maigret most likes to sniff. The aroma of tasty simmered dishes, fragrances of little white wines, of Calvados or a foamy beer, leave Maigret filled with delight; scents of *choucroute* in the brasseries, or *"a fragrant whiff in which lingered for him the quintessential Parisian dawn, the smell of café crème, of warm croissants, with a slight hint of rum "* (*Cécile est morte*, CEC: 1st part: 1). And then there are all the smells of the *Brasserie Dauphine*, *"among the odors always floating in the air of the brasserie, there were two which dominated the others ... that of pernod, around the bar, and that of coq au vin which came in puffs from the kitchen"* (*Maigret et le corps sans tête*, COR: 6).

FLAVORS AND IMPRESSIONS OF TASTE

Food, as we know, plays an important role for Maigret. Not only because it represents an oral pleasure, synonymous with symbolic rumination, but also because it's an important part of the world of odors, and of the world of flavors to which it is linked. The smells of food—Maigret sniffs them everywhere, in markets, shops, restaurants, his apartment... And these odors, which blend the flavors and tastes, are also an important reflection of his memories (see *Maigret's favorite meals* below)

Maigret is sensitive to the smell of drinks, of which some are particularly dear to him ... the anise seed smell of *aperitifs*, the fragrances of *eau-de-vie*, and above all, the smell of coffee, which both reminded him of his childhood and the tender attentions of his wife, waking him in the morning with a cup. (*see Drinks—an array of beverages* below)

But he also likes the sourish taste of white wine, the sharp taste of *choucroute*, and the crispy taste of fries.

And the flavor of the air is important to Maigret, its flavors differing according to the seasons: *"the air smelled strongly of spring, with puffs so warm and fragrant"* (*Mademoiselle Berthe et son amant,* ber: 2). In summer, *"The air was tasty like fruit, with cool puffs against a warm background"* (*Maigret se fâche,* FAC: 5) In winter, *"cold air, tasty, which you could drink like spring water"* (*La maison du juge;* JUG: 3). And again, the *"dusty flavor"* of the fog, the flavor of the rain, *"so fresh and flavorful that, from time to time, he stuck out his tongue to snap up a couple of drops, which had a special taste"* (*Maigret tend un piège,* TEN: 2). Or the flavor of the snow... *"[Maigret] wanted to stick out his tongue to catch one of those tiny flakes floating in the air, with the dull taste he remembered "* (*Un Noël de Maigret,* noe: 2).

SENSATIONS ON THE SKIN

Maigret also apprehends the world around him by collecting tactile impressions; his skin absorbs the warmth or coolness of the air, the moisture of the fog or rain, and the descriptions of these sensations are particularly eloquent for the reader, who is able to "feel" these impressions himself: *"There was still a bright sun, but with a dry little coldness that sent steam from your mouth, and froze your fingertips"* (*L'amie de Madame Maigret,* MME: 3); *"The water fell in bursts, icy, whipping your face and hands, sticking your wet clothes to your body"* (*Maigret et le tueur,* TUE: 1); *"Maigret ... was bathed in warmth, his skin moist and voluptuous as only under the first suns of April"* (*L'écluse n° 1,* ECL: 1); *"He had taken a few steps in the darkness, in the fog which clung to his skin like an ice pack"* (*L'inspecteur Cadavre,* CAD: 7); *"Outside, the cold became even more biting, and the flakes, tiny and hard, almost invisible in the halo of the streetlamps, stung your skin, where they seemed to want to imbed themselves"* (*Les scrupules de Maigret,* SCR: 6).

Maigret's Drinks—An Array of Beverages

At the Quai des Orfèvres they'd teased him about this habit. If, for example, he began an investigation with Calvados, he'd continue with Calvados, so that there'd been cases on beer, cases on red wine, and even a few on whisky [Maigret se trompe, TRO: 7].

If a good part of Maigret's investigations have been "beer cases," certain others have been a veritable "orgy" of alcoholic diversity. For example, in *Liberty Bar,* Maigret absorbs successively an anise aperitif, whisky, vermouth, wine, *gentian,* rum, an unidentified drink, beer, and even a bottle of Vittel (mineral water), which is probably useful to help handle all that! In *Maigret,* the list isn't bad either—marc brandy, beer, Armagnac, white wine, Champagne, red wine, brandy and water, Pernod, Calvados, rum and—Vittel!

Among the "Calvados cases," we note *Maigret et la vieille dame.* The "brandy cases" are often those where Maigret investigates in bars or nightclubs, as for example, *Maigret au Picratt's.* An example of a "white wine case" is *Maigret en meublé,* where Maigret often goes to drink at the Auvergnat near Mlle Clément's boarding house. "Pernod cases" bring to mind the heat typical of summer days, as in *Maigret et la Grande Perche.* The "whisky cases" often have an American connection (for example *Maigret, Lognon et les gangsters*). We also find "grog cases," as when Maigret is down with the flu, as in *Maigret et le marchand de vin.*

In the last part of the Maigret saga, Simenon more frequently makes reference to the health of his aging Chief Inspector, and in particular his drinking habits. Even before the Chief Inspector's stay in Vichy, Dr. Pardon had warned him about excess, suggesting that he drink a little less, an injunction not so easy to follow for Maigret, who finds in drink—and in food—a source of inspiration to resolve his cases.

BEER

"He treated himself to a glass of beer. He'd promised Dr. Pardon not to overdo it. But could you call it overdoing it to drink, over the course of a day, three glasses of draft beer?" "Maigret drank his beer. The first of the day. He counted them. When he'd meet Pardon, he'd tell him the numbers, not without pride." (Maigret et l'homme tout seul, SEU: 1, 2)

Indispensible accompaniment to the sandwiches of interrogations, and of *choucroute* in brasseries, thirst quencher for summer days, imbibed while leaning on a zinc counter, beer is the first drink mentioned in the saga, and the most frequently consumed by Maigret in his investigations. The overall average number of beers per novel across all the texts is three. If we consider this as a function of publishing periods, we find it at 2.5 for Fayard, 5 for Gallimard, and almost 3 for Presses de la Cité. Which is to say, the novels of the Gallimard period are an epoch where Simenon had his Chief Inspector drinking heavily (did the privations of war at the time of writing, increase the writer's craving?), and, on the other hand, despite his good intentions, Maigret does not drink much less, in fact, no less at all, during the last years of his investigations. In a third of the novels, Maigret drinks more than three beers per novel (more often, four or five), and there are very few novels in which Maigret drinks no beer at all. Finally, we can note one more amusing thing: the novel *Maigret et l'homme tout seul* is one of those where Maigret imbibes the most beer, while paradoxically, he spends his time being careful not to drink too much. If you examine the text in detail, it's no less than

10 beers (!) that Maigret drinks in this novel: three on the first day of the case, two the second, one on the fourth, one on the fifth, and three on the eighth. On his behalf, we can admit that he never surpassed the daily average dose of three that he had decided on.

FRUIT BRANDIES (*EAUX-DE-VIE*)

Maigret's choices are rather eclectic at the beginning of the saga. From the Fayard period until the beginning of the Presses de la Cité period, he consumes "*fil-en-six*," *mirabelle, genièvre, gentiane* and kummel. Then, after *L'amie de Madame Maigret*, the Chief Inspector generally drinks *prunelle*, the sloe brandy his wife gets from her family in Alsace, and that consumption will usually be "domestic," it's something he drinks at home, in his apartment on Boulevard Richard-Lenoir. As if the consumption of these brandies was under the authority of his wife, the *prunelle*, a family product, was necessarily of high quality. But it's also a sort of ritual that Maigret observes during the course of his investigations, which consists of him taking a little glass of alcohol from the buffet in the dining room before leaving the warmth of his family home to plunge once more into his investigation. The *prunelle* is an emblem of the security of his home, a reassuring object, a symbol of everyday life, when Maigret is plunging into an unknown world. Thus, in *Les scrupules de Maigret*, after Maigret has scanned numerous psychiatric works to try to understand the case of Marton, "*In the end, he rose, having had enough, tossed the book on the table and, opening the buffet in the dining room, brought out the carafe of prunelle, and filled one of the little glasses with the gilt edges. It was like a protest of good sense against all the learned mumbo-jumbo, a way of once more planting his two feet firmly on the ground*" (SCR: 3).

We recall that in *Les mémoires de Maigret*, Louise had insisted that her husband make a certain correction: "*Simenon spoke of a certain bottle which we always had on our buffet at the Boulevard Richard-Lenoir ... and which my sister-in-law brought us from Alsace on her annual visit. He wrote carelessly that it was prunelle. Now this was raspberry brandy. And for an Alsacien, that was, apparently, a serious difference*" (MEM: 8). Alas! No offense to Louise, and in spite of the correction made by her husband Jules, he continued, nevertheless, to imbibe the *prunelle*, for apparently Simenon was not too upset by Mme Maigret's remark; indeed, it's always *prunelle* that the Chief Inspector drinks in the novels which follow *Les mémoires* and, in *Une confidence de Maigret*, it's *prunelle* that Mme Maigret puts in the *coq au vin*, while the raspberry only appears in two novels. But perhaps the key to the puzzle is given us in *Maigret et le voleur paresseux*, where Maigret finds in his buffet both the raspberry *and* the *prunelle*. And if the buffet contains these two, it contains also, according to other novels, Calvados. And if Maigret, after all, preferred *prunelle* to raspberry? In reality, we'll find an answer in *Maigret et le marchand de vin*: "*Towards noon, Maigret murmured, hesitantly, 'I think I'm going to have myself a glass of prunelle.' She didn't object, and he opened the buffet. He had a choice between prunelle and raspberry brandy. Both came from his sister-in-law in Alsace. The raspberry was more fragrant…*" (VIN: 5)

ARMAGNAC

As Jacques Sacré has written, in his book, *Bon appétit, commissaire Maigret*, Armagnac "*appears as a noble alcohol, taken only on certain occasions or in certain locales*," and so its consumption by the Chief Inspector is somewhat less than that of the other "strong drinks," like cognac, Calvados, and marc. Very seldom present in the Fayard novels, it is then regularly imbibed in the Gallimard and Presses de la Cité periods, slowing down towards the end of the saga, the state of his health and the age of the Chief Inspector being probable causes, not to mention the benevolent recommendations of his friend Pardon.

In *Maigret*, the Chief Inspector takes an Armagnac with Amadieu, and this drink provokes "*a gentle feeling of well-being, giving the sensation that all his accumulated fatigue was gradually dissolving*," alcohol as therapy, in a way. A "deluxe" Armagnac is the one Maigret has in the company of Forlacroix in *La maison du juge*; Armagnac, a noble alcohol, is symbolic for this distinguished-looking judge, who lives in a harmonious house: "*From a Renaissance chest, he removed a silver platter, a decanter, and some crystal glasses, and these objects, under the well-calculated lighting, gave off sumptuous reflections, providing an atmosphere of refined peace and comfort*" (JUG: 2). Another old Armagnac in *Cécile est morte*, providing a grand finale to the dinner at Mélanie's, a fine Armagnac, since the *patron* who proposes it to them is a native of Gers and is provided by the vintners of his district. The alcohol plunges the Chief Inspector—and his guest, the American criminologist—into a state of well-being, permitting them to savor relaxedly Juliette Boynet's letters. "*They were blissfully hot. The Armagnac perfumed the air and their palates.*"

But, little by little, especially towards the end of the Presses de la Cité period, Armagnac seems to have lost its attraction for the Chief Inspector. Thus, in *Le voleur de Maigret*, it's without pleasure that he drinks it, and the quotations speak volumes: "*You'll accept, at least, an old Armagnac? He had* to accept." "Had he perhaps drunk too much, him too? In any case, he couldn't finish his enormous glass of Armagnac." And if he accepts a last glass at Parendon's (*Maigret hésite*), it's with a certain restriction… "What can I offer you? My cognac isn't famous but I have a 40-year old Armagnac…." "Very little, please…" Decidedly, Armagnac has fallen out of favor. But was it ever really in? As noted above, this, by far, of the four strong alcohols consumed by Maigret, is the one least favored, Maigret preferring Calvados, and above all, cognac. So it's not so surprising that he gives this response to Parendon, who has remarked on the poor quality of his cognac. Lacking cognac, he drinks— but not too much—Armagnac.

COGNAC

This is the strong alcohol most often consumed by Maigret, either as cognac or fine, the two terms apparently designating the same drink. Besides being Maigret's preferred strong alcohol, it has a special function, which Paul Mercier has so well demonstrated in his book *La botte secrète de Maigret: le verre de cognac*: that of an auxiliary in the interrogation of a suspect. "The secret weapon" is contained in a bottle in the famous closet in Maigret's office at the PJ. We'll say no more about the subject, but refer you to Paul Mercier's book.

CALVADOS

Another alcohol Maigret likes is Calvados, with its touch of earthy tang. However, the meeting of Maigret and Calvados got off to a rather bad start…. The first *calva* that the Chief Inspector imbibed was in *La nuit du carrefour*, at the inn in Avrainville. The pitiful meal served by the *patron* was crowned with a "*synthetic Calvados*" with nothing to recommend it. Maigret didn't touch it again until the end of the Fayard period, and, in *Maigret*, the Calvados at the Tabac Fontaine was just one second-rate among others. For variety, Maigret "*had drunk all kinds of drinks, beer, coffee, Calvados, and Vittel water.*" A *calva* washed down with Vittel water doesn't suggest too much quality of the alcohol. This is no doubt the reason this drink will never have the prestige of Armagnac, nor the essentiality of cognac, but will long remain much more functional, serving as a simple after-dinner drink, or a glass taken on the go, or forming a part of the collection of liqueurs in the buffet at the Boulevard Richard-Lenoir, awaiting the *prunelle*.

It's from *La première enquête de Maigret* that Calvados will take on another function, serving as a tool for the Chief Inspector to imbibe during a case; it's in this novel that he experiments for the first time with the "trick," that he'll develop, a technique he'll use again later, being assisted by other drinks as well. Installed on the Rue Chaptal, at the well-named *Vieux Calvados*, the young Maigret begins his first stakeout by drinking cider. If this drink is lighter than a strong alcohol, it has nonetheless a certain effect... "*He'd never drunk cider for breakfast. This was his first experience and, contrary to his expectations, his chest was pervaded with warmth.*" Convinced by the result, he lets himself get carried away by other temptations, and accepts—rather easily—moving to something more serious. He doesn't protest when Paumelle pours him a Calvados, no more than he refuses to renew the experience every half hour of the morning. After the third glass, the Calvados begins to take effect. "*He began to feel comfortable, and even rather perky.*" For that matter, he continues, "*Calvados! There was nothing else to do. He'd stay with it to the end.*" At the end of the day, after having a cider again, "*Maigret felt hazy, after all those Calvados of the day,*" he discovered for the first time the magical effect this imbibing brought about. "*However, after a moment of low spirits in the afternoon ... perhaps caused by the difficulty of absorbing all those little drinks since the morning, Maigret felt more composed. Something was happening in him that he didn't yet recognize, and he never suspected that the 'trigger' which had been produced would become so familiar that it would one day be legendary at the Quai des Orfèvres. It was hardly more than a comfortable warmth throughout his body, a slightly more intent way of walking, of looking at people, the light and shadow, the carriages and streetcars around him*" (PRE: 4).

Calvados's origins, tied to the soil, makes it an alcohol with a specific social stamp, plebian, as opposed to other more "aristocratic" spirits, "*Maigret had taken a Calvados after his dinner, intentionally, perversely, for he was going to be plunged into a world where Calvados is hardly drunk, let alone marc. Whisky, champagne, fine Napoléon*" (*Maigret voyage*). From *marc* to *whisky*, a social scale which is symbolically represented by the alcohols consumed at each level.

MARC

It's consumed by Maigret slightly more often than Armagnac, but less than Calvados. It's the little glass you take to fortify yourself, like the glass of brandy Maigret offers his nephew come to seek his assistance in *Maigret*, "*First off, you'll have something to drink. His uncle took the bottle of brandy and two glasses from the cupboard... 'To your health! Above all, try to calm down a little'*" (MAI: 1). Marc, like Calvados, and perhaps even more so, is socially marked. It's the alcohol of the people, of the rural world. Maigret often drinks it when he's on a case in the provinces. And the consumption is often more than one glass, so that the smell of the place permeates, the unique odor of a little provincial café. "*It was hot. The little glasses had been refilled three or four times, and an odor of marc mixed with the smell of the pipes.*" (*La maison du juge*, JUG: 8).

A striking example is found in *L'affaire Saint-Fiacre*. Maigret, during his first visit to the steward Gautier, is offered a glass from "*a bottle of marc whose label proclaimed its venerable age.*" This venerability, which authenticates the taste of the alcohol, contrasts nonetheless with the whisky the Chief Inspector had just drink at the château with Maurice de Saint-Fiacre. And this contrast is doubly symbolic. At the château, they drank *whisky*, at the steward's, *marc*. But even more interesting, the whisky at the château was "imported" by Jean Métayer, for "*In my time, there was no whisky at the château.*" says Maurice de Saint-Fiacre, while the marc, although lower on the social scale, "*dates from the former count*," the steward tells Maigret. This inversion of the origins of the two alcohols marks symbolically the sociological upheaval which has occurred at the château, that the true master, Maurice de Saint-Fiacre, has deserted, ceding his place to the young secretary/gigolo. And, underlying everything is also the idea that the steward has appropriated the "*patron's reserves*" (since it's a bottle of *venerable marc of the former count*), he has covertly bought the farms of the domain, building himself a fortune on the ruins of Saint-Fiacre.

WHISKY

Whisky, as said above, is the "brand" at the top of the social scale. So for the plebian Maigret it is not his favorite drink. He only consumes it under certain circumstances, with certain people, in certain situations. Whisky is also the cosmopolitan label, travel, foreign things. The first occasion for Maigret to drink whisky is at a bar—American, as it should be—La Coupole, with the Crosby couple (*La tête d'un homme*). Next, he has it at the mayor of Concarneau's (*Le chien jaune*), at the Château de Saint-Fiacre (*L'affaire Saint-Fiacre, see above*), at Brown's villa and at Jaja's (*Liberty Bar*), with O'Brien in New York, of course (*Maigret à New York*), with Pyke on the Blue Train (*Mon ami Maigret*), with Harry Cole in America, equally expected (*Maigret chez le coroner*), and then a whole series of glasses in *Maigret, Lognon et les gangsters* (*Indeed, when you fight against the American underworld, you use the same weapons!*). He has another at the bar in the Savoy in London (*Le revolver de Maigret*), at the bar at the George-V (*Maigret voyage*), at Norris Jonker's (*Maigret et le fantôme*), the bar of the Hôtel du Louvre (*Maigret et l'affaire Nahour*), and finally at the Batille's (*Maigret et le tueur*).

WINE

Wine is, after beer, the drink most frequently consumed by Maigret. Ranging from the little white swallowed at the corner of a bistro counter, to the great wines tasted with Dr. Pardon at their memorable dinners. For the details, see the book by Jacques Sacré, who has created a "menu of Maigret's wines."

CHAMPAGNE

Champagne is little appreciated by Maigret, who only drinks it in a few rare novels. It's often a drink which is imposed on him, and he only drinks it when he can't avoid it. Thus, in *Pietr le Letton*, at Pickwick's Bar, "*They set before him, authoritatively, a bottle of champagne.... Maigret, who hated champagne, drank it in little sips, to quench his thirst.*" (LET: 7). In *La première enquête de Maigret*, it's Dédé who forces him to drink "*flute after flute of champagne*," which doesn't stop Maigret from celebrating with "sparkling wine" his nomination to Chief Inspector Barodet's squad.

APERITIFS

The aperitif Maigret likes best is the "anise seed drink," in the form of Pernod or pastis. He sometimes drinks martinis or vermouths, and, much more rarely, absinthe, some rare cocktails, and *mandarin-curaçao*, which celebrated Maigret's nomination to Chief Inspector Guillaume's squad (*Les mémoires de Maigret*), and which Maigret drinks, as a sort of commemoration, after the Director of the PJ had placed him on "temporary leave" (*Maigret se défend*). We note that Pernod is often consumed during the fine seasons, spring or summer, as a sort of pre-vacation celebration, because of its Mediterranean evocation.

RUM

This is an alcohol that Maigret usually drinks in the form of grog, a drink which serves to warm body and soul, and a good excuse to fight off an oncoming cold or flu. Grog is drunk during rainy investigations alongside a canal or river (*Le charretier de La Providence, Chez les Flamands*), or in the fog at the edge of the sea (*Le port des brumes*); or during the autumn rains (*Maigret et l'homme du banc, Maigret se trompe, Maigret et les témoins récalcitrants, Maigret et le fantôme*), or winter frosts (*Les scrupules de Maigret, Maigret et le voleur paresseux, Maigret et le client du samedi*). We note that the last grogs that Maigret consumes are made for him by his wife (*Maigret et le tueur, Maigret et le marchand de vin*), while Maigret is coming down with a cold, the "medicinal" function seemingly recognized by Mme Maigret herself.

COFFEE

Coffee is a drink often consumed by Maigret. Drunk only occasionally in the Fayard and Gallimard novels, especially when accompanied by croissants in the guise of breakfast in a bar, or in the "watered" form (mixed with alcohol), coffee is found much more regularly in the Presses de la Cité period. On the one hand because we more often see Maigret getting out of bed, awakened by the odor of the cup of coffee prepared for him by his wife, and on the other because coffee, along with an after-dinner drink, often crowns the end of a good meal, whether at a restaurant, at home, or at the Pardons.' However, these meals are mainly confined to the second half of the saga, where they are much more often detailed.

WATER AND VARIOUS OTHER DRINKS

Mineral water is an exception—but who'd be surprised at that?—in the drinking habits of the Chief Inspector. He only drinks it in three novels.... In *Liberty Bar*, he orders a bottle of Vittel, from which we understand that he needed to cleanse his stomach, which he had filled, in a single day, with numerous glasses of vermouth, as well as wine, coffee, whisky and gentian! Once more, in *Maigret*, the Chief Inspector orders a Vittel water, after his coffee, Pernod, beer and Calvados. The third time, obviously, is in *Maigret à Vichy*, where it's the only drink he's authorized outside of coffee, after having confessed his little sins to the doctor who examined him.

> *"And wine? a half-liter, a liter a day?"*
> *"Yes... No... More... With meals, usually, I only drink two or three glasses.... At the office, sometimes a glass of beer that I have brought up from the Brasserie Dauphine..."*
> *"Aperitif?"*
> *"Often enough, with one or another of my colleagues.... In the evening, I don't mind a glass or two of prunelle that my sister-in-law sends us from Alsace..."* [VIC: 1].

In almost the same register as the water we find *tisanes*, herb tea, a drink reserved for "sick days." Maigret submits to *tisanes* prepared by his wife, in exchange for a few puffs on his pipe. Happily, he's not often really ill, and he usually succeeds at fighting off the flu with grog. Finally, we find in four novels, some unusual drinks for the Chief Inspector. First, the voyage to America requires Coca-Cola in *Maigret à New York* and *Maigret chez le coroner*, then, for more local color, cider at the Trochu's in *Maigret et la vieille dame*. And lastly, a unique *"Vichy-fraise, strawberry Vichy water, but it made him feel sick"* (*La première enquête de Maigret*), and he never tried it again. We realize that this consumption, the choice of drinks is never trivial for Maigret, but reflects the Chief Inspector's state of mind, the progress of the investigation, or the milieu into which he is plunged. And if Maigret drinks so much, particularly alcohol, we mustn't forget that he has a metaphorical need to "drink in" the world around him.

Maigret's Favorite Meals

Maigret doesn't really become a gourmet until fairly late in the saga. In the Fayard period, the Chief Inspector is usually satisfied with sandwiches, or snacks eaten on the run, and it's hardly much better in the Gallimard novels. It's actually not until the end of the Presses de la Cité period that Maigret spends much of his investigation enjoying tasty meals, and moreover, the "mythical" dishes most loved by Maigret, *blanquette de veau, choucroute, fricandeau à l'oseille, coq au vin* and *andouillette*, for the most part don't appear until the later novels.

SANDWICHES

But our Chief Inspector, if he appreciates these good dishes, is constrained by his job to being satisfied more often with sandwiches (which perhaps explains why…). This is the food most frequently mentioned in the texts. And we also find that the largest majority of these sandwiches are eaten during interrogations taking place in Maigret's office. Most of the time the sandwiches are brought up by a waiter from the Brasserie Dauphine, Joseph or Justin, carried on trays covered with *demis* of beer. The first food Maigret eats in the saga, sandwiches from the Brasserie Dauphine, appears in *Pietr le Letton*. Maigret likes them crusty, with ham or *pâté*. And the sandwich is, above all, an essential ingredient of the police interrogation. So we find in the story *L'affaire du boulevard Beaumarchais*, during a long night of interrogation, Maigret opening the door of his office, *"Lucas! … Maigret called out, looking over his inspectors like someone who couldn't see clearly. Dash out and get me some sandwiches…. Stop at the Brasserie and have them send up some demis…."* And there's the key to the puzzle: the sandwich Maigret chews, first in *"large mouthfuls,"* actually serves to clarify the mystery for him, to make the truth come out, so he can "see it clearly." To share sandwiches and beer is like sharing "bread and wine," to enter into communion with the man being interrogated, symbolically inviting him "to sit down at the table," as Maigret does with Prosper Donge in *Les caves du Majestic*, Alfred Jorisse in *Maigret et l'homme du banc*, Pierrot the musician in *Maigret se trompe*, and Adrien Josset in *Une confidence de Maigret*. The ritual "sandwiches and beer" are so much a part of his interrogations that Maigret will reproduce the setting outside of his office. So in *Maigret à New York*, in an investigation the retired Chief Inspector leads far from his old Parisian office, he recovers the memory of the ritual; having brought together Parson, Little John and Mac Gill in his hotel room to have them witness his telephone call to Daumale, he sets the scene. He orders whisky, then "*About to hang up, he changes his mind, 'Add some ham sandwiches.' Not because he was hungry, but because that was his habit at the Quai des Orfèvres and it had become like a ritual*" (NEW: 9).

BLANQUETTE DE VEAU (VEAL RAGOUT)

Maigret discovers this dish rather late, and it's only mentioned on four occasions in the texts. The *blanquette* is savored for the first time in the Brasserie Dauphine in *Un échec de Maigret*, and Maigret likes it to the extent of ordering it again in *L'ami d'enfance de Maigret* and *Maigret et le marchand de vin*, where it is "*perfectly creamy, the sauce a golden yellow, very aromatic*." And in *La folle de Maigret*, it's Mme Maigret who prepares it—she's certainly not going to let herself be outdone by the Brasserie Dauphine!

CHOUCROUTE (SAUERKRAUT)

As Jacques Sacré writes, "*Choucroute, omnipresent flower of the brasseries of Paris … accompanied, above all, by beer, plenty of beer. Choucroute, the rich and invigorating dish true to the image of the Chief Inspector.*" It's the next most often cited dish in the novels after sandwiches. *Choucroute* is also a pleasure that can be shared with all sorts of guests: an American criminologist (*Cécile est morte*), an old *clochard* (*Signé Picpus*), or certainly Lucas (*Maigret et son mort*), Lapointe (*Maigret et les braves gens*) or Mme Maigret (*L'amie de Madame Maigret*). *Choucroute* "*garnie*" is accompanied by sausages ("The beer was good, the *choucroute* possible, very possible, and he ordered another pair of sausages—too bad if it wasn't very *Grand Siècle*!" Maigret in Versailles, in *La Maison du juge*, JUG: 6). And with salt pork, it's especially delicious when it's Mme Maigret who prepares it—naturally, since she's from Alsace!

FRICANDEAU À L'OSEILLE
(VEAL LOIN WITH SORREL)

It's "*one of my favorite dishes*" says Maigret in *L'auberge aux noyés*, though we rarely see him eat it in the saga. Too tired in *Signé Picpus*, he turns it down when prepared for him by Mme Maigret, but makes up for it in *Maigret et son mort* with one prepared by Irma, and in *Maigret s'amuse* and *La folle de Maigret*, made by Mme Maigret.

COQ AU VIN
(STEWED CHICKEN IN WINE SAUCE)

Another plate to be shared with company: an American criminologist … again! (*Cécile est morte*), an American FBI agent (*Maigret à New York*), a street tough (*La première enquête de Maigret*), the Pardons (*Maigret se défend*), and Mme Maigret (*Maigret et le tueur, Maigret et l'homme tout seul*), who has moreover a little "trick" to make the dish more delicious: she replaces the traditional glass of cognac or Armagnac with plum brandy from Alsace!

ANDOUILLETTE
(SMALL SAUSAGE MADE OF CHITTERLINGS)

The meat dish most frequently cited in the texts, as Jacques Sacré writes, "*The champion is, as you'd expect, andouillette, provincial dish and pride of the Loire where Maigret likes so much to eat. Andouillette is also a classic in the little bistros of Paris, one of their trademarks.*" "Rediscovered" by Maigret in *Maigret s'amuse*, when he returns with Mme Maigret and the Pardons to a restaurant on the banks of the Marne that he'd frequented years earlier, he likes it, and orders it again in numerous novels in the remainder of the saga, accompanied by fries or mashed potatoes.

DESSERTS

Maigret isn't a great lover of sweets, preferring the invigorating force of a *pâté* sandwich or the sharp aroma of a *choucroute*. Here are, however, some of Maigret's desserts found in the texts.

Cakes and pies: a "tiny piece of almond cake" at the Hôtel de la Loire (*Monsieur Gallet, décédé*), and another almond cake at the Brasserie Dauphine (*Maigret et Monsieur Charles*); a cake served with three different kinds of cream, at the lunch at Van Hasselt's (*Un crime en Hollande*); Anna's rice tart (*Chez les Flamands*); Mélanie's mocha cake (*Cécile est morte*); the strawberry cake at a restaurant on the Place des Victoires (*La folle de Maigret*); Mme Pardon's rice cake (*Une confidence de Maigret*); the plum tart at *Chez l'Auvergnat* (*La patience de Maigret*); Dr Bresselles' sister's apple pie (*Maigret à l'école*); the marzipan tart (one of Mme Maigret's specialties) (*Ceux du Grand Café*).

Crèmes: Mme Maigret's citron cream, a "masterpiece" (*Le fou de Bergerac*), and again from her, a chocolate cream (*L'amoureux de Madame Maigret*) and a "creamy caramel crème" (*Cécile est morte*).

Pastries: Mme Chabot's *profiteroles* (*Maigret a peur*), the *mille-feuilles* eaten with Ricain (*Le voleur de Maigret*), the *baba au rhum* at a little restaurant on Rue de Miromesnil (*Maigret hésite*) and at the inn at Meung (*Maigret et le tueur*).

Other desserts: *crêpes Suzette*, eaten at Les Halles with Mr Pyke (*Mon ami Maigret*), and *œufs au lait* (*Maigret et le corps sans tête*), yet another of Mme Maigret's specialties!

Maigret's Humor

It would be a mistake to imagine that Maigret is always gruff and grouchy. Our Chief Inspector, in fact, is not lacking in humor, but his irony often escapes his listeners. Consider these examples:

In *Le notaire de Châteauneuf* (not: 1), M. Motte is trying to find a way to explain Maigret's presence at his home without revealing his true identity… "'I can't introduce you as the famous Chief Superintendent Maigret.' Maigret seldom made fun of people, and yet he couldn't resist. With the utmost seriousness he murmured: 'Shall I wear a false beard?'" A little further along, the notary tries to find a suitable name to give his guest: "*Mister what…?*" and Maigret suggests, "*Legros?*" [*maigre* = 'thin'; *gros* = 'fat, heavy'].

In *La maison du juge* (JUG: 5), Maigret, a prisoner of the rainy Vendée, waits impatiently for an urgent phone call from Nice (where it is no doubt fine and sunny!), which is slow to arrive. "*[Maigret] looked at the time…. What are they doing, these Nice guys, under their cut-out tin sun?*"

In *Maigret se fâche* (FAC: 2), Malik has dragged home a reluctant Maigret: "*…if you're so inclined, I'd love to have you spend a few days with us. Do you play tennis? Horseback riding perhaps? 'Why didn't he ask me if I played golf or went water skiing?'*"

In *Le revolver de Maigret* (REV: 6), Maigret, who has to leave for London, which has put him in a bad mood, gets a phone call from the presiding magistrate, whom he doesn't care for: "*What can you tell me?—I can tell you that I don't have time, that I'm taking a plane for London in 25 minutes.—For*

London?—Right.—But what have you discovered that...—Sorry, I have to hang up now ... the plane won't wait.... He was in such a mood that he added, 'I'll send you a postcard!' At which point, of course, he had hung up."

In *Maigret à Vichy* (VIC: 4), Maigret, who is there for the cure, has to keep to a diet, and the nourishment he's obligated to ingest hardly pleases him... "*They'd eaten the noodles which served for hors-d'œuvre and they'd just served them scallops* [nature!] *when Maigret was told he had a phone call. 'Hello!—'Is this a bad time? Are you in the midst of eating?' [Maigret] had recognized Lecoeur's voice and grumbled, 'If you can call it eating!...'*"

And we can mention for the pleasure of it, the lengthy scene in *Maigret et son mort* (MOR: 3), when Maigret, staying home because of the flu, gets a phone call from Judge Coméliau. The scene is too long to repeat in its entirety, and so we'll only offer this remarkable morsel the Chief Inspector presents to the judge, so juicy to anyone aware of Coméliau's stuffy primness. "*Tell me, your honor, did you ever happen to push a dried pea up your nose?*"

Maigret Dreams

Maigret's dreams are relatively important in the saga, and they always have a connection with the Chief Inspector's investigation at the time. They are the "mises en abyme, *the telescoping mirrors of the story of the case; they recapitulate the particulars, but regrouping the elements ... as of function of Maigret's interior life, his unconscious*" (in Els Wouters, *Maigret: «je ne déduis jamais». La méthode abductive chez Simenon*). These dreams, which grant us entry, in a way, into the thoughts of the Chief Inspector, bring him even closer and make him even more human, in what they reveal about his character. Here are the subjects of some of Maigret's dreams, drawn from the texts: In *Le fou de Bergerac*, Maigret, immobilized in bed by his wound, dreams that he's a beached seal, immobilized at the edge of the sea. In *Maigret et la jeune morte*, he dreams that he's playing chess with Lognon, "*who awaits, confidently, the opportunity to put Maigret into checkmate*," as in reality Lognon was trying to find Louise's murderer before Maigret. In *Maigret et les vieillards*, he dreams that he's a little boy surrounded by old people, when in reality he was trying to understand the bygone world which was that of Princess V. In *Maigret et les témoins récalcitrants*, the long dream where he explains to the judge about the house and life of the Lachaumes, as he would have liked to explain it in reality. And in *Maigret et le voleur paresseux*, somewhat the same sort of dream, where Maigret tries to explain the murder of Cuendet to the Prosecutor.

4

At Home

A Visit to the Maigrets' Apartment

The Quai des Orfèvres and the apartment on the Boulevard Richard-Lenoir are a like two poles between which the Chief Inspector navigates during the course of his investigations, leaving the one in the morning to go to his office, returning from the other after his day of work. At the Quai des Orfèvres, it's the daily routine of the investigation, where his faithful inspectors await him. The Boulevard Richard-Lenoir is his haven of rest, "*a bourgeois apartment where the good odors of simmering dishes await him, where everything is simple and neat, clean and comfortable*" (*Les mémoires de Maigret*, MEM: 7). On the one hand, the Quai des Orfèvres and the streets of Paris, the many places Maigret discovers in the course of his investigations, cases in unknown areas he must become familiar with; on the other, the Boulevard Richard-Lenoir, where he finds his daily life, reassuring, at the side of Mme Maigret, where he can forget the torments of his exhausting quest for a truth which sometimes eludes him: "*it was good to find once more the voice of Mme Maigret, the smells of their apartment, the furniture and things in their places*" (*Maigret a peur*, PEU: 9). We note the indispensable presence of Mme Maigret in the apartment, of which she's like the soul; as proof of which, without her, that which is the essence of the apartment no longer exists, and Maigret, in the absence of his wife, avoids entering a "*chez-lui*" which isn't one anymore. "*Maigret didn't like to stay in Paris without his wife. He ate, without appetite, in the first restaurant he came to, and he sometimes slept in a hotel to avoid going home*" (*La guinguette à deux sous*, GUI: 4); "*Was it only for the investigation that he set himself up on the Rue Lhomond, or because he hated to go back to an empty apartment?*" (*Maigret en meublé*, MEU: 2).

In the beginning of the saga, Simenon was satisfied to have his Chief Inspector merely make brief stops at home, stopping only to pick up a suitcase before departing, or just taking the time for a cup of hot coffee, without speaking with his wife. It's also true that a large portion of the Fayard novels took place outside of Paris, and so Maigret hardly had the opportunity to stop at the Boulevard Richard-Lenoir. Nonetheless, it already constituted, from this first period, a place of "R&R" that the Chief Inspector, after his odysseys in the provinces or outside the country, would return to at the end of the novel. After having described somewhat Maigret's apartment in the Gallimard period, Simenon began the Presses de la Cité period with the Chief Inspector in retirement, and so we have to wait until *Maigret et son mort* to enter further into the intimacy of the domicile of the Maigret couple. From that point, Simenon won't stop adding little descriptive touches to their Boulevard Richard-Lenoir home, this "*small and warm*" apartment, "*hushed*," with its "*slightly syrupy tranquility*," but oh so necessary to the "replenishment" of our Chief Inspector. If, most often, Maigret only stops at home at meal times, or to sleep (though these moments, as we have said, are essential for his balance), he sometimes spends more time there, as when he has the flu or when he's on vacation. The cases where he sets up a kind of "branch office," as in *Un Noël de Maigret*, are rarer, but he sometimes has visits there from "clients" he would usually see at the PJ: Jo the boxer and Ferdinand the garage owner in *Maigret et son mort*, Boubée in *La colère de Maigret*, Bureau in *Maigret et le tueur*, Pigou in *Maigret et le marchand de vin*, and Planchon in *Maigret et le client du samedi*.

So let's follow the Chief Inspector when he leaves his office. After having traversed on foot (at least in nice weather) the route which takes him home (probably strolling along the quays and then crossing the Place de la Bastille), Maigret reaches No. 132 (at least that's the address given in *Maigret et son mort*) Boulevard Richard-Lenoir. He enters the building, climbs to the fourth floor (or the fifth, depending on the novel), and the door opens before he can take his key from his pocket; Mme Maigret, without really paying attention (or at least so she makes it seem), always hears his steps on the stairs, and she's always ready to greet him.

Maigret, even before hanging up his overcoat on the coat rack in the entryway, heads for the kitchen, because "*his first concern, on reentering the apartment, no matter the time, is to go into the kitchen to uncover the pots on the stove*" (*Maigret et son mort*, MOR: 8). Then, having taken off his coat and hat, he'll probably go into the dining room, and warm his hands in the heat of the stove, installed in spite of the radiators, because Maigret has always liked stoves.

When they first moved in, the Maigrets still had no bathroom, and their little dining room served as a living room. Later, enlarging their lodgings by taking over the apartment next door gave them the possibility to install, in addition to a bathroom, a living room, complete with a fireplace. But Maigret doesn't like it, and the couple hardly ever set foot in it, only entertaining their occasional visitors there, preferring the dining room where they welcome their close friends and family. *"It was there that Maigret had his pipes and his armchair, and Mme Maigret her sewing machine"* (*Le revolver de Maigret*, REV: 1). It's in this dining room, separated from the living room by a glass door, that we discover a round table, lit by a hanging lamp. The furniture is rustic, dark oak, dating from the time of their marriage. And there's a pendulum clock in a dark oak case, with a copper pendulum. Maigret is usually installed in *his* armchair, near the window. Within arm's reach, on an end table, a pipe (the others in a rack), some newspapers, the telephone, and, depending on the circumstances, a cup of herbal tea for the times of cold or flu, or a little glass of sloe gin (or raspberry liqueur), that Maigret has poured from one of the carafes lined up on the dining room's glass buffet. As for Mme Maigret, she prefers to use an armless chair, feeling "trapped" by an armchair. It's also in the dining room that the Maigrets take their meals, the open window *"letting in the odors of outdoors, the familiar sounds of the Boulevard Richard-Lenoir"* (*La patience de Maigret*, PAT: 1). The meals themselves have been set to simmering—over gas heat—by Mme Maigret, in the room which is reserved for her *by definition*, the kitchen. For proof that this is Louise's domain, we find not a single description of the kitchen in the saga; as is often the case in the novels, the action is seen from Maigret's viewpoint (particularly the descriptions of places, scenery, and other atmospheric circumstances). The Chief Inspector cannot describe this kitchen to us, for he only visits it briefly when he returns home, to lift the covers of the casseroles. We never see him cook anything, nor help wash the dishes (that said, he is a typical man of his generation, that of the years about which the novels were written).

However, some modernity does arrive to the apartment. Simenon, coordinating the time of the writing with the time of the action, introduces a television into the Maigrets' apartment. Modern times change habits, and the Maigrets rearrange—a little—the set up of the rooms: the television is placed in the living room (which finds thus a certain usefulness!), and the dining room table is placed so the couple can watch while they eat. But the attraction of this novelty hardly lasts, and after having passed the stage of neophytes fascinated by everything which crosses the little screen, they become more selective, choosing a good western, skipping the variety show singers, then more often only listening to the news, and finally preferring to return to the cinema.

In the last novels of the saga, Maigret has "reconciled himself" to some extent to the living room, which, incorporating the dining room, is now set up as a larger living room, where Maigret still has his armchair, now of leather, near the window, and the room is lit by a lamp and an overhead fixture.

Besides the bathroom, there is also a guest room in the apartment, used but rarely, particularly by Mme Maigret's sister. Then a clothes cabinet and, later, a little desk that Maigret had installed. The curtains are mesh, and the windows can be covered by shades or shutters. The floor is parquet, with a rug in the dining room.

Finally, the apartment contains a bedroom, the most private place, but which is paradoxically the first room described in the saga (in *Pietr le Letton*, LET: 19), and one of the rooms where we meet the Maigret couple most often (holding aside the dining room, important as it is, since it's around meals that many of the bonds are established between Maigret and his wife). It's in the bedroom that Maigret finds his wife when he returns from a case in the middle of the night, and it's there that Louise comes to awaken him in the morning, bringing him his coffee in bed. And it's there, finally, that many of the novels begin, particularly towards the end of the saga, when Maigret is awakened in the middle of the night by the ringing of the telephone. If Simenon risks showing us, at the beginning of the novel, the Maigrets in bed; it's with, of course, all the restraint and propriety that we expect from them. Simenon never makes the slightest overt allusion to the sexuality of the couple, which exists, beyond any doubt (see for example in *Maigret s'amuse*, when Maigret recalls to his wife a certain "*little woods, in the Chevreuse valley*"), but of which the relationship is imprinted with tenderness and complicity. We understand that the Maigrets are united, and there's no need to show it further. The "*deep, serious kiss*" (*Au rendez-vous des Terre-Neuvas*) that Maigret plants on his wife's forehead before going to sleep, is sufficient for us to understand the intensity of their relationship.

In this bedroom, papered with bouquets of roses, the Maigrets sleep in a large bed with an eiderdown cover of red silk and a large feather pillow. The room also contains a mirrored armoire, and a wing-chair. It has two windows, opening on the Boulevard Richard-Lenoir, and the shutters never close tightly. On Mme Maigret's night table, the alarm clock, for she's the first to rise, to prepare her husband's coffee—we don't actually dare to suggest male chauvinism at the Maigrets, considering how Louise adores "pampering her big infant of a husband" (see *Les mémoires de Maigret,* MEM: 4). On Maigret's night table, the telephone, which he brings from the dining room to hook up in the bedroom. And if the phone doesn't ring during the night, Maigret can start his day by peacefully taking his breakfast with his wife. "*It's 8:25 in the morning, and Maigret gets up from the table finishing his last cup of coffee*" (*Maigret se trompe,* TRO: 1). A last piece of "maternal" advice from Mme Maigret... "*You haven't forgotten your umbrella?*," and Maigret is on his doorstep, Boulevard Richard-Lenoir, lighting his pipe, "*already tastier than other mornings."* There's the first fog of autumn, waiting for him to dive into a new case.

Place des Vosges

Readers of the story *L'amoureux de Madame Maigret* or the novel *Maigret se fâche* will probably be surprised to discover that the Maigrets live at the Place des Vosges. Simenon himself eventually explained this "incongruity." Indeed, in *Les mémoires de Maigret* (MEM: 8), he wrote, through the intermediary of his Chief Inspector, "*In many of his books, Simenon had us living in the Place des Vosges without furnishing the slightest explanation. It's true that for a few months we did live there. But we weren't in our own home. That year, our landlord had finally decided to undertake the renovation the building had long been in need of. They promised us it would take no longer than three weeks. After two weeks, they'd gotten nowhere, and just at that moment, the workers went on strike, and it was impossible to know how long it would last. Simenon was leaving for Africa where he planned to spend a year. "While you're waiting for the work to be finished, why not set yourselves up in my apartment in Place des Vosges?" And that's how we wound up living there, at No. 21, to be exact, without being unfaithful to our fine old boulevard.*"

Simenon might have found some pleasure in conveying the idea that the Maigrets had lived at "his house," since we find the same affirmation in *Maigret se défend* (to Vivier who gives him Mlle Motte's address, Rue des Francs-Bourgeois, Maigret replies that he knows the building, for he'd "*lived for a while quite nearby, at Place des Vosges*"). In *Maigret et le clochard* ("*During the few months that Maigret had lived in the Place des Vosges, while his building on Boulevard Richard-Lenoir was being remodeled, they had often, he and his wife, walked around the Île Saint-Louis in the evening*"). And in *Maigret et le tueur* ("*He knew the Île Saint-Louis fairly well since they had lived at Place des Vosges, and during that time, in the evening, they'd sometimes stroll, arm-in-arm, around the island*").

The Man from Meung

Besides the apartment on the Boulevard Richard-Lenoir, the Maigrets have a second *pied-à-terre*; it's the little house in the country they'd bought at Meung-sur-Loire. For Maigret, it's the "house of his dreams," not only the house to evoke in Maigret his childhood memories (odors and plays of light), but also the material symbol of the Chief Inspector's retirement. This is where he'll pass his "old days," forgetting the long stakeouts at the corner of a rain-soaked street, to cultivate tomatoes, strawberries and vegetables for salad, to fish and play innumerable hands of cards at the corner café.

The house at Meung, if it's tied at first to the Maigrets' weekend activities, is nonetheless the Chief Inspector's "retreat," in the first sense of the word, the house he goes to to "retire" from active life, a new sanctuary for a Chief Inspector tired (?) of chasing malefactors. Is he actually as content as all that to quit the Quai? Nothing is less clear! It's true that we sense, towards the end of the saga, a certain "enough-is-enough" spirit in the Chief Inspector, for the tedious sides of his métier (magnified by the "takeover by youth," reduction of police powers, doubts Maigret has about the legal system, etc.). Nevertheless it's with sadness and nostalgia that he reflects on the moment when he'll have to give up what had been his daily lot for so long: the little white wine at the counter, the odor of the soup in the concierge's lodges, the barges passing under the Pont Saint-Michel, his office blue with pipe smoke. Besides, let's not forget that it's Simenon himself who decides—not his Chief Inspector!—that Maigret should henceforth live at Meung. We see in *Les mémoires de Maigret* (MEM: 8), "*There was the time, also, when, without warning, he had me retired—which I wasn't, and until which I still had numerous years of service. We'd bought our house at Meung-sur-Loire and spent our Sundays there whenever I was free, to work on it. He came to visit us there. He was so taken with the setting that, in the following book, he anticipated the actuality, aging me shamelessly and settling me in there definitively. 'That changes the atmosphere a little,' he told me when I spoke to him about it. 'I've started to have enough of the Quai des Orfèvres.'*"

The house at Meung, an "*old house which resembled a rectory*"—which doesn't displease Maigret—has little square-paned windows. It's surrounded by an orchard with cherry trees, poplars, plum trees, and a plane tree, and a garden with low walls covered with trellises and pierced with a little green door. In his "parish priest's garden," Maigret grows lettuce, melons, tomatoes, peas and eggplant. Between the garden and the house is a partly-covered courtyard, paved with red tile, furnished with an iron table, a green-pained bench, a deckchair with red and yellow stripes, a sideboard, an old cook stove, and a rattan armchair. To enter, you strike a copper door-knocker. There's a hallway paved in gray or blue, then a dining room, with a pot-bellied stove and the Chief Inspector's armchair, then the kitchen, low, with a heavy-beamed ceiling, the floor covered with red tile and bluish stone, with plastered walls. The kitchen has a fireplace, a cupboard filled with provisions and bottles of alcohol, straw chairs, a standing shelf with copper saucepans, a beech table, and a staircase decorated with copper balls and steps of polished oak leading to the second floor. There the bedroom is found, furnished with a dresser and standing closet, as well as a bathroom. Characteristic of the house is its mixed odors: wood smoke, goat's milk, wax, cut hay, ripening fruit and simmering dishes, midsummer grass. Alongside the house is a packed-earth shed, filled with tools, where Maigret keeps his fishing gear. Besides the gardening, the Maigrets keep a goat, and a cat prowls the house. Beyond the turn in the road you can see the Loire, on the banks of which Maigret has a green-painted skiff he uses to go fishing.

Once retired, how will Maigret occupy his days? Besides the gardening (perhaps a way to find again a little taste of his country childhood, and to reconnect with the land), above all Maigret likes to fish. It's something he knows well, for he'd gone fishing during those rare free periods he'd been left by his cases: trout fishing in Alsace (*La guinguette à deux sous*), roach in the Seine (*La colère de Maigret*). Maigret is a fairly good fisherman; in one morning's fishing, he caught three pike in the Loire (*Maigret*), and another day, it was one pike and enough perch for frying (*Ceux du Grand Café*). It was even this familiarity with fishing that allowed him to understand M. Blaise's trick in *Signé Picpus*.

Outside of fishing, Maigret also plays cards: bridge, Pope Joan, manille and above all belote. He also sometimes plays billiards. And sometimes, does some reading: Fouché's *Memoirs*, or even Dumas, when Alexandre rejoins Georges…

> *"What's that over there?" "Where?" "In the road, opposite your windows, in that doorway … a man wrapped in a cloak."* … *"Ah! This time," cried d'Artagnan, leaping for his sword, "this time he won't escape me!" And drawing his sword from its scabbard, he dashed out of the room… "Wait! Where are you running off to like that?" the two musketeers cried to him together. "The man from Meung!" replied d'Artagnan, and he disappeared* [Alexandre Dumas: *The three musketeers*].

Maigret at the Movies

In addition to Maigret's leisure activities at Meung, there's another recreation the Chief Inspector enjoys, but this more often in Paris: the cinema. If Maigret likes going to the movies, it's not so much for the film itself—he's simple enough in his taste on that point—he likes westerns, and comedies from the 20s and 30s, Chaplin, and Laurel and Hardy. In fact, what he likes about the movies, is going there accompanied by his wife.

At the beginning of the saga we encountered few allusions to the cinema. It was while following Pietr le Letton that he entered a movie theater, where a "puerile film" was showing. Maigret hardly glances at the screen, satisfied to mull over his investigation. It's somewhat the same "technique" he uses in the memorable scene in *Cécile est morte*, where we see "*Maigret, his hands in his pockets, pipe in his teeth, strolling down Boulevard Montparnasse, looking grouchy. He stops in front of a movie theater*" (CEC: 2nd part: 2). He asks for a seat in the balcony, settles himself in, encased in his overcoat, and "*in that state of physical numbness, his thoughts, like in dreams, sometimes going to the absurd, followed paths that pure reason wouldn't have discovered.... And that's how he thinks without thinking, in snatches, by pieces of ideas which he doesn't try to put end to end*" (CEC: 2nd part: 3).

What Maigret likes about the movies is a certain ambiance, another way of brushing up against his fellow men... "*Maigret wasn't fussy about films. In actual fact, he preferred everyday films over any of the big productions, and, deep in his seat, he'd watch the images go by without concern for the story. The less pretentious the theater, the thicker its atmosphere, people laughing at the funny parts, eating chocolate bonbons or peanuts, lovers entwined, the happier he was*" (*Maigret, Lognon et les gangsters*, LOG: 5).

But, except for a "change of pace" when he was too involved in an investigation, it's above all for the pleasure of sharing a good moment with Mme Maigret that the Chief Inspector goes to the movies. And it's especially in the Presses de la Cité novels, where Mme Maigret takes on greater importance, that we see the couple going off, arm in arm, to a local movie house, on the Boulevard des Italiens or the Boulevard Bonne Nouvelle, or, more rarely, to one of the big theaters on the Champs-Elysées. And, in addition to the entertainment he derives from the film, he enjoys as well the tradition of the intermission, when he buys candy for his wife, and while she eats, "*smoking a half pipe in the lobby, while looking vaguely at posters of upcoming films*" (*Les scrupules de Maigret*, SCR: 6).

Madame Maigret

Basically, she was delighted with the picture Simenon had drawn of her, as a good "granny," always at her stove, always polishing, always pampering her big baby of a husband [*Les mémoires de Maigret*, MEM: 4].

Mme Maigret in the Saga

In the Maigret saga, Mme Maigret cannot be ignored. Indeed, what would Jules be without Louise? A Chief Inspector of the police, maybe not too bad, but certainly a man incomplete. Mme Maigret is the guardian of the haven of Boulevard Richard-Lenoir, one of the two poles between which Maigret navigates, the other being, of course, the Quai des Orfèvres. On the one side, his work is a confrontation with worlds not always easy to understand; on the other, some simple pleasures, sensory and basic, odors of simmering dishes, the tranquility of a cozy home, the little attentions of a loving spouse.

Mme Maigret appears at the beginning of the saga—she is, in fact, present in *Pietr le Letton*, first by allusions to her made by her husband, then an appearance "in person" in the last chapter. We could say that from this novel the tone was set. Her first mention is in the third chapter, when Maigret decides to take the train for Fécamp, and he says to Torrence, "*It's not worth going home and waking my wife.*" You might think there was a certain lightness, even cynicism, on the part of the husband, but there was none. The life of the couple is set up in a way that Mme Maigret knows that she is there to wait for her husband, to be present, preferably with a good meal on the fire, in case he returns unexpectedly. Since he forgets (more or less unconsciously) to call to say where he is, she's the one to get the information. Which is the case for her second appearance, in Ch. 6. Maigret, back from Fécamp, returns to the Quai and asks, "*'My wife hasn't called?' 'This morning. We told her you were out on a case....' She was used to it. He knew that he could return home and that she'd be content to welcome him, stirring her pots on the stove and filling a plate with some fragrant stew. She might ask, but only after he was at the table, and she was gazing at him, her chin between her hands.... 'Everything okay?....' At noon or five o'clock, he'd find his meal ready all the same.*"

Having sketched the essentials of Mme Maigret's function (especially as it appears in the beginning of the saga; we'll see later on that it will be enriched, as, in parallel, that of the Chief Inspector is enriched and refined), we see her as Penelope, patiently awaiting her husband, reheating for as long as it takes the meal she'd prepared, and worrying about him without pushing, without asking the details of his work. That's how we find her in the last chapter, when Maigret finally comes home, with an additional component— besides doing the cooking, she also becomes a nurse. The Chief Inspector, having finished his case, finally decides to take care of his wound, and to rest. As for Mme Maigret, "*she scurried around the apartment, content, pretending to grumble, for appearances sake, stirring whatever was in the pot, moving buckets of water, opening and closing the windows, checking from time to time.... "A pipe?..."* A little before that, and not without a preliminary treating of the nurses to a glass of plum brandy from Alsace, and asking two dependable questions of her husband: "*Did they hurt you*" and "*Can you eat?,*" she permitted herself to question him about the conclusion of his case, knowing full well that she'd get but a minimum of information. But that would be enough for her. "*Mme Maigret shrugged her shoulders. 'It's really useless being the wife of an officer of the Police Judiciaire!' But she said it with a smile.*"

Mme Maigret is present (ranging from a simple mention in the text to a character integrated into the action) in 69 novels and 18 stories, a large majority of the texts in the saga. She's missing from five of the Fayard novels (*Le charretier de La Providence, Le chien jaune, Un crime en Hollande, Le port des brumes,* and *L'affaire Saint-Fiacre*) and one from the Gallimard period (*L'inspecteur Cadavre*), but she's present in *all* of the Presses de la Cité novels. If we examine the average number of chapters per novel in which Mme Maigret appears, for the Fayards, we count one chapter out of three where she is mentioned; for the Gallimards, we move to one out of two; and for those from Presses de la Cité, we arrive at two out of three. And so we note a marked increase in her presence throughout the saga. We note further that Mme Maigret is already present in two of the Fayard novels (*Au rendez-vous des Terre-Neuvas* and *Le fou de Bergerac*), where she accompanies her husband to the locale of his investigation, something rather rare, for in most of the novels where she's present, the investigations take place in Paris, and Maigret meets her when he returns from work. When Maigret leaves Paris, he's usually alone (except for *Maigret en vacances* and *Maigret à Vichy,* for obvious reasons).

Another interesting point to examine is where in the novel Mme Maigret appears most frequently. In general, we note that for the first two periods, she's generally present at the end of the novel. It's there that her husband finds her at the completion of a case, a way for him to "take stock," to draw a conclusion, to find again the haven of his home—the rest of the warrior, in a sense. In contrast, for the Presses de la Cité period, if we also find this component, it's balanced by another. Indeed, we see more and more, as we advance through the saga, novels opening on a familiar and familial scene, where Maigret is breakfasting with his wife before leaving for work, assuming he hasn't been awakened by a phone call in the middle of the night, with Mme Maigret getting him a cup of coffee and a warm scarf before he escapes into his nocturnal investigation. And we note also the increasingly more important role played by Mme Maigret—the scenes where the Chief Inspector returns home for dinner, to sleep, and in a way, to "decompress," are more and more numerous. Mme Maigret is not merely "the lady who waits by her stove" (even if she continues to stir the invigorating dishes which her husband needs get back in balance), but she becomes more and more of a confidante, with whom Maigret shares more than a simple meal.

Physical and Psychological Aspects

Mme Maigret—to the same extent as her husband—is not described in detail. If Maigret is hardly more than a silhouette—an overcoat and hat—leaving the reader to construct his own representation, and actors to embody him by slipping into his image, Mme Maigret is also evoked in bold strokes, sketched, rather than described. We know that she wears curlers at night (a typical portrait of a homemaker in the years between 1930 and 1950!), that she hardly wears make-up, just using a little powder, wearing a "*slightly sweet perfume*" for special occasions. She's happy wearing an apron when she's at home, but also when she's installed with her husband at a hotel, ("*Even when staying at a hotel, she wore an apron to feel a little more at home, as she said.*" *Le fou de Bergerac*, FOU: 3). These are cotton aprons, blue. To go out, she wears a hat: a hat with a green feather, a straw hat, or a little white hat, and she wears white gloves. She wears dresses, of course (and not slacks), like the women of her day, by preference, floral patterns, light cotton in summer, wool in winter. She's happy in pink, but also in blue. She was, moreover, wearing a pale blue dress when Maigret met her for the first time (*Les mémoires de Maigret*).

Physically, she's rather plump, probably blonde (a slightly stout Alsatian), her hands a little pudgy. Since her youth she'd always had the same build: "*She was a big girl, fresh, like you see in cake shops, or behind the marble counters at dairies, a big girl, full of vitality*" (*La première enquête de Maigret*, PRE: 2), "*a young girl, slightly chubby, her face very fresh, and in her eyes, a sparkle that you didn't see in those of her friends*" (*Les mémoires de Maigret*, MEM: 4).

One of the things Maigret valued most about her was that she was cheerful, even merry. He loved to find her in the morning, *smelling fresh and soapy, all fresh, coiffed, wearing a pale apron*, or *already fresh and alert in a flowered housecoat*.

It's not until *Les mémoires de Maigret* that the name Louise is attributed to Mme Maigret. And in fact, it appears to be the only novel in which her first name appears, since in the others, her husband always calls her "Mme Maigret." We recall that in the story *L'amoureux de Madame Maigret*, her husband calls her "Henriette," like Simenon's mother, but also like Henriette Liberge, Simenon's "Boule."

Mme Maigret's Family

On the family side, Mme Maigret is originally from Alsace, where the couple sometimes spends their vacations, near Colmar, where she happily helped make jams and liqueurs. The family includes a number of cousins, one of whom lives in Nancy, and eleven aunts, one living in Quimper. Mme Maigret also has family on the Isle of Ré. A good part of the Alsatian branch worked for the Highways department. But the family relationship that is of most interest in the novels is Mme Maigret's sister. For the Maigret researcher, this sister continues to raise questions, for she has, depending on the novel, different names, as does her husband, whose family name also changes with the texts. One way to clarify (?) the situation is to say that Simenon wasn't always overly concerned about consistency with regard to the name of Mme Maigret's sister. Another possibility is that the "sister" of Mme Maigret is actually "sisters," in other words, that there are more than one. This is the premise of the little game that we've played below, in examining the texts concerning this character. Get your pencil ready!

We learn, in *L'ombre chinoise*, that Maigret's sister-in-law arrived from Alsace with the plum brandy, along with her husband André, who ran a brick-yard. In *Mon ami Maigret*, the couple, on a visit to the Maigrets, has the last name Mouthon. Apparently they have no children. In *Maigret en meublé*, Mme Maigret is in Alsace caring for her sister Hortense, who's recovering from an operation. In *La danseuse du Gai-Moulin*, the Maigrets receive a card from a sister who's about to have a new baby. In *Le fou de Bergerac*, the sister-in-law in Alsace gives birth to a daughter; she's had three children in four years. In *Maigret*, we have the appearance of Philippe Lauer, a police inspector, who comes from the Vosges and is Mme Maigret's nephew. In the same novel, the sister-in-law's husband is named Emile, and he works in an office. In *Félicie est là*, the sister-in-law, Elise, comes from Epinal (in the Vosges) with her husband and children. In *Maigret et l'inspecteur Malgracieux*, mention is made of Maigret's nephew, Daniel, who has a wife and daughter, and who works at Police Emergency Services. He could be Philippe's brother, and in this case, the baby announced in the card in *La danseuse du Gai-Moulin* could be either Philippe or Daniel. In *Maigret et son mort*, Mme Maigret's niece is called Aline (possibly the baby born in *Le fou de Bergerac*?).

In *Maigret s'amuse*, the sister-in-law lives in Colmar with her husband Charles and their children, while in *Maigret et le clochard*, Mme Maigret's sister, Florence, lives in Mulhouse, her husband works in the Highways department, and they also have children. There's no reason why this couldn't have been one couple who moved from Colmar to Mulhouse. In *Jeumont, 51 minutes d'arrêt!*, we find another nephew, Paul Vinchon, an Inspector on the Belgian border. Could he be Florence's son?

In *Mademoiselle Berthe et son amant*, there's yet another nephew, Jérôme Lacroix, an inspector in the PJ, who has a wife and a son. In *L'homme dans la rue,* Mme Maigret sister comes from Orléans (could she be Jérôme's mother?). In *L'amoureux de Madame Maigret,* Mme Maigret has gone to meet her sister who lives in Paris, and in *Maigret et son mort,* the sister, Odette, apparently single, is invited to dinner. But, in *Une confidence de Maigret,* the Maigrets have no family in Paris; has Odette moved? And if so, does she live in Orléans?

Got it?!

Here's the situation as we can imagine it: Mme Maigret has four sisters: Hortense, who lives in Alsace, married to André Mouthon, with no children; Elise, who lives in Epinal, married to Emile Lauer, with three children, Philippe, Daniel and Aline; Florence, who lived in Colmar and then moved to Mulhouse, married to Charles Vinchon, with a number of children, of whom one is Paul, an inspector on the Belgian border; and Odette Lacroix, who lived in Paris then moved to Orléans, probably a widow, and who has a son, Jérôme… *Voilà!*

MME MAIGRET AS PENELOPE

As mentioned above, the first image that Simenon shows us of Mme Maigret is that of a spouse at home, watching her pots, awaiting the return of her valorous warrior. A long, and often fruitless wait, since the Chief Inspector sometimes forgets to call to advise her that he won't be back (*"Mme Maigret, once more, would wait in front of the two place settings set out on the round table. She was really used to it! And it hadn't helped to install a telephone…. Maigret would forget to call." Cécile est morte:* CEC: 1st part: 2). We note all the same, that over time, his character becomes more refined, a certain delicacy appears, and the phone calls become more frequent (see *Mme Maigret on the telephone,* below).

Like Penelope, Mme Maigret also practices the "needle arts." If she doesn't weave, she sews, embroiders, knits—works of patience which help pass the time waiting for her husband to return. Like Penelope as well, she welcomes her champion's return without recrimination, but with concern. A concern shown with a few simple questions, but which reflects none the less the tenderness she feels for her husband. And these questions always revolve around the same themes, those already present at the beginning of the saga: physical and emotional health, appetite, and the progress of the case. *"Did you work everything out? … You've been walking around in the rain again. One day you'll suffer for it and you'll be sorry! Did you at least eat well, in Givet?"* (*Chez les Flamands,* FLA: 11); *"As usual, Mme Maigret opened the door of the apartment before he turned the knob. She didn't mention that he was late. Din-*

ner was ready. 'You haven't caught cold?'" (Maigret se trompe, TRO: 4); "'Is that you?' It must have been hundreds, if not thousands of times that she'd asked that question in a sluggish voice when he'd returned in the middle of the night, that she'd fumbled to light the lamp on the night table, then gotten up, in her nightgown, darting a glance at her husband to see what kind of mood he was in... 'You're not hungry? Should I make you something?'" (Maigret et le fantôme, FAN: 1).

And when sometimes Maigret just stopped at home briefly, in the middle of a case, though it was something his wife hardly appreciated, she was careful to say nothing... "While he ate his lunch at the Boulevard Richard-Lenoir, his wife couldn't get a word out of him.... She understood from his mood that it would be pointless to ask what time he'd be home" (Cécile est morte, CEC: 2nd part: 2); "He was still 200 yards from home.... She understood immediately that things weren't going well with his case, and not to ask any questions" (Maigret et le tueur, TUE: 3). Furthermore, she knew her husband so well that she really didn't need to ask him many questions: "When I came home, my wife had no more than to look at me, without asking anything, to know how everything was ... and she knew the meaning of my bad moods, my certain way of sitting down, when I came home at night, of filling my plate, and she didn't push" (Les mémoires de Maigret, MEM: 6); "She could detect the slightest change in his mood and, while she didn't ask him any direct questions, she tried nonetheless to discern what was bothering him" (Les scrupules de Maigret, SCR: 2); "When the Chief Inspector got home.... Mme Maigret needed but a glance to gauge the state of his spirits" (Maigret et l'affaire Nahour, NAH: 7); "When he got home, he didn't try to hide his bad mood. With Mme Maigret, it was, moreover, impossible" (L'ami d'enfance de Maigret, ENF: 4).

Mme Maigret on the Telephone

The more years of writing that pass, the more Simenon describes in depth the relationship of the Maigret couple. As a consequence, their phone calls are more and more frequently used to symbolize the links which unite them. In the first half of the saga (Fayard, Gallimard, and the beginning of the Presses de la Cité period), it's Mme Maigret who calls her husband, because he'd often forgotten to tell her he wouldn't get home. Since then it's Maigret himself who calls his wife to warn her that he won't be home for lunch, dinner, or even to sleep, and the phone calls become more numerous in the second part of the Presses de la Cité period. And sometimes Maigret calls his wife for other reasons: to suggest that they spend the weekend in the country, and occasionally—rarely—to invite her out for a drink or for dinner, or perhaps to announce that *in fact* he will be home for lunch or dinner! We also note that it's rare for Maigret to ask someone else to call his wife for him. When it does happen, it's either because he doesn't have time himself, or doesn't want to speak because he's in the middle of resolving a problem.

Maigret, who's not very outgoing, only uses a few words of affection when he speaks with his wife. The rare times he calls her "*Dear*," except for in *Le fou de Bergerac* (FOU 8), are on the phone (*Chez les Flamands*, FLA: 7, and *L'Etoile du Nord*, eto: 3). When Maigret picks up the phone to call his wife, he often opens by saying, "*Hello, is that you?*" or "*Is that you?*," as a sort of "*odd habit, as he had certainly recognized his wife's voice*" (*L'ami d'enfance de Maigret*, ENF: 2), "*as if he didn't know that it couldn't be anyone else, and as if he didn't recognize her voice!*" (*La colère de Maigret*, COL: 6). The contents of the conversation between Louise and Jules revolves most often around the same subjects, from "*I won't be back for lunch*" and its variations, to "*What are we having to eat?*" and other versions. Maigret hardly mentions his cases to his wife, who sometimes risks a timid, "*Something wrong?*" or "*There's nothing bad?*," questions to which she furthermore receives no answers.

Contact instrument *par excellence*, the telephone allows Maigret to maintain the link with his wife, to connect his life in the office with that of his home. And even if this link is light and often "mundane" in its expression, it's nonetheless real. Mme Maigret knows well that she shouldn't expect great discourse from her husband when he calls… "*The first thing Maigret did on entering the Brasserie Dauphine, was to head for the phone and call his apartment. 'I know,' said Mme Maigret before he'd opened his mouth. 'You won't be home for lunch. I was expecting it…'*" (*Maigret et Monsieur Charles*, CHA: 3). The phone call to his wife is above all to reassure her…. The Chief Inspector is thinking of her and the delicious meal she'd prepared for him, but his investigation comes first. And so, she contents herself with keeping his meal warm, and waiting for the next phone call, hoping to hear, "*Hello, is that you, Madame Maigret?*," a little phrase filled with tenderness and affection.

Mme MAIGRET THE COOK

Mme Maigret is a good cook, which by now almost goes without saying; to the extent that there's even been a book published (by Robert Courtine) of Mme Maigret's recipes. From the simple "*ragoût odorant*" [fragrant stew] at the beginning of the saga (see the extract from *Pietr le Letton* cited above, in Mme Maigret in the saga), to the everyday "*fricot sur le feu*" [stovetop stew] mentioned in *La nuit du carrefour*, we move little by little to more precise notations, like the quiches, which scent the whole house in *Chez les Flamands*, or the various "*en-cas pour homme alité*" [snacks for the bedridden] that Mme Maigret makes in *Le fou de Bergerac*—"*un bon bouillon de poule*" [a good chicken soup], a "*crème au citron* [lemon cream], *which was a pure masterpiece*," and some less attractive herbal teas, but which Maigret swallows in exchange for a few puffs of his pipe. Then, in *Liberty Bar*: "*Would you like to me to make a 'morue à la crème' [cod with cream]?*" "*You can't imagine how much!*" (LIB: 11). And we find again the same degree of enthusiasm from the Chief Inspector for the dishes prepared by his wife in *Maigret*: "*What kind of soup have you made?*" *he shouted, seating himself on a crate.*" "*Tomato.*" "*All right!*" (MAI: 10). It sometimes happens that in spite of the culinary efforts of Mme Maigret, the Chief Inspector becomes so wrapped up in his case that he can't do justice to the dishes served... "*He rested his elbows on the table, crumbled the bread onto the tablecloth, chewed noisily, and all that was a bad sign.... Had he even noticed that he was eating a creamy caramel custard?*" (*Cécile est morte*, CEC: 2nd part: 2)

Happily, this was not the rule, and in general, Maigret had rather a tendency to appreciate his wife's cuisine: "*...and God knows Mme Maigret knew how to simmer a stew!*" (*Maigret à New York*, NEW: 1). And how could we not share his opinion, reading a few examples: boiled chicken, "*with a fine red carrot, a fat onion and a bunch of parsley*," which unfortunately would burn in the pot (*L'amie de Madame Maigret*, MME: 1), coq au vin with Alsatian plum brandy (*Une confidence de Maigret*, CON: 8), macaroni and cheese, "*filled with finely diced ham, and sometimes, a truffle cut even finer*" (*Maigret et le clochard*, CLO: 4), "*Alsatian sauerkraut with pickled pork, especially tasty*" (*Maigret et l'affaire Nahour*, NAH: 3), tarragon chicken topped with asparagus tips (*L'ami d'enfance de Maigret*, ENF: 2), baked mackerel, slow cooked in white wine, with plenty of mustard (*Maigret et le tueur*, TUE: 3), a roast with heads of celery and mashed potatoes (*Maigret et le marchand de vin*, VIN: 5), and "*a pretty pink leg of lamb, with just a drop of blood dripping near the bone*" (*Maigret et l'homme tout seul*, SEU: 6).

MME MAIGRET THE HOUSEWIFE

Mme Maigret not only has the talents of a cook, she's also a woman who likes to care for her home, who maintains the cleanliness of her household, as we see her "*shaking a rug where a nurse had left footprints*" in *Pietr le Letton*, "*airing out the sheets*" of the unmade bed in *La nuit du carrefour*, "*scouring the brass*" in *Cécile est morte*, "*waxing the floor*" in *Maigret se défend*, and "*ironing*" in *Maigret et le marchand de vin*.

We have to view these images, not as "compulsive cleanliness," but rather the manifestation of Mme Maigret's not feeling comfortable except in a place she has succeeded in fashioning into her image, reflecting her "inner cleanliness," a certain serenity, which is certainly one of her character traits that pleases her husband the most, even from the beginning of their relationship. We recall their first meeting (*Les mémoires de Maigret*), and how Louise knew how to put young Jules at ease in the episode of the petits fours. Beneath her "sweet grandma" exterior, we feel a certain force in this woman, a will which doesn't manifest itself in a vehement manner, but by acts which fit her personality. In *Au rendez-vous des Terre-Neuvas*, no sooner had the couple settled into the hotel, then Mme Maigret began by "*rearranging the room to her liking*," in *Le fou de Bergerac*, "*...she upset the kitchens. She gave recipes to the chef, and made copies for him to file.*" While the gentleness of her character is real, it doesn't stop her from wanting to run her household as she wishes, to be the sole mistress of her home. "*She didn't want a maid and was happy with a cleaning lady in the morning for the heavy work*" (*L'amoureux de Madame Maigret*, amo: 1). "*She allowed a cleaning lady, certain days of the week, but only for the heavy work, and even then she often redid it after her*" (*Maigret et les braves gens*, BRA: 4). Moreover, when her husband had the misfortune to propose that they get a maid, because he was afraid of her wearing herself out, she was hardly appreciative. "*In her mind, it was a little as if he wanted to take away one of her prerogatives, one that she held dear to her heart*" (*Les scrupules de Maigret*, SCR: 2).

Mme Maigret the Nurse

Kitchen and household, the range of talents of Mme Maigret doesn't stop there. She also combines a gift for nursing, which, given what we've already seen of her, isn't surprising. From the beginning of the saga, she will care for her husband's wounds, as we have seen above. We find her again in the nurse's role in *Le fou de Bergerac*, as a nurse with all the qualities: calm, skillful, patient, caring... "*Mme Maigret accepted the situation as she accepted everything, without surprise, without excitement. She'd been in the room for an hour, and it had already become her room, for she'd brought all her little things, her personal touch.*" (FOU: 2). Her husband, moreover, appreciated his wife in this role, and he would sometimes "cheat" with a bad cold, pretending that it was the flu, since then he could lead his investigation while staying in his room, which sometimes turned out to be useful: "*Let's say that here, at home, with my wife to care for me, I feel more relaxed thinking about the case and leading the investigation*" (*Maigret et son mort*, MOR: 3). And that goes far back into the history of the couple... "*She nursed him tenderly. You could say she coddled him. However, he had the impression that she wasn't fooled.... She loved to make him herb teas, poultices, to make broth and eggs with milk. And she liked to carefully close the curtains and walk on tiptoes, sometimes opening the door to see if he were asleep.*" (*La première enquête de Maigret*, PRE: 9).

MME MAIGRET THE COLLABORATOR

An initially less evident facet of Mme Maigret, is her role in her husband's work. Even if, in general, and especially at the beginning of the saga, he had kept her outside of his investigations, over the course of time, he would sometimes share certain details, taking her as confidante to his moods. Further along in the saga, the more we find Maigret speaking of the progress of his case with his wife along with seeing him spending more time at the Boulevard Richard-Lenoir. Nevertheless there are times when she's led to play a more important role in a case (as in *L'amie de Madame Maigret, L'amoureux de Madame Maigret, Le fou de Bergerac, Maigret et le clochard,* and *Maigret et le fantôme*). As stated above, she questions her husband, even if she doesn't always get an answer. Still, a simple question on her part can sometimes give him the chance to draw a conclusion to his investigation, in order to "move on." Thus, in *Pietr le Letton*, at Maigret's return home at the end of the novel, once he's cared for and installed in his bed, his wife asks about Anna Gorskine. If Maigret doesn't give her any details, he nevertheless formulates a sort of conclusion, in the form of the sentence, "*Life is so complicated, you see....*" In *Au rendez-vous des Terre-Neuvas*, it's Mme Maigret's questions that allow her husband to express what he feels about Le Clinche's situation. In *Liberty Bar*, also at the end of the novel, on Maigret's return home, his wife asks him, "*What was it about, this affair?*" And Maigret answers "*A love story!*" And the rest of the dialogue follows the same pattern. Mme Maigret asks questions about the case, and her husband (for once!) explains about the protagonists. In *Les scrupules de Maigret*, when the Chief Inspector is reading a psychiatric work, his wife asks, "*You have a difficult case?*" He's content to shrug his shoulders and grumble, "*A story of madmen!*" In *La folle de Maigret*, when the Chief Inspector returns home from his office, "*Mme Maigret opened the door as soon as he reached the landing, as always. 'You seem preoccupied.' 'Quite. I'm struggling with an affair about which I don't understand a thing,'*" and later in the dialogue, Mme Maigret asks questions about the murdered old woman.

MME MAIGRET THE SPOUSE

Alongside all these "functions," Mme Maigret has also the role of spouse, that is, the other half of a couple. The relationship between the two characters is strong, even if it's not manifested by grand demonstrations, nor great discourse. Some small affectionate gestures, the exchange of simple words, but which reflect no less the deep tenderness uniting the couple. *"It was a serious kiss, deep, which he placed on the brow of his wife, already asleep"* (*Au rendez-vous des Terre-Neuvas*, REN: 6); *"And he kissed her hand, with a tenderness hidden by playfulness"* (*Le fou de Bergerac*, FOU: 8); *"There were rituals that had taken years to establish, and to which he held more than he would have liked to admit ... his wife had a special gesture of taking his wet umbrella from his hands at the same time as tilting her head to kiss him on the cheek"* (*Maigret chez le ministre*, MIN: 1); *"He slid under the warm sheets, turned out the light, and found in the darkness, without fumbling, his wife's lips"* (*Les scrupules de Maigret*, SCR: 6); *"That was part of the tradition. Mme Maigret automatically took her husband's arm, and, on the empty sidewalk, they walked slowly into the quiet of the night"* (*Une confidence de Maigret*, CON: 4); *"This dinner was very nice though, full of intimacy, of subtle understanding between him and his wife"* (*Maigret et le voleur paresseux*, PAR: 6); *"Arm in arm they headed towards the Boulevard Bonne-Nouvelle, and they were feeling fine, with no need for conversation"* (*Maigret et le client du samedi*, CLI: 2); *"It was a soft, quiet evening, with long silences between the sentences, which didn't prevent them from feeling very close to each other"* (*Maigret et le clochard*, CLO: 4). Maigret, moreover, even if he doesn't make a show of it, knows well that he needs the presence of his wife to exist fully... *"In fact, in a normal time, what would he talk about with his wife when he was with her? Nothing, really. Then why, all day long, did he miss her so much?"* (*Les vacances de Maigret*, VAC: 1); *"She didn't call him "sweetheart" and he didn't call her "dearest." What purpose would it have served, since they felt like they were in some sense the same person?"* (*Maigret et le fantôme*, FAN: 6); *"He had rarely wanted so much to go home and see the tender and cheerful eyes of his wife"* (*Maigret se défend*, DEF: 4).

This relationship between the couple, based on trust and complicity, was built from their first meeting. We can recall, in *Les mémoires de Maigret*, the "gaffe" of young Jules, consuming, to compose himself, the petits fours at the Highways Division party, and discovering nevertheless, a knowing look from one of the guests... *"At that moment, in the darkness, I saw a face, the face of a young girl in blue, and on her face, a soft expression, reassuring, almost familiar. You would have said that she'd understood, that she was encouraging me.*" (MEM: 4). And thus appeared in Maigret's life this calm and serene being, the "resource person" with whom he deposits his worries and troubles, this character essential to his equilibrium.

There is, however, a drama in the history of the Maigret couple ... they'd lost a little daughter, either at birth, or a little afterwards. We learn nothing further from the few allusions in the text. We know however, that that's what provokes the "nostalgia of paternity" in Maigret, nostalgia which he compensates for in his relationship with his inspectors, and which no doubt explains his especially indulgent attitude with regard to the young delinquents, as, for example, Paulus (*Maigret en meublé*), Antoine (*Maigret et le corps sans tête*), or Lecoeur (*Maigret et l'homme du banc*). It's also why he "compensates" by calling his inspectors "my children," who are somewhat his "spiritual sons," particularly young Lapointe. As for Mme Maigret, she overcomes her "great sadness" of not having children by redirecting all her affection to her husband, whom she "pampers" and whom she watches over with motherly attention.

Dr. Pardon

In his affections, Maigret, outside of his wife and "children"—his inspectors—cultivates few friendships. He has his "old accomplices," Dr Paul and Moers, but these are rather professional encounters, "work relationships," in a way. With no family in Paris, and Madame Maigret's family far off in Alsace, the Chief Inspector and his wife had hardly any "evenings with friends" until the day that Jussieu, head of the Forensic Laboratory (the only appearance in the novels of this character in that role), takes Maigret with him to Dr. Pardon's. Pardon is a General Practitioner, who worked for five years as an intern at Sainte-Anne's, and had since set himself up as neighborhood doctor in a popular district. Very quickly, the two men got along very well, sharing the same view of life, and the same passion for traditional cuisine. Indeed, Pardon regularly invites some of his colleagues for a "Doc's dinner," where "*a single dish was served, preferably a regional dish.*" (*Le revolver de Maigret*, REV: 1). First there was the *cassoulet*, then the *coq au vin*, couscous, Dieppe sole, cod *brandade*, and others. And each time, there was also "*a surprise, perhaps an extraordinary wine, maybe a liqueur, or ... a Pineau des Charentes*" (REV: 1).

Pardon is three years younger than Maigret, "*small, somewhat plump, with a very large head and bulging eyes*" (*Le revolver de Maigret*, REV: 2), He has brown hair starting to gray, and at 45, he was almost bald. He smokes cigarettes and cigars. He's scrupulous, meticulous, very simple, but has "*extremely subtle delicacies.*"

He lives in the Picpus district, but it's difficult to exactly locate the street of his building. Simenon has him live sometimes on the Boulevard Voltaire, sometimes Rue Picpus, sometimes Rue Popincourt. But what's certain is that it's not far from the Maigrets' apartment, since they walk to the Pardons' (a five-minute walk, according to *Le revolver de Maigret*). We also know that the Pardons' apartment is not on the ground floor, because they take an elevator to get there, and that there's a balcony with "*wrought iron arabesques.*"

Pardon has a "calling" for his métier—as has no doubt Maigret, which brings them closer—working 12 to 15 hours a day (his waiting room never emptied), often called out in the evening—especially when the Maigrets are invited! Also like Maigret, he suffers the disillusionments of the limits of his work. Maigret freely asks his opinions on difficult cases, or his assistance when a case involves physicians, and while the two men are friends, that doesn't stop Pardon from being the doctor with him; it's Pardon who sends Maigret to take the cure at Vichy, and it's on his advice that Maigret attempts to drink less.

The relationship between the two men becomes very quickly a friendship—he's the only man that Maigret considers his "friend"—and he occupies a more and more important place in the novels, appearing in 26 out of the 49 of the Presses de la Cité novels—quite a high number, considering his relatively late appearance in the saga.

Two more things connect Maigret and Pardon: For one, they have the same type of wife: "*If Mme Pardon was thin and the Chief Inspector's wife stout, they had, both of them, with regard to their husbands, the same unassuming attitude.*" (*Le revolver de Maigret*, REV: 2). As a result they themselves became friends, as their husbands were, with the difference being that they called each other by their first names (Mme Pardon was Francine), while the men used their family names and "*vous.*" That's also why we see, at their traditional dinners, the two women moving off to some corner while their husbands discuss work. The two women also have in common their taste for knitting, and above all, their culinary talent. Which brings us to the second element shared by Maigret and Pardon, their taste for good food. Their meetings are situated, most of the time, under the sign of gastronomy. The monthly dinners are the occasion for Mmes Pardon and Maigret to challenge their cooking skills, and it's at the Pardons' that Maigret enjoys calf's head *en tortue, épaule de mouton farcie, canard au sang, bœuf bourguignon.* And afterwards it wouldn't be at all astonishing for Pardon to send Maigret for the cure! On her side, Mme Maigret offers her guests *pintadeaux en croûte,* and she reveals to her friend the secret of her *coq au vin*... *"I've always wondered how you make it.... There's a slight aftertaste, hardly perceptible, which gives it its charm, and which I can never quite identify." "But it's really so simple.... I suppose you add a glass of cognac at the last moment?" "Cognac or armagnac ... whatever's handy...." "Well, for me, although it somewhat unorthodox, I add some plum brandy from Alsace.... That's the whole secret!"* (*Une confidence de Maigret*, CON: 8)

On the family side, the Pardons may be happier than the Maigrets. They have a daughter Alice, or Solange, who has two children, and Mme Maigret will be the godmother of the first. Her husband is a veterinarian or an engineer, depending on the novel.

And lastly, we note that it's thanks to Dr Pardon that Maigret meets Prof. Tissot, the psychiatrist who will help him in the Moncin case (*Maigret tend un piège*). Indeed, Pardon has the habit of inviting, in addition to the Maigrets, *"some colleague or another, almost always interesting men, either because of their personality, or their research, and it was often opposite some important person, say a famous professor, that the Chief Inspector found himself seated"* (TEN: 2), which didn't displease him at all, quite to the contrary... *"It didn't take long for them to feel with Maigret that they were on common ground, and some of these after-dinner conversations, aided by an ancient liqueur, in Dr. Pardon's peaceful living room, with the windows almost always open on the crowded street below, lasted fairly long into the night.... Their way, for them and him, of being interested in man, of viewing his sorrows and failures, was almost the same"* (TEN: 2).

(See *Maigret and the world of medicine* in *Part III. The Saga*)

Maigret Has the Flu ... Bedridden Investigations

Maigret is no "super-cop," always in top physical shape; more than once in the saga, he's had to lead an investigation when he was wounded, bedridden, or down with the flu. His "weaknesses" only serve to make him even more human.

And it's right from the start of the saga that we discover that the Chief Inspector is a "man like any other." Indeed, in *Pietr le Letton*, he's shot by a member of Pietr's gang. Wounded in the chest, he nevertheless continues his investigation (for he is, after all, a hero), stoically enduring the pain. In *Le fou de Bergerac*, he's shot once again, but this time it's more serious. Hit in the left shoulder, he has to remain in bed for a little over two weeks. Fortunately, Mme Maigret is there to pamper him, and the Chief Inspector makes the most of the opportunity, finding a way to carry out his investigation—in an unusual and original way, to say the least. Sending his wife out to report to him on the places and circumstances, he himself, based in his bed, imagines the characters, draws parallels, and shuffles thoughts that are like pieces of ideas. He doesn't "reason," he "gropes around," assembling images, half dreaming, half feverish. "*He was dreaming less now. Even when he closed his eyes under a sunbeam, Maigret's ideas were a little clearer. But he continued to juggle the characters created or reconstructed by his imagination*" (FOU: 2).

In *La première enquête de Maigret*, after receiving a violent blow to his head, he's treated briefly at the hospital, and then brought home, where Mme Maigret, once more, but with a certain pleasure, takes on the nurse's role. As for Maigret, he takes advantage of his condition to "reflect" on his case in his own way. He draws lines and shapes on a piece of paper, representing characters and places, and he constructs hypotheses. After getting up to continue his investigation, and discovering that he was expected to "let it disappear," he finds himself once more in bed with a fever, which Maigret would put to good use. "*He sank down into his damp bed, in a good odor of sweat. It was his way of withdrawing into himself. He didn't yet know that this would become one of his habits, that he'd often resort to this method when he found himself discouraged or ill at ease. The change was produced almost on command. Instead of his ideas becoming clearer, they blurred.... He slipped into a half-sleep, reality taking on new forms, mingled with childhood memories*" (PRE: 9). A situation we find again in the story, *Le témoignage de l'enfant de chœur*, where this time, it's the flu that has him stuck to his bed. Here too, his fever is mixed with childhood memories, which he will use to understand the actions of the altar boy. "*He was alone, hot, wet, deep in his bed ... he was not yet Maigret the Chief Inspector, he was the altar boy.... And it would be a lovely thing, no run-of-the-mill investigation, conducted from his bed*" (cho: 2). We find this "tactic"—knowing how to utilize a cold or the flu to advance the progress of his investigation—elsewhere in the saga, employed by Maigret when he was stalled in an investigation, as in *Maigret et son mort...* "*It happened from time to time like that, when an investigation wasn't moving forward as he'd like, he'd go to bed, or to stay in his room*" (MOR: 3).

5

"Methods"

"I don't think anything..."

"You think she was the one who..."
"You're forgetting that I don't believe anything until the close of a case."
And he added with a skeptical smile,
"And even then!" [*Maigret et l'affaire Nahour*, NAH: 4].

Mention is often made of Maigret's "motto," which would be, "*I don't believe anything (at all)*," an illustration, not so much of his skepticism, as his refusal to judge Man, whatever he may be. It's true that it's a formula the Chief Inspector often uses, with some minor variations, as for example the answer he may give to the question, "*What do you think?*," a question often asked him by self-assured judges inclined to organize people into perfectly clear-cut categories. To that question, the Chief Inspector has the habit of simply dropping a laconic, "*Nothing!*," which in fact tells a lot about his way of considering an investigation: he doesn't think, he thinks nothing, in the sense that he doesn't analyze a murder as if it were a puzzle that could be resolved by a series of brilliant deductions. And sometimes he replies simply, "*Nothing at all!*," one of his favorite phrases, "*that he often repeated when he was floundering in a particularly dense case*" (*La maison du juge*). As he says to his colleague Pijpekamp (*Un crime en Hollande*): "*You, you think something! You even think lots of things! While I, I believe I don't think anything at all...*" (HOL: 5). No, Maigret doesn't "think" in the way a Hercule Poirot uses his little gray cells. To Descartes's "*I think, therefore I am*," the Chief Inspector could counter with his own; he's not a "thinking" being, in the sense of a man who defines himself by logic, but a being of trial and error: "*I don't think anything. I seek*" (*Maigret et l'homme du banc*).

"Put yourself into someone else's skin"

One of the things that makes the Maigret novels so original, and which distances them greatly from "classic" detective stories, is the Chief Inspector's efforts to put himself into someone else's place, and to try to understand how that one feels. What's even more original is that this "empathy" includes gestures, attitudes which Maigret takes, and his mimicry, you might say, of the one he's interested in. This is particularly true in the novels where the Chief Inspector seeks to understand the past of a victim, for this past should reveal the reason for his murder.

In *Maigret et son mort*, we not only see Maigret going into the cafés from which Albert Rochain telephoned him, but even, once he's discovered Albert's own café (*Au Petit Albert*), (MOR: 4), installing himself there: "*the Chief Inspector ... seemed to truly move in. In less than half an hour, it was as if he were at home,*" drinking, as Albert did, a *Suze*, he spent the night... "*He tried on the house like trying on new clothes.*" It was by trying to put himself into the place of "his dead man," by acting like him, making, in a way, the same movements, that Maigret ended up understanding why he'd been killed.

In *Maigret et la jeune morte*, the Chief Inspector similarly "follows" Louise Laboine, seeking to understand her. It's not by brilliant logical deductions that he discovers the truth, but because he'd gotten to know Louise, from the inside, you might say, by his extraordinary ability to "put himself into someone else's skin." It's the same way Maigret works to understand Jules Lapie in *Félicie est là*, when he tries on Peg-Leg's straw hat, and, as the Director of the PJ said, he "*moved into an investigation like into a pair of slippers*" (*Félicie est là*, FEL: 2); or in *Maigret et l'homme du banc* (BAN: 5), "*He thought so much about Louis that he ended by behaving like him, even making the same facial expressions.*"

And again, in *On ne tue pas les pauvres types* (pau: 3), when Maigret has discovered Tremblet's "hideout," what's the first thing he does? "*Before anything else, to replace the water in the cages, and fill the canaries' feeders.*" In other words, he puts himself in the victim's place, he "acts like him." These are the same impulses he obeys in *Maigret et le corps sans tête* (COR: 7), when he returns at night to the Calas café to reflect in a relaxed way on the hypotheses of his investigation, observing the places where Aline spends her life: "*his eyes fixed on the counter, on the glasses, the bottles ... he asked himself if he wasn't about to find the answer to his question.*" And we find it again in *La colère de Maigret* (COL: 5), when the Chief Inspector "puts himself in the footsteps" of the victim to understand what happened to him. "*One would have thought that Maigret was playing the nightclub owner, and that, in spite of the difference in their size and weight, he was trying to imitate Emile Boulay.*"

Maigret Takes Notes

Maigret's notebook, even if it doesn't have a very important place in his investigations, nonetheless plays its role, and it's found throughout the texts. What's it like, this notebook? It's *a common laundress's notebook, with a black oilcloth cover, a little 10-sou notebook, quadrille-ruled*, held together with a rubber band, and filled *with notes in all directions, one on top of the other*. If we could manage to decipher these notes, here's what we might be able to read there: Maigret's to-do list, facts to verify at the beginning of his investigation (in *Monsieur Gallet décédé*); information he could obtain on important people in Concarneau (*Le chien jaune*); people's opinions of the Peeters family (*Chez les Flamands*); the time of Dr. Janin's arrival at L'Aiguillon (*La maison du juge*): the words 'hat' (*Signé Picpus*) and 'red car, Sébile' (*Félicie est là*); the names of the members of the Czech gang, and the dates of their attacks (*Maigret et son mort*); phone calls in and out of Porquerolles (*Mon ami Maigret*); notes on the people he questioned in *Maigret en meublé*; notes on the patient cards of Serre, the dentist (*Maigret et la Grande Perche*); phone numbers of three advertising agencies on Rue Réaumur (*Le revolver de Maigret*); notes on Point's collaborators (*Maigret chez le ministre*); Mme Josselin's maiden name (*Maigret et les braves gens*); and notes on Nina Lassave's death (*Maigret et l'homme tout seul*).

Sometimes Maigret tears a page from his notebook to send a message to one of his collaborators. For example, he asks Lucas by note if Gassin is armed, (*L'écluse n° 1*), and he gives a note to Inspector Dunan to order a raid (*Félicie est là*). Lastly, we know that Maigret writes in his notebook with a pencil, and not with a pen.

And since we're talking about the writing, we note that Maigret's handwriting is not the most elegant, as with his *huge forefinger*, he grinds his pen into the paper, making *fat, squashed down strokes*, but also, "*in contrast, the writing was very small, but thick, so that from a distance it looked like a row of blotches*" (*Chez les Flamands*, FLA: 7).

Maigret's Drawings

In the course of an investigation, Maigret, sometimes lost in thought, sometimes while on the phone, doodles on a piece of paper a more or less shapeless drawing, but one whose unconscious meaning reveals nonetheless the "functioning" of the Chief Inspector's mind.

Thus in *Maigret*, the Chief Inspector is trying to understand what has

taken place in the *Floria*, the murder case in which his nephew was impli-
cated... "*Maigret, with the zeal of a schoolboy, drew a rectangle, and, about in
the middle of the rectangle, a little cross.... Down at the bottom of the rectangle
he drew another, smaller one, the desk. And in this desk, finally, a dot, representing the revolver. This was of no value. It didn't mean a thing. This affair
wasn't a geometry problem. Maigret persevered all the same, crumpled his paper
into a ball, and started his drawing on a new sheet. Only, he no longer thought
about the meaning of the rectangles and crosses*" (MAI: 2). In *L'amie de Madame
Maigret*, the Chief Inspector is trying to reconstruct the sequence of events
of the case. On the date Gloria Lotti went to Concarneau—"*In the margin,
Maigret playfully drew a woman's hat with a veil...*" And in *La folle de Maigret*,
the Chief Inspector, in his office, is mentally trying to summarize the case,
examining reasons for the crime, all the time reflecting... "*He was doodling
on a sheet of paper and suddenly realized that it more or less looked like an old
lady*" (FOL: 4).

In *La maison du juge*, Maigret telephones to Nantes, then to Nice, to get
information on Janin and Mme Forlacroix. In the background remains the
unconscious memory of the glimpse of Lise Forlacroix in her bed. "*He gave
his instructions in a few words, and, when he was finished, he glanced mechanically at the paper resting on his desk, and saw that what he had drawn was
clearly a fleshy mouth, the lips well-defined and sensual like in a painting by
Renoir. He tore the sheet into little pieces and threw them into the fire*" (JUG:
5). We'll leave the pleasure of interpreting this last gesture to the psychiatrists.
Similarly, in *Maigret et les braves gens*, the Chief Inspector is listening to the
telephone report of Torrence, who'd just searched the maids' rooms in Josselin's building. He'd discovered in one of the rooms, "*a young woman, stark
naked ... very dark, with immense eyes, clearly Spanish or South American.*"
And what does Maigret do while he's listening? He draws "*mechanically on
a blotter, the torso of a woman.*"

Maigret Draws His Gun

At first glance, it would appear that Maigret almost never carries a
weapon; his image is hardly that of the "fast-shooting cop." And when we
examine the texts, this impression is confirmed: Maigret's revolver is only
mentioned in 11 novels. Moreover, he only carries his gun in the Fayard novels,
the novels closest to "detective stories," in the classic sense. In *Pietr le Letton*,
Maigret follows Pietr on the rocks of Fécamp, but "*without thinking of drawing
his gun.*" In *Le chien jaune*, Maigret and Leroy observe the pathetic scene of

the reunion between Léon and Emma: "*Why had Emma clasped her hands? … Her face was distorted by a troubled expression of fear, pleading, pain.… Inspector Leroy heard Maigret cock his gun. They were only about 15 yards away. A sharp crack, a broken window and the colossus would be in no condition to do any harm*" (JAU: 7). Of course, Maigret wouldn't shoot.… In *La nuit du carrefour*, in the scene where Mme Goldberg gets shot, Maigret dashes after the person who fired, and "*while running, the Chief Inspector takes his gun from his pocket.*" But he doesn't shoot. He won't make use of his weapon until the end of the novel, when he'll shoot at the inner tubes containing drugs in Oscar's garage, then later through Michonnet's empty window. In *Le fou de Bergerac*, Maigret chases the unknown man from the train, reaches into his pocket for his revolver, but doesn't have time to get it out before he himself feels the shock of a bullet. In *Maigret*, the Chief Inspector picks up Audiat's trail, but he's followed himself by Eugène's car. "*It was too late to turn back. And further, he had no desire to.… His only precaution was to take his gun from his pants pocket and ready it*" (MAI: 6). If he didn't shoot at that moment, he would later, when, at Cageot's, Cageot understood that he'd been trapped by Maigret's trick. "*At the word "telephone," Cageot glanced at the receiver. At the same moment there was a blast, an odor of burnt powder filled the room, and a bluish cloud spread across the floor. Maigret had fired. The bullet had hit Cageot's hand, causing his gun to fall*" (MAI: 10).

In *Maigret et son mort*, Maigret is armed during Bronsky's turbulent arrest… "*He took his gun from a desk drawer, assuring himself that it was loaded, as Colombani watched him with a faint smile. 'You want me with you?…' 'You have your piece?' 'Always in my pocket.' Not Maigret … it was rare*" (MOR: 9) But the Chief Inspector didn't make use of it, preferring to fall with all his weight on his adversary. In *Maigret au Picratt's*, during the arrest of Oscar Bonvoisin, there's a gun, first mentioned three times to punctuate the action: "*There was no sound, no sign of life inside. The Chief Inspector nonetheless had his gun in his hand.… He went back down when he heard steps outside, and glued himself to the wall, his gun pointed towards the door.… He placed one of his men at each side of the third door, and rested his hand on the knob, holding his gun with the other*" (PIC: 9) However, he only made unintended use of his weapon; having discovered Bonvoisin, instead of shooting him, he "*held his gun by the barrel, and tried to hit him with the butt.*" In *Maigret, Lognon et les gangsters*, Maigret, who wasn't armed when he was followed by Cinaglia in the streets of Paris, decides to carry his gun when it turns into a fight; since the gangsters want to "play American style," he can use their technique. Maigret takes drastic measures and goes to arrest them at Maisons-Laffitte: "*Maigret … had taken an automatic from his drawer and was checking that it was loaded…. His pockets were weighed down with two automatics.* [one was for Torrence]." And this time, Maigret would make use of his weapon; Cinaglia, who'd seen Maigret through the window, was about to shoot him "*At the same moment, Maigret pressed the trigger of his own gun, and as in a Hollywood film, Charlie's gun fell to the floor, while his hand hung limp.*" (LOG: 7). In *Le revolver de Maigret* (REV), besides mentioning the famous American revolver, which "*he had never used,*" we find also this sentence the Chief Inspector says to Alain Lagrange, "*I'm unarmed … it's a mistake to think that all the inspectors and Chief Inspectors of the PJ are armed. In reality, they have no more right to be than any other citizen.*" Finally, in *Maigret et l'indicateur* (IND), the Chief Inspector has to arrest Manuel Mori: "*A little later, Maigret returned to his office and did something unusual: he took his automatic from a drawer and slipped it into his pocket.*"

It's clear—Maigret only rarely uses a gun, essentially when it's an affair involving "tough guys," and above all for defense. Four shots in the entire saga, one into some inner tubs, and one into a window, we see easily that the Chief Inspector is not a believer in "strong arm tactics."

6

Work Places

Quai des Orfèvres: A Visit to Maigret's Office

Maigret's office is not only his workplace, where he assembles the elements of a case (reading reports, using the phones and the centralizing information), but it's also a gathering place, where he meets with his faithful collaborators, and a "confessional" where he directs his "clients" to their final confession. And we recall that it was chronologically the first place described in the saga, the setting for the opening scene of *Pietr le Letton* (LET). Let's follow the path Maigret takes at the Quai des Orfèvres on his way to his office.

THE STAIRCASE

"*He hurried under the arch of the P.J. where there was always a draft, making straight for the stairs, encountering the characteristic odor of the building, the pale green light of the still-lit lamps*" (*Maigret et les témoins récalcitrants*, TEM: 1). When Maigret arrives at the Quai, he greets the orderly with a wave of his hand, crosses the *glacial* porch, *always dark*, surmounted by a "*stone arch where it's always colder than elsewhere*" (*Maigret voyage*, VOY: 8), then crosses the equally *glacial* courtyard and starts up the staircase. This staircase is not insignificant in the Maigret saga. The Chief Inspector ascends and descends it innumerable times in the course of his investigations, and Maigret has his own way of taking the stairs—most often, climbing slowly, *heavily, with slow steps, his step heavy*, both because he anticipates the difficulties of an investigation ("*Maigret had a way of climbing the stairs to the second floor of the Quai des Orfèvres, seemingly indifferent at first, at the base of the stairway, where the outside light was fairly direct, then more preoccupied as he penetrated the gloom of the old building, as if the cares of the office enveloped him as he approached*" [*L'amie de Madame Maigret*, MME: 2]), and because this "ascension" towards his office is like the beginning of an almost invariable ritual; after the staircase, there comes the length of the hallways, the greeting of the old usher, the traditional showing his face in the inspectors' room, and finally entering his own office.

More prosaically, the climbing of these stairs is also slow for Maigret because he bears a certain weight, and not just psychological! Which is why he climbs the stairs "*breathing heavily*," arriving at the top "*always slightly out of breath*," and in the end he's had enough of this climb, if we can believe his comment in his last case (according to the chronology of the writing), "*They've modernized the place, grumbled a breathless Maigret, but they didn't come up with the idea of installing an elevator*" (*Maigret et Monsieur Charles*, CHA: 1) An elevator?! Heaven forbid! What would become of the poetry of the staircase, "*with the slanted rays of the sun like you see in a church*" (*Les mémoires de Maigret*, MEM: 7).

What's this stairway like? It's *large, vast, wide, grayish, drab, poorly lit*, with a weak bulb here and there, but above all dusty, with a very special dust, "*like a fog of dust in the sun*" (*Maigret et la Grande Perche*, GRA: 3). And if the stairway manages "*even in summer, on the brightest morning, to be sad and gloomy*" (*Maigret aux assises*, ASS: 4), what can be said of its condition in fall and winter where its deadly drafts always reign, "*wet footsteps mottle the stairs* " (*Maigret et l'homme du banc*, BAN: 1), where "*a damp draft ran through it and the wet footsteps on the stairs didn't dry*" (*Maigret aux assises*, ASS: 4). On these stairs, Maigret has unchanging habits: that of sniffing with pleasure, the familiar odor, of looking deeply into the stairwell behind him, and of mechanically casting a glance into the waiting room at the top of the stairs, on the second floor, on the left, at the entrance to the hallway where the Chief Inspectors' offices are lined up.

The Waiting Room

Maigret calls it the "glass cage," because one side is glass. And as the door is also on this side, it's also glass. On the other three walls, covered with light green wallpaper, are aligned black frames containing photographs of policemen "fallen in the line of duty." The room has a fireplace, on the mantle of which is enthroned "*a Louis-Philippe clock, exactly like the one in Maigret's office, and running no better than his*" (*Les caves du Majestic*, MAJ: 11). In the middle of the room, a table covered with green cloth, so that it resembled a billiard table. Visitors could sit, as they chose, on armless chairs or in armchairs, equally covered in green velvet, equally uncomfortable. In spite of the windows, a lamp is always lit in this room. And this electric light, no doubt fairly dim, made the room "*poorly lit*," with the green of the furniture and walls giving everything a *"gloomy, depressing"* atmosphere. Maigret wondered why they'd chosen that green shade *"whose reflection gave faces a cadaverous tinge."* (*Cécile est morte*, CEC: 1st part: 2). In fact, this depressing green tint and the glass walls had a certain usefulness: overwhelmed by this atmosphere *"yellowish and sad like in a little provincial railway station"* (*Les scrupules de Maigret*, SCR: 2), witnesses—and above all suspects—became more talkative, relieved at finally being seen after having been left *simmering* long enough for them to become *well-done* and ready '*to spill the beans.*' And so it's often intentional that the Chief Inspector lets his visitors *stew* in this room to which the inspectors have given various names—*"the aquarium,"* because of the glass walls and greenish tint, and from the impression the police must feel of watching their visitors "in a goldfish bowl," or the *lantern*, or the *icebox*, a metaphor which, like *purgatory*, suggests well this idea of the interminable wait the visitors suffer, a wait imposed and desired by Maigret, to the end of *"making them talkative"* and *"having them reach the end of their resistance."*

THE HALLWAY

We find Maigret again at the top of the stairs. After pushing open the glass door, we discover a vast, long hallway, an immense corridor with many doors, as dusty, damp, and poorly lit as the stairway, where a single lamp served as a nightlight and it lit the long dusty perspective of *"this hallway, the grayest, the most drab on earth, today touched by the sun, at least in the form of a sort of luminous dust"* (*Maigret et le corps sans tête*, COR: 2). This hallway, so animated during the day—*"you could hear the inspectors coming and going ... doors slamming, telephones being used in all the offices"* (*Cécile est morte*, CEC: 1st part: 1); so calm and deserted at night—*"Was it possible to be any more at home in the vast premises of the Police Judiciaire, than dead in the middle of the night ... he opened the door of his office and contemplated the long perspective of the corridor, where but two dim lamps were lit ... the night drew on thus, in the intimate heat of these vast premises that the darkness seemed to shrink, and where only five were working or moving about"* (*Maigret et l'inspecteur Malgracieux*, mal: 2).

THE OFFICE OF THE DIRECTOR
OF THE PJ AND THAT OF THE INSPECTORS

Now that we're in the hallway, we can push open any of the various doors, and find ourselves, for example, in the office of the Director of the PJ. Maigret likes this room, situated at the end of a long hall. Preceded by a waiting room furnished with armchairs and an enormous round settee covered with red velvet, we enter the office through an upholstered door. It's lit by a number of lamps, one of which, with a green shade, is set on the mahogany desk, where we also find a crystal globe serving as a paperweight, and a copper inkwell. There are two mahogany bookcases.

We open another door, and we're in the inspectors' room... "*He could have called Lucas by phone, but, when it was one of his inspectors, he preferred to get up from his chair, to go and open the door which communicated with their office. It was not to check on them, but in a way, to take the temperature of the house*" (*Maigret et les témoins récalcitrants*, TEM: 4). We can access this office either from the hallway or from Maigret's office, where one of the two doors opens directly into it. Maigret likes to go "*prowling in the inspectors' room*" (*Les scrupules de Maigret*, SCR: 4) when an investigation is "stalled," as if to absorb some energy. "*He felt empty, useless. Yet, by habit, he pushed open ... the door of the inspectors' office*" (*Maigret se défend*, DEF: 4), "*To kill time, he ... made a little tour of the inspectors' room...*" (*Maigret aux assises*, ASS: 4). Maigret had done this innumerable times, the act of opening the door to the inspectors' room, to the extent that it had become a sort of ritual... "*In spite of a day's surprises, there were almost ritual actions he did without thinking, like, after lighting his pipe, pushing open the door to the inspectors' office*" (La patience de Maigret, PAT: 1). He prefers this direct contact with his men rather than calling them on the intercom.

What's it like? It's a large, wide room, where each Inspector has his place (Maigret had had his there also, in his beginnings) before an ink-stained wooden table, (on which Torrence had once amused himself by carving his initials). The room had to be large, for as many as 20 Inspectors could be there. Besides the tables, the room is furnished with green-shaded lamps, chairs, luminous globes, telephones, and above all, typewriters, whose clacking could often be heard from Maigret's office. In this room typically reigns great animation, a continual coming and going... "*During this time, fifty other cases lay claim to the inspectors. They come in, go out, telephone, type their reports...*" (*Maigret et son mort*, MOR: 2); and sometimes—extremely rarely—you find but two watchmen playing cards. We note also that Lucas, being a Sergeant, has the right to his own office, besides his space in the Inspectors' room.

CRIMINAL RECORDS AND THE LABORATORIES OF FORENSIC IDENTIFICATION

Before heading into Maigret's office, while we're still in the hallway, let's take the stairs up to the attics, and the laboratories of Forensic Identity. Here we find the Criminal Records room, where "*on miles of shelves are aligned the dossiers of all those who have fallen afoul of the law.*" (*Maigret et la jeune morte*, JEU: 6). The employees there are dressed in long grey smocks, working with more than *80,000* files, stored in iron cabinets, and holding the fingerprints of all those who have passed through the anthropometric services. The room is next to the laboratory of Forensic Identification, separated from it by a spiral staircase, "*poorly lit, resembling one taken from a château*" (*L'amie de Madame Maigret*, MME: 5).

To access the laboratories, Moers's empire, we have to go through "*a complex network of corridors and stairways*" (*Pietr le Letton*, LET: 3) narrow and tortuous. We push open the door with the frosted glass panes, and enter the area of anthropometry, a gray-painted room, furnished with benches where those arrested during the night left their clothing, with an anthropometric chair used for measurements, and photographic apparatus. The photographs are developed in a little adjoining room, lit by a neon lamp. "*Another stairway, on the left, narrower than the first, leads to the laboratory*" (*Maigret*, MAI: 4), where "*specialists ... begin their meticulous work on various objects*" (*L'amoureux de Madame Maigret*, amo: 2). The laboratory, with mansard windows, is an immense room with a sloping ceiling, whose roof was partly windowed, explaining why it was overheated in summer, and a mansard window. What do we find in this room? First of all the famous articulated mannequin used for reconstructions. And then test-tubes and projectors, all sorts of complicated equipment used by the dozen or so technicians and specialists in gray or white smocks. In the corner of the room, we find Moers's table, lit by a lamp "*which he moves towards or away from his work by pulling on a piece of wire*" (*L'amie de Madame Maigret*, MME: 5), and which is covered with diverse and sundry objects ... "*loupes of all sizes, scrapers, pliers, bottles of ink, chemicals, as well as a clear glass screen lit by a strong electric lamp*" (*La tête d'un homme*, TET: 4), "*all a set of delicate instruments*" (*Maigret tend un piège*, TEN: 4). We note that Maigret does not dispute the utility of material clues; he knows very well that they "*need specialists in nine cases out of ten, if not just for fingerprint issues*" (*Maigret et l'indicateur*, IND: 4), and he has often been assisted in his investigations by the work of Moers and his men, which has permitted him to confirm his intuitions. We cite here, among so many examples, the red wax found under Calas's fingernails (*Maigret et le corps sans tête*), the wood dust in Moss's clothing (*L'amie de Madame Maigret*), the coffee stains on the letter written by Radek (*La tête d'un homme*). More than once, Maigret has gone upstairs, as he says, to the attic, not only to see how the investigations were proceeding, but also because he "*liked the atmosphere of these rooms under the roof, where they worked far from the public, in a peaceful ambiance*" (*Maigret et l'indicateur*, IND: 4).

Maigret's Office

"*My guest regarded my pipes, my ashtrays, the black marble clock on the mantle, the little enamel basin behind the door, the towel which always smelled like a wet dog.... And I can still see young Sim coming into my office in the morning, as if he'd become one of my inspectors, politely telling me 'Don't trouble yourself...' and sitting himself down in a corner.*" (*Les mémoires de Maigret*, MEM: 1). So, shall we do as "young Sim," and push open the door to Maigret's office, found at the end of the corridor, the second door, the next to the last on the left? We turn the white porcelain knob. It's first of all a light and an odor which strikes us: "*Pipe smoke floated in the air of the office where the rays of the sun shone in obliquely. The air began to smell of ham, beer, coffee.*" (*Maigret et les vieillards*, VIE: 7) There was always the odor of a cold pipe, of tobacco. Behind the door there's a hook or a peg where the Chief Inspector hangs his jacket. His overcoat is on a coat-hanger. But most often, he keeps his hat and coat in the cupboard ("recess, nook, recess in a wall, compartment, closed by a door and constituting a fixed wardrobe."—as defined in the *Petit Robert* dictionary). In Maigret's office, this "recess in a wall" must have been all the same somewhat sizeable, since the Chief Inspector can lean halfway into it, and it contains "*an enamel basin, a hand-towel, a mirror and a suitcase*" (*Pietr le Letton*, LET: 6), and shaving materials, a razor, shaving cream and a towel. Described since the beginning of the saga, this cupboard has great importance throughout the investigations; we often see Maigret washing his hands there, and above all, taking out the famous bottle of cognac which he keeps "*less for himself than for certain of his clients who sometimes have need of it*" (*Les scrupules de Maigret*, SCR: 8); and if he serves a glass (or two!) to Ferdinand Voivin (*L'affaire du boulevard Beaumarchais*), Ernestine (*Maigret et la Grande Perche*), Helen Donahue (*Maigret, Lognon et les gangsters*), Jef Schrameck (*Maigret et l'homme du banc*), Emile Lentin (*Un échec de Maigret*), Jenny (*Les scrupules de Maigret*), Adrien Josset (*Une confidence de Maigret*), Mme Josselin (*Maigret et les braves gens*), Norris Jonker (*Maigret et le fantôme*), Francis Ricain (*Le voleur de Maigret*), or Louis Mahossier (*Maigret et l'homme tout seul*), it sometimes happens that he has need of one himself.

The floor of Maigret's office is covered with a rug. On the wall, behind the desk, a map of Europe, one of Paris, and in a black and gold frame, a photo of the Association of Station Secretaries from when Maigret was 24. We might expect "*a desk covered with files, with two or three telephones ringing at once, inspectors coming in and out, witnesses or suspects slumped in chairs*" (*Les scrupules de Maigret*, SCR: 1). But today, the morning is calm, and we find the Chief Inspector "*seated at his desk, the stove humming at his back.*

On his left, the window, which the fog covers like cheesecloth; before him on the mantle, the black marble Louis-Philippe clock, the hands stopped for 20 years at noon" (Les caves du Majestic, MAJ: 8).

His Desk

On his desk, pipes, of course, and heaps of files and reports, through which Maigret must sometimes rummage, for *"order wasn't Maigret's strong point"* (*Stan le Tueur*, sta: 3). We also find a large glass ashtray, but since it's usually filled with ashes, Maigret has the habit of emptying his pipe into the coal scuttle. Always on the desk, within arm's reach, Maigret has a telephone, a telephone directory, and a calendar. And there's also a lamp there, with a green shade, which blocks the light and casts strange reflections on the faces of "clients" seated opposite the Chief Inspector, *"leaning towards the circle of light of his lamp which illuminated an annotated file"* (*Maigret et le voleur paresseux*, PAR: 4). Maigret is usually satisfied with the *"greenish light"* diffused by his desk lamp, and doesn't bother with the ceiling lamp, *"so that the edges of the room remained in shadow and only faces were illuminated"* (*Maigret et le marchand de vin*, VIN: 6), and the bulb had no shade, which gave a harsh light. Greenish light, harsh light, like that of a lighthouse illuminating the windows of the PJ at night, a sign that interrogations were taking place, a battle between a man driven to the brink of a confession and the Chief Inspector seeking a truth. Finally, the man is sent to the Dépôt, the photographers jostling each other, the journalists rushing *"towards Maigret's office, which resembled a battlefield. Glasses, cigarette butts, ashes, torn papers, the air smelling of tobacco already cold."* (*Maigret tend un piège*, TEN: 1). Under his desk, Maigret has available an electric button, allowing him to buzz for the usher or an inspector. Finally, the desk has drawers, in which Maigret keeps a rather sundry collection of objects: some telegrams, papers on a suspect, a cold pipe, some cigarettes, packets of drugs, a revolver, photographs of a crime scene, the key to the door between the PJ and the Palais de Justice, a list of the nightclubs and cabarets of Paris.

The Mantle and the Clock

The mantle is of black marble, the top decorated with a bust of the Republic; and on it a black marble clock with bronze ornaments, flanked with candlesticks. While it was stuck for years at noon (MAJ: 8), somehow Maigret had gotten it to run, though as often as he'd adjusted it, it usually seemed to be 10 minutes fast, or 15 minutes slow. This clock had been made by a certain F. Ledent—his signature was visible in beautiful script on the pale face—

supplied 50 or 100 years earlier to all the administrations and ministries, and all the offices of the PJ. Whether fast or slow, the clock nonetheless marked the time in Maigret's office, and he refers to it when he remembers the time a visitor had come, or when he'd responded to a more or less disagreeable phone call, or to know that it's time to go home, or to call his wife to tell her that he'd get something to eat at the Brasserie Dauphine.

The Stove

In spite of the fireplace (moreover, probably Maigret had never made a fire there, and it was rather just for show), Maigret has in his office a stove, no doubt the accessory, besides his pipe and overcoat, most indispensable for his character. We recall further that this stove was "born" at the same time as Maigret himself… *"During the rest of the day, I added to my character certain accessories … a pipe, a bowler hat, a heavy overcoat with a velvet collar. And, as there was a damp cold in my abandoned barge, I gave him, for his office, an old cast iron stove"* (Simenon: *La naissance de Maigret [The Birth of Maigret]*, foreword to the *Complete Works* from Éditions Rencontre).

Why did Simenon endow Maigret with this mythical stove? The answer given by Simenon is no doubt insufficient by itself. Another reason is probably that Maigret doesn't use his stove simply for the heat it gives off, but also because he likes to poke at it, either to compose himself during a difficult interrogation, or to occupy himself while he reflects on a difficult case… *"I must admit that I harbored a certain fondness for that huge stove, whose iron bars I loved to see glowing red in winter, and which I used to stoke up to the brim. This was not so much an inveterate habit as a trick to keep my composure. In the middle of a difficult interrogation I would get up and poke the fire at length, then throw in noisy shovelfuls of coal, looking quite bland, while my client stared at me in bewilderment"* (*Les mémoires de Maigret*, MEM: 1). The stove appears from the beginning of the saga, since the novel *Pietr le Letton* opens with this sentence. *"Chief Inspector Maigret, of the First Flying Squad, lifted his head, had the impression the roaring of the cast iron stove planted in the middle of his office and connected to the ceiling by a fat black pipe, was weakening. He … got up heavily, adjusted the key, and tossed in three pieces of coal. After which, standing, his back to the fire, he filled a pipe."*

Chronologically the first object mentioned, the stove has from the beginning an important place in the investigations; not only does it allow the portrayal of Maigret in one of his favorite attitudes, but it's also an essential element of the environment in which the Chief Inspector operates. This stove has a very important place in *Pietr le Letton*—Maigret passes his time refilling it, warming himself at it, and it's the reason his office, in this case, strongly evokes the feeling of a sanctuary of well-being to which Maigret always returns after one of his excursions into the cold and damp of November. We find him in this same pose in *L'ombre chinoise* (OMB: 4), "*he planted himself with his back to the fire in his characteristic pose when he need to reflect.*" Maigret et son mort (MOR: 1) begins with Maigret stoking the fire in "*the last stove in the PJ, which he had struggled to keep during the installation of central heating at the Quai des Orfèvres.*" Waiting for the phone call from Albert, he suppresses impatience by "*talking, smoking his pipes, stoking, from time to time, the stove*" which was so full you could see below it *a little red disk.* But the administration will win out, and eventually remove his dear stove, and Maigret can merely express his regrets. "*If Maigret still had his coal stove, which they'd allowed him for so long after the installation of central heating, but had finally taken away, he would have stopped from time to time to fill it, to stoke it and make a rainfall of red cinders*" (*Les scrupules de Maigret*, SCR: 1). Henceforth, no more stoking, no more coal, no more roaring of the stove. Maigret would have to content himself with the gurgling in the pipes, the scalding radiators that the person in charge of heating hardly knew how to adjust correctly, so that the heat was stifling in Maigret's office, and he could no longer doze tranquilly, numbed by the heat of his stove.

The Window

The window of Maigret's office is double, side-by-side, and can be closed with curtains or a linen shade. But it's rare that Maigret closes the curtains, for the importance of this window is not so much the light it allows into the room, but rather that it's an opening onto the outside, a way for Maigret to regard the scenery of the Seine—"*He planted himself in front of the open window and saw 'his' view of the Seine, with as much joy as if he hadn't seen it for weeks*" (*Maigret et l'indicateur*, IND: 5); and to hear the sounds of his city— "*from time to time he raised his head like a schoolboy, turning toward the unmoving foliage of the trees, listening to the rustling of Paris which took on a particular sonority on the hot days of summer*" (*La colère de Maigret*, COL: 1). What does Maigret see from his window? Two essential elements: the Seine and the Saint-Michel bridge; and all the descriptions of the views from his office window revolve around these two elements. "*He watched, dreamily, the Seine flowing beyond the trees, the passing boats, the bright spots of women's dresses on the Pont Saint-Michel*" (*Maigret et le clochard*, CLO: 4). On the Seine, the indispensable barges... "*In a kind of bluish-green dust, the Seine flowed, almost black, and a bargeman was hosing down the deck of his boat moored at the quay. A tug glided silently by with the current, going off to seek its string of barges ... the tug from earlier was coming back upriver, whistling*" *before passing under the bridge, followed by seven barges*" (*Le revolver de Maigret*, REV: 5).

The scene from his window also gave Maigret indications of the weather. "*The curtains had not been drawn, so you could easily see the drops of rain roll down the black panes, starry in the reflections of the lamps of the quays*" (*L'affaire du boulevard Beaumarchais*, bea), "*he interrupted himself with a sigh to go and open the window. He'd hardly had time ... to return to his place and savor a spring breeze which gave a particular flavor to his pipe, when his papers started to rustle, rising to finally scatter throughout the room.*" (*Maigret et la jeune morte*, JEU: 5), or the time of day ... "*you could see the windowpanes progressively darken, the view dissolving into points of light which seemed as far away as the stars*" (*Maigret et la Grande Perche*, GRA: 7), "*The Seine took on the aura of a milky fog which whitened and made the day, revealing the empty quays*" (*La nuit du carrefour*, NUI: 1).

Finally, for Maigret, this window has another function. It's thanks to the window that he can take one of his favorite poses, that of *planting himself in front of the window*, a position he adopts numerous times, either for reflection, or to "change his thinking" ("*The Chief Inspector went to stand for a moment in front of the open window, as if to take a bath of reality by regarding the passers-by and the cars on the Pont Saint-Michel, a tug with a large white cloverleaf on its stack*" [*Le voleur de Maigret*, VOL: 3]), or yet to listen to the end of an interrogation. He also used it often when filling a new pipe.

But this manner of planting himself so often at the window has perhaps also another meaning... "*In his office, as on the Boulevard Richard-Lenoir, Maigret had the habit of walking up to the window and staying there, looking at nothing in particular, the windows across the way, the trees, the Seine or the passers-by. Was it perhaps a sign of claustrophobia? Everywhere, he instinctively seeks contact with the outside*" (*Maigret se défend*, DEF: 6), "*And where does it come from, his mania, in the office, of rising at any time to go and plant himself before the window? ... He liked his office, but he couldn't spend two hours there before he seemed to need to escape. In the course of an investigation, he wanted to be everywhere at once*" (*Le voleur de* Maigret, VOL: 6).

Chairs, Armchairs, Beer and Sandwiches

To receive visitors, Maigret sets out chairs, some of green velour (which he supplements, when the visitors are numerous, with chairs borrowed from the inspectors' office), armchairs, of which some are also of green velvet, but he prefers to have his clients installed directly in the light in front of him, in an uncomfortable chair, so that they feel somewhat discomfited, which "helps" them speak.

Maigret himself is in *his* armchair, where he happily seats himself, or sinks into for a nap, "*leaning back in his armchair, his vest unbuttoned, a pipe gone out in his teeth*" (*Les caves du Majestic*, MAJ: 8), adopting sometimes a pose which speaks volumes about his rapport with his client. Thus in *La tête d'un homme* (TET: 9), facing Radek, "*The Chief Inspector, feigning indifference, leaned back in his armchair, put his feet up on the desk and listened with the distracted air of sometime who has the time, but doesn't take great interest in the conversation,*" or in *L'ombre chinoise* (OMB: 4) with Mme Martin: "*He was leaning backwards, in a coarse enough pose, and he was smoking his pipe in delicious little puffs.*"

One last element forms an integral part of the decor of Maigret's office, and that's the immense tray covered with demis and piles of sandwiches which the waiter from the Brasserie Dauphine would bring so many times during the course of his famous interrogations, where the office was the theater. Indeed it's hard to imagine those long nights at the PJ without the presence of the sandwiches and beers that Maigret and his men ingest, whether they're hungry or not, since this food forms an inevitable part of the ritual. "'*Who will take care of ordering some beer at the Brasserie Dauphine? And some sandwiches!' It was a sign that one of the big nights at the PJ was beginning*" (*Maigret et son mort*, MOR: 9); "*Maigret's office, in the end, looked like a barracks, with empty glasses, plates of sandwiches on the table, pipe ash almost everywhere on the floor, and scattered papers*" (*Maigret et l'inspecteur Malgracieux*, mal: 3).

Here we are at the end of our visit to Maigret's office. The Chief Inspector's day is finished, we're going to let him "*descend the stairs all alone, his back heavy,*" then "*stop on the first landing to slowly light the pipe that he's just filled*" (*Maigret tend un piège*, TEN: 8). "*As always at that hour, there's a draft, and the stairway is damp and cold*" (*Maigret et le fantôme*, FAN: 1). But no matter—Maigret, after having taken a last glass at the Brasserie Dauphine, will return to the warm atmosphere of his apartment on the Boulevard Richard-Lenoir. Louise awaits him, with a nice little dish simmering. We'll leave him there for today, his silhouette disappearing into the fog at the end of the street.

Emergency Services

Besides 36, Quai des Orfèvres, there's another important location for police work—the premises of *Police-Secours*, Emergency Services, located in the Préfecture de Police building. *Police-Secours* is mentioned in many novels, sometimes when Maigret receives a call from them, sometimes when he calls them himself to learn if something has happened in Paris, or sometimes he just goes over, to "take the pulse" of the capital.

The first mention of this locale occurs in the story *L'Etoile du Nord*, where it's a call from the officer on duty at *Police-Secours* which will clinch Maigret's investigation. The novel *Signé Picpus* opens at *Police-Secours...* "*Three minutes to five. A white bulb lights up on the immense map of Paris which covers one entire section of wall. A worker sets down his sandwich, inserts a plug into one of a thousand holes of a telephone switchboard.*" (SIG: 1). Further along, the locale is described as a "*room which is like the brain of Police-Secours.*" It's there that Maigret has come to await the announcement of the possible murder of a fortune-teller.

The story *Maigret et l'inspecteur Malgracieux* begins at *Police-Secours*. Maigret, "*bored, alone in his office,*" awaiting an important phone call, crosses the street. "*It was comfortable, a little heavy, in the vast room of Police-Secours, where Maigret had come for refuge.*" There he found his nephew Daniel, with whom he exchanged some family news. There follows next in the text a lengthy explanation of Maigret's relationship with the place... "*Maigret had always liked this immense room, calm and neat like a laboratory, but which was, however, the very heart of Paris. At every intersection in the city, there are red-painted devices, with a glass that has simply to be broken to connect automatically with the police station of the district by telephone, as well as with the central station. Does someone call for help for some reason or another? Immediately one of the lights goes on on the giant map. All day long, all night long, the dramatic life of the capital comes thus to be written in little lamps on a wall. Maigret had always maintained that young inspectors should be required to serve at least a year in this department to learn the criminal geography of the city.*" It's precisely the breaking of the glass of a call box which is the origin of the investigation which unfolds for Maigret.

7

Collaborators

While Maigret, in his investigations, is the "team captain," the one who, *"each morning, puts everyone in his position, and follows the leads"* (*Les mémoires de Maigret,* MEM: 2), he is nevertheless surrounded by collaborators, to whom he entrusts parts of his investigations. Whether in Paris, the provinces, or sometimes out of the country, our Chief Inspector has had to work, over the course of his career, with a relatively significant number of policemen.

The Faithful Four

A Paternal and Friendly Relationship

Among his closest collaborators, Maigret has formed special bonds with four of them, his "faithful four," Lucas, Janvier, Lapointe and Torrence, an entourage serving him as both assistants and confidants. Thanks to this "front line" of loyal collaborators, he can escape the curse of nostalgia for his lost paternity. And so it's a privileged relationship that Maigret has with these four men, that of a "boss" and his team, that of an "almost father" with his "almost sons," a relationship of a man with other men.

These four characters are different and recognizable entities, endowed with their own characteristics marking their individuality, which not only permits giving an authenticity to the part of Maigret's life which takes place in his office, but still offers the Chief Inspector a diversity in the manifestation of his feelings. Thus, Maigret will behave with Lucas as with his second, the one who stands in for him, while with Janvier, and then with Lapointe, it's the notion of paternity that will be more in play, Maigret "chaperoning" the two men in their apprenticeships of their métier. The case of Torrence is a little different. In the beginning, second to Maigret at the start of the saga, after a "chance mishap," as we will see further along, he is replaced in this

101

function by Lucas, and "Fat Torrence" will later take on another role, while not as close to the Chief Inspector, still important however for the touch of humor which he brings to the novels.

If we speak of the "faithful four," it's not by chance, since we find the term in the texts themselves: "*Lucas understood that it was serious.… Maigret was phoning for him, was going to take Torrence off the stake-out and pick him up on the way, so automatically Lucas thought of Janvier, the other faithful, as if it would have been abnormal for the operation to take place without him.*" (*Maigret, Lognon et les gangsters*, LOG: 7). A very clear distinction is made between these four inspectors and Maigret's other collaborators, qualifying the four men as Maigret's "personal team," calling them his "*favorite inspectors*," his "*closest*," "*his most intimate*" collaborators.

If Maigret calls all his collaborators by a familiar "*mes enfants*" [my boys], it's to Lucas, Janvier, Torrence and Lapointe that his preferences go without a contest. He has a very close relationship with these four men, at once friendly ("*Outside of his closest collaborators, like Lucas, Janvier, Torrence and, more recently, young Lapointe, for whom Maigret had a real affection, the Chief Inspector had no friends except Dr. Pardon*" *Maigret et l'affaire Nahour*, NAH: 1) and paternal, particularly with Janvier, and later Lapointe, as we'll see further along. Maigret has not only transferred onto them the affection he couldn't give to a son, but he also appreciates them because with them there's no need to use long sentences; a glance is often enough for understanding. No need for the Chief Inspector to give long explanations ("*In Paris he would have had his team around him, fellows who knew his methods, and with whom he would hardly have had to speak*" *La maison du juge*, JUG: 3), and he sometimes lets them in on his "cogitations," for which they show their appreciation.

From their side, the devotion of the Faithful Four to their boss is almost cult-like. "*Torrence, who had no less than a veritable worship of the Chief Inspector*" (*Maigret à New York*, NEW: 8); "*There were three at the Quai … who granted the Chief Inspector an admiration bordering on worship: Lucas, the eldest, Janvier, who had been, some time back, as young, inexperienced and ardent as Lapointe, the third member, 'little Lapointe' as they called him*" (*Maigret voyage*, VOY: 2).

The Use of "*Tu*"

The closeness of the relationship between Maigret and his men is also denoted by the Chief Inspector's use of the familiar "*tu*" with them. Maigret uses "*tu*" sparingly, and those he addresses this way are rare, ignoring its special use by the police with certain "clients," petty thieves, streetwalkers, pimps, etc., who constitute the "professionals" of crime with whom the police deal most often, and with whom they are, in a way, on an equal footing. Outside of "professional" use, Maigret hardly uses "*tu*," which he essentially reserves for his wife. Even with Pardon, his only real friend, the Chief Inspector uses "*vous*." With his old schoolmates, he generally prefers "*vous*," permitting a certain distance. Finally, only his close collaborators have the right to a familiar "*tu*," and even so! While Maigret uses "*tu*" and "*vous*" almost equally often with Moers, with his more or less close collaborators—district inspectors, men in his brigade or provincial inspectors—he sometimes uses "*tu*," sometimes "*vous*," depending on his affinity, and on his mood of the moment.

With the Faithful Four, things are less evident than they may seem. While we might expect them to receive Maigret's "*tu*," he sometimes uses "*vous*," and the explanations given by Simenon himself are rather contradictory. Presented by the author in the novels of the last part of the saga, these "clarifications"—which they aren't exactly—show us rather that Simenon is not very clear about this use of "*tu*," and at the very least he doesn't seem to have taken the trouble to reread his novels before making his affirmations. But rather, let's examine the facts…. The first "explanation" of Maigret's use of "*tu*" with his collaborators is given in *Les scrupules de Maigret*… "*Except for Janvier, with whom he'd always used* "tu," *Maigret only used* "tu"—*and only with certain people—in the heat of action, or when he was very preoccupied*." (SCR: 6). Now let's look at the second explanation, found in *Maigret et le voleur paresseux*: "*There were a few like that, that the Chief Inspector used* "tu" *with, first off the old-timers, with whom he'd started, and who, at that time, used it to him too … though now they didn't dare, calling him Monsieur Chief Inspector, or sometimes* "Boss." *There was also Lucas. Not Janvier, he couldn't say why. And finally the very young ones, like little Lapointe*." (PAR: 3). Hmm, so with Janvier, does he use "*tu*" or not? Let's look at the third explanation, given in *Maigret et le tueur*: "*Of all his collaborators, Lucas went back the furthest, and Maigret sometimes used* "tu" *with him. Also with Lapointe, because he'd started out quite young, and he still seemed like a precocious kid*." (TUE: 3). Good, that seems to clear it up for Lapointe and Lucas, while.

Finally, the fourth explanation is in *Maigret et l'homme tout seul*: "*[Janvier] was the only one with whom Maigret used* "tu" *regularly. He also used* "tu" *with little Lapointe, the last to join the team. As for others, he used* "vous," *except sometimes when he was distracted or in the heat of action*" (SEU: 5). It would seem that Janvier would generally receive "*tu*," but if we take another, rather telling example, we find that the contradiction still exists. In *Maigret et le marchand de vin* (VIN: 6), when Maigret has regrouped his team in his office to review the Pigou affair, we see the Chief Inspector giving each his orders, and so he says to Janvier, "*You (Vous) Janvier, you (vous) go select six men who spell each other…*"; to Torrence, "*For you (vous), Torrence…. Your (votre) sector is the Place des Vosges…*"; to Lucas: "*Lucas, for now…. You (Toi), Lucas, you (tu) will cover the Quai de Charenton*."; and to Lapointe, "*You (Tu) stay, at my disposition…. You (Tu) will also organize our information….*" This hardly clarifies the problem of the use of "*tu*." And so we've attempted a somewhat more detailed analysis of the texts, and tried to formulate a possible rule for the Chief Inspector's use of "*tu*" with his Faithful Four.

Out of the 56 novels where **Lucas** is spoken to by Maigret, the Chief Inspector uses "*tu*" in 48, "*vous*" uniquely in one sole novel, and in 7 novels, he uses both forms. The first thing to note is that "*tu*" is clearly the form most utilized by Maigret, which seems natural enough between two men of whom one is the "oldest collaborator" of the other. The only novel where Maigret only uses "*vous*" is *Le charretier de La Providence*, and that's probably explained by the fact that it was the first novel, in the chronological order of the writing, where Maigret truly worked with Lucas. From the following novel, *Le pendu de Saint-Pholien*, Maigret used "*tu*" with his inspector. If we examine the 7 novels where the Chief Inspector uses both forms, we note the following points: First, in *La tête d'un homme*, Maigret uses "*tu*" and "*vous*" equally, using "*tu*" in the heat of action or when he is moved or excited. Here, for example, an extract from Ch. 2, where Maigret gives a simple order to Lucas, "*Listen (vous), my friend! … I want you (vous) to dash over to the offices of the 'Sifflet,' Rue Montmartre…*," and an extract from Ch. 3, when Heurtin attacks Dufour at the Citanguette. Maigret, who had witnessed the scene from afar, orders Lucas: "*Quick! … Take (tu) a car…. Dash (tu) over there….*" In the novels *La nuit du carrefour, Les caves du Majestic, Signé Picpus, Maigret voyage* and *Les scrupules de Maigret*, Maigret generally uses "*tu*" with Lucas, and he only uses "*vous*" in a very clear context—when he addresses him in someone else's presence, for example, a suspect he's interrogating—and this use of "*vous*" is in a way "official." Thus in *Signé Picpus*, Maigret is interrogating Le Cloaguen about his visits to Mlle Jeanne, "*Then Maigret got up, headed toward the door to call Lucas, and in a rough voice, "What's this, Sergeant…. I notice that your (vos) information is incorrect…. You (vous) certainly told me, Sergeant, that Mlle Jeanne never used cards*" (SIG: 5). Lastly, in *Maigret et le clochard*, where Lucas only appears on two occasions, when Maigret sends for him to get the belongings of the clochard at the hospital, and when the inspector arrives, Maigret uses "*vous*" at first, "*Come (vous) into my office for a moment. It was to send him to Hôtel-Dieu…. No doubt they'll send you* (vous) *from office to office…. You'd* (vous) *best arm yourself with some kind of impressive letter*" (CLO: 3), Then, when Lucas returns with the clochard's things, and comments on them, Maigret asks, "*Did you (*tu*) take his prints?*" (CLO: 4). In this case, Maigret's use of "*vous*" is probably because he's distracted

Of the 44 novels where Maigret directly addresses **Janvier**, he uses "*tu*" in 39, "*vous*" in one sole novel, and both forms in 4. Here again, the use of "*tu*" appears to be the form most commonly used by Maigret, explained both by Janvier's age at the beginning of the saga (a young man of 25 in *La tête d'un homme*), and then by the paternal relationship which Maigret maintains with him (*see below*). In the only novel where he uses "*vous*" exclusively with the inspector (*Maigret et le marchand de vin*), Janvier appears very infrequently, and the only scene in which Maigret addresses him directly is cited above. We could speak here also of an "official" use of "*vous.*" In the novels where Maigret uses both forms, we find in *Une confidence de Maigret* the "official" form, as for Lucas, when Maigret speaks to Janvier in the presence of a third party, and in the three other novels, *Signé Picpus, Les vacances de Maigret* and *Maigret et le tueur*, Maigret generally uses "*tu*" with Janvier, using "*vous*" only sometimes when he's "distracted."

The rapport between Maigret and **Torrence** being more complex (*see below*), this complexity also occurs in the use of "*tu*" and "*vous.*" Of the 31 novels which apply, Maigret uses "*tu*" with Torrence in 23 cases, "*vous*" in 6, and in 2 he uses both forms. He began by using "*vous*" with Torrence in *Pietr le Letton*, then used "*tu*" when the inspector reappeared in the Gallimard novels. He uses "*vous*" uniquely in *Les scrupules de Maigret, Maigret et les témoins récalcitrants, Une confidence de Maigret, Maigret et le marchand de vin* and *La folle de Maigret*, and finally Maigret uses both forms in *Maigret et les braves gens* and *Maigret et l'homme tout seul*—though we note that in these two novels, "*vous*" is used much more often than "*tu.*" Consider in *Maigret et les braves gens* (BRA: 3), this sentence referring to Torrence, "*He didn't use 'tu' with him, though he'd known him much longer than Lapointe.*"

In the case of **Lapointe**, things are much clearer. In the 34 novels considered, we find only one example of "*vous,*" in *Les scrupules de Maigret,* where, we note, Maigret generally uses "*tu*" with the inspector, using "*vous*" on only two occasions, a little by "distraction." The use of "*tu*" is obvious with Lapointe, whom Maigret has truly "taken under his wing," and who is for him an incontestable "substitute for paternity."

We can thus conclude, with regard to the use of "*tu,*" that it's most used for the Faithful Four, that it seems evident that Maigret uses this form of address in view of the bonds which unite him to his inspectors, and that the "*vous*" indicates, for him, a way of distancing himself, used by the Chief Inspector according to circumstances. The "*tu*," familiar, friendly and paternal, is reserved by Maigret for his closest, and the Faithful Four, without a doubt, form part of the Chief Inspector's "family."

Portrait of Musketeer Good Lucas

After having appeared briefly in *Pietr le Letton*, where his name was mentioned by Torrence, he rejoins Maigret in *Le charretier de La Providence* as an inspector for "he almost always worked with Maigret," then became sergeant from *Le pendu de Saint-Pholien* on. He had, in a way, taken the place of Torrence, killed in *Pietr le Letton*, and "resuscitated" by Simenon in the Gallimard novels. Described as Maigret's "*second*," his "*best collaborator*," his "*best sergeant*," he is the "*right arm*" of Maigret, whom he often replaces in the office when the Chief Inspector is absent. Described further as the "*oldest collaborator*," he's the one who will take Maigret's place when he retires.

OTHER APPEARANCES

Alongside his "official" presence in the Maigret saga, the name Lucas appears as well in some novels published under pseudonyms. First, in the four novels signed Christian Brulls: *L'inconnue*, *Fièvre*, *Les forçats de Paris*, and *L'évasion*. In the last two, the name Lucas is only mentioned, while in the first two, Lucas plays a more important role: In *Fièvre*, he's an inspector under the orders of Chief Inspector Torrence, while in *L'inconnue*, the roles are reversed; it's Lucas who's the Chief Inspector, and Torrence his inspector. Lucas also appears in two novels signed Georges Sim, *La fiancée du diable* and *Matricule 12*, in which he is Chief Inspector.

Further, Simenon also sets Lucas in some stories and novels signed in his own name, the novels *Les suicidés*, *Le testament Donadieu*, *L'homme qui regardait passer les trains*, *Monsieur La Souris*, *L'outlaw* and *L'enterrement de Monsieur Bouvet*, and the stories *Philippe* (in the collection "*Les 13 coupables*"); *L'énigme de la Marie Galante* (in the collection "*Les sept minutes*"); *La piste de l'homme roux*, *La Bonne Fortune du Hollandais*, *L'amiral a disparu*, *La sonnette d'alarme*, *Le château de l'arsenic*, and *L'amoureux aux pantoufles* (in "*Le petit docteur*"); *L'arrestation du musicien*, *Le vieillard au porte-mine*, *Le ticket de métro*, *Le prisonnier de Lagny*, *Le club des vieilles dames*, *Le docteur Tant-Pis*, and *Le chantage de l'agence O* (in the collection "*Les dossiers de l'agence O*"). In *Les suicidés*, *L'outlaw* and *L'enterrement de Monsieur Bouvet*,

Lucas is an Inspector (in *L'outlaw* he's under the orders of Chief Inspector Lognon), while in the three other novels cited, and in the stories, he is Chief Inspector.

Physical Description

Small, plump, pudgy, "almost as fat [as Maigret], but shorter" (*Le port des brumes*, POR: 7), so that the Chief Inspector appeared "twice as large and substantial as Lucas" (*Maigret, Lognon et les gangsters*, LOG: 4). The sergeant tried to copy his Chief's ways... "*Lucas, insisting on resembling Maigret in all points, placidly puffed a pipe*" (*Signé Picpus*, SIG: 8); "*Lucas was almost his replica, with a smaller head, shoulders half as broad, and a face which he could hardly render stern. Without boastfulness, perhaps without realizing it, by mimicry, through admiration, he had wound up copying his Chief down to the smallest gestures, in his attitudes and expressions.... Even his way of sniffing the glass of plum brandy before it reached his lips...*" (*Un Noël de Maigret*, noe: 4). His short, portly silhouette, his short legs, his appearance of "*a fat little man who walks with a bounce*" (*Maigret s'amuse*, AMU: 7), "*trailing his left leg a little*" (*Maigret chez le ministre*, MIN: 4), making you think "*of one of those foolish dogs which seem to have sausages for legs*" (*Maigret et son mort*, MOR: 5). These "canine" comparisons return frequently, in *Signé Picpus*, when Maigret learns of Mascouvin's accident—"*Lucas was standing near him, a Lucas who averted his look and who had the air of a beaten dog*" (SIG: 2); in *La pipe de Maigret*, when Maigret goes to look for Joseph at Chelles—"*Lucas brought up the rear with the indifference of a Newfoundland dog*" (pip: 3); in *Maigret au Picratt's*, Arlette's aunt is accompanied by Lucas to the morgue—"*She was taller than the sergeant, very cold, and, in the hallway where she led the way, she seemed almost to be leading him on the end of a leash*" (PIC: 5); in *Maigret en meublé*, Maigret rejoins Lucas at Cochin where Janvier has just been operated on—"*Little Lucas took several steps towards him, with the sideways gait of a beaten dog.*" (MEU: 1). We note that aside from the comic effect of this description, the comparison can also be "moral," suggesting loyalty.

The portrait can be further completed in saying that Lucas, beardless, usually closely shaven, except when he'd spent the night on the job, wore a "*Charlie Chaplin mustache*" (or at least that's what we learn in *L'arrestation du musicien!*). With the passage of time, he's going bald.

As for dress, Lucas wore the same sort of clothes as his boss: a hat, straw in summer, a Panama which, on his head, looked like "*a native hut or a lampshade*"! (*Maigret et la Grande Perche*, GRA: 1); a black overcoat, long and full, which made him look like a candle-snuff, according to Torrence!

(*L'arrestation du musicien*), a jacket, a vest, and when he was in a good mood, a bright tie, in fact, "*whimsical, blue with white polka dots*" (*L'amoureux aux pantoufles*).

And finally we note that if sometimes Lucas smokes cigarettes, he prefers, loyally emulating his chief, to smoke a pipe, which he does evidently "*with a placidity mirroring that of the Chief Inspector*" (*Félicie est là*, FEL: 7).

CHARACTER PORTRAIT

Conscientious, obstinate, patient, meticulous, trying—in vain!—to appear severe, with good intuition and tact, overlooking the fact that "*everyone could easily guess his profession*," his qualities are appreciated by Maigret, who will happily see his sergeant succeed him in his position of Chief Inspector.

And once named Chief Inspector, Lucas will continue to take for his model his former boss, adopting the same attitudes. "*Chief Inspector Lucas asked his questions benevolently, always with an air of not attaching much importance to them*." (*Monsieur La Souris*); "*Lucas, during this time, put on a mindless look, stuffing his pipe, hesitating to light it*" (*ibid.*); "*If he played at being a tough guy, it was, however, with a gleam of gaiety in his eye*" (*L'amoureux aux pantoufles*).

RELATIONSHIP WITH MAIGRET

The two men are very close, understanding each other without the need for long explanations. A wink of the eye or a glance could be enough, for Lucas knew his boss well. If Maigret sometimes treated Lucas like an idiot, he still maintained his affection for him, translated into words as "*good Lucas*," *vieux* [old friend], *mon vieux* or *mon vieux Lucas*, while Lucas continued to call him "Boss," even after Maigret retired.

PERSONAL INFORMATION

Lucas's first name never appears in the Maigret saga. Nonetheless, we know it, thanks to information found in *Le testament Donadieu* ... his first name is André. He's 10 years younger than Maigret. Married, his wife panics over nothing, and doesn't like to have people over for dinner. He has a brother-in-law who works as an accountant's assistant, has family in Pau. A second cousin of his wife's works as a concierge at the Sorbonne. It's never mentioned in the texts whether Lucas has children; one sole allusion to a possible descendant is made in *L'énigme de la Marie-Galante*. He lives on the Left Bank.

NOTABLE ACTIONS

He did the tailing of Victor Gaillard (*La guinguette à deux sous*), Gassin (*L'écluse n° 1*), Victor Poliensky (*Maigret et son mort*), and Marton (*Les scrupules de Maigret*). On stake-outs, we find him disguised as old and lame to watch the Polish gang (*Stan le Tueur, Cécile est morte, Maigret et son mort*), and he did the surveillance on Félicie's house (*Félicie est là*). He participated in the eventful arrests of Nicolas (*La pipe de Maigret*), the gangsters (*Maigret, Lognon et les gangsters*), the art thieves (*Maigret et le tueur*), and Jo Mori (*Maigret et l'indicateur*). He organized the information for the Steuvels case (*L'amie de Madame Maigret*), the Ward case (*Maigret voyage*), and was in charge of the Mazotti case (*La colère de Maigret*).

Portrait of Musketeer Little Janvier

He appears in the saga for the first time in *La tête d'un homme*, where he is assigned to trail Heurtin after his "escape" from the Santé Prison. In the Fayard period, he only returns once, for a brief appearance in *La guinguette à deux sous*. From the Gallimard novels, and especially those of the Presses de la Cité period, he will take an important place, that of one of the favorite inspectors of Maigret, who will have for him an almost paternal affection, waiting for his "second son" who will be Lapointe.

OTHER APPEARANCES

Parallel with the Maigret saga, Simenon puts Janvier to work in other novels: *Monsieur La Souris, Cour d'assises, L'outlaw*, and *La vérité sur Bébé Donge*; in two stories in the collection *Les dossiers de l'agence O, L'arrestation du musicien* and *Le chantage de l'agence O*, as well as in the story *Sept petites croix dans un carnet*, in the collection, *Un Noël de Maigret*.

While in *Cour d'assises* his name is merely cited as an inspector of the Sûreté of Nice, in *La vérité sur Bébé Donge* he's an inspector on the Flying Squad at Cahors. In *L'outlaw*, he's back in Paris, working as an inspector for Chief Inspector Lognon. In the three stories, he's an inspector at the PJ, and especially in *Sept petites croix dans un carnet*, he works with Chief Inspector Saillard, a "double" of Maigret. Finally, in *Monsieur La Souris* he has become a sergeant, under the command of Chief Inspector Lucas.

PHYSICAL DESCRIPTION

Tall and thin, blond or red-headed, with a slightly chubby face and pink skin, always closely shaven, he becomes a little pot-bellied with age, and has a gangly walk.

For dress, he also follows the "classic" line of Maigret and Lucas: raincoat or overcoat, hat, jacket, and tie. For his suits he likes light colors.

He smokes cigarettes, a bad habit, especially at night, which isn't good for him (see *Maigret en meublé*)!

CHARACTER PORTRAIT

Quite young when he joins the squad, he makes the blunders of a beginner, as in *La tête d'un homme*, where he tries to put on a casual air when he's on a stake-out, and is almost brought to tears when he's shaken off by Radek, who gets him drunk. It should be said that he has a slight weakness for alcohol!

But little by little he'll improve with age, and his qualities will assert themselves; he's meticulous, with a naturalness that makes him less obviously a policeman, likes delicate tasks, and is filled with excitement when he succeeds at a mission.

RELATIONSHIP WITH MAIGRET

As has already been said, Maigret has an affection for Janvier which tends to the paternal… "*Besides Lucas—his right arm—Janvier had always been his favorite inspector. He got him when he was still very young, like Lapointe today, and he took to calling him 'little Janvier.'*" (*Maigret en meublé*, MEU: 1). And on his side, Janvier also felt for his boss an attachment almost filial, knowing his methods and style, like Lucas ("*Someone from the Quai des Orfèvres, a Lucas or a Janvier, would not have needed to observe Maigret for long to understand.*" *La maison du juge*, JUG: 9), exchanging winks or knowing looks. Maigret's affection translates, as for Lucas, into the use of terms like "*my old Janvier,*" "*old man,*" and "*my little Janvier.*"

We also note once more that this affection reaches such a depth that it doesn't end with Maigret's retirement… "*Then Janvier, the good Janvier— what good men they all were that day, and how good it was to be with them again, to be working together like in the old days!*" (*Maigret se fâche*, FAC: 5).

PERSONAL INFORMATION

We know Janvier's first name from *Maigret en meublé*—Albert. He's 20 years younger than Maigret. Janvier's family and children hold a fairly significant place in the novels, and it's one of the facets by which Simenon has created a particularly "living" character. It's also something which helps to establish a chronology of Maigret's investigations, for we learn in the string of the novels, of Janvier's marriage, and the births of his children. Janvier's wife is named Marie-France. In *Maigret et son mort*, he's only been married a year; in *Mon ami Maigret*, his wife gives birth; we learn in *Maigret et la Grande Perche* that it's a boy; in *Maigret au Picratt's*, the child is still an infant; in *La pipe de Maigret*, Janvier awaits a new child; in *Maigret en meublé*, he already has two children and is awaiting a third (as he hopes for a girl, we can deduce that the first two were boys!); in *Le revolver de Maigret*, he has three children, with the last less than a year old; in *Maigret et le clochard*, his wife gives birth to her fourth; in *Maigret chez le ministre*, the child is newborn, and we learn that his daughter is called Monique (she will later marry an engineer! (see *Les mémoires de Maigret*), and one of his eldest will be called Pierrot. We also learn that on Sundays he sometimes takes his family to Chelles, Vaucresson, his sister-in-law's or his mother-in-law's, and that his wife's sister had married Joseph, who'd been a waiter at the Brasserie Dauphine. Janvier lived at first on Rue Réaumur, then had a house built in the suburbs.

Notable Actions

Janvier was in charge of tailing Heurtin and Radek (*La tête d'un homme*), Ellen Darroman (*Les caves du Majestic*), Félicie and Jacques Pétillon (*Félicie est là*), and Alfonsi (*L'amie de Madame Maigret*). He'd disguised himself as a café waiter for the surveillance of the Polish gang (*Stan le Tueur*), and he'd also done the surveillance of Le Cloaguen's apartment (*Signé Picpus*) and Louise Filon's (*Maigret se trompe*), among others. Maigret sent him to gather information on Maria Van Aerts (*Maigret et la Grande Perche*), Pierrot (*Maigret se trompe*), Blanche Lamotte (*Maigret chez le ministre*), Marton (*Les scrupules de Maigret*), and Marinette Augier (*Maigret et le fantôme*). He participated in several eventful arrests, that of Oscar Bonvoisin (*Maigret au Picratt's*), Eugène Benoît (*Maigret chez le ministre*), Manuel Mori and Line Marcia (*Maigret et l'indicateur*). He assisted Maigret in the Combarieu affair (*Le client le plus obstiné du monde*), where the two men carried out an investigation a little as if they were "on a binge"! Janvier was shot in the right lung (*Maigret en meublé*). And finally, he was in charge of the Jave case (*Maigret s'amuse*).

Portrait of Musketeer Fat Torrence

If Maigret felt like a "father" to his inspectors, in the same way that M. de Tréville felt himself the father of his musketeers, Torrence is without a doubt Maigret's Porthos. He has a physical presence and good nature hidden beneath a real "bad guy" exterior.

Torrence appears officially in the Maigret saga in *Pietr le Letton,* where he's a sergeant under Maigret's command, and his principal collaborator. Inopportunely killed by the pen of Simenon, who will "exonerate himself" later ("*I believe that somewhere or other Simenon makes him die in place of another inspector who was in fact killed by my side in a Champs-Elysées hotel*" [*Les mémoires de Maigret,* MEM: 8]), and will resuscitate him at Maigret's side. He thus reappears in the story *L'homme dans la rue,* then in the Gallimard novels, and those of the Presses de la Cité. But there remains some residue of this "murder" of Torrence, and he never recovers his premier position with Maigret. If he's nonetheless one of Maigret's favorite inspectors, we must recognize that the Chief Inspector has a more distant relationship with him, using "*vous*" with him more often (*see above*), assigning him less important tasks than his other faithful, for he's often relegated to jobs "in the background," simple tails or stake-outs, when he's not just the driver. It must also be said that in Simenon's portrait, Torrence doesn't manifest the same "depth of judgment" as the other three faithful, or at least he doesn't have the same ability in his work. With regard to this, this sentence in *Maigret et l'homme tout seul* is significant: "*Normally, he would have taken Janvier with him, but he needed someone completely trustworthy and capable of taking initiative at the Quai des Orfevres during his absence*" (SEU: 1). Lucas, absent from this story as he's on vacation, cannot replace Maigret, and it's Janvier that Maigret chooses instead. Further, if we consider the collection *Les dossiers de l'agence O,* in which Torrence appears (*see below*), he's far from first rank in the level of his intellectual abilities.

OTHER APPEARANCES

Torrence plays a relatively important role in some novels outside the Maigret saga, and he's a character that Simenon seemed to like well enough in his first police novels. In novels published under pseudonyms, Torrence appears as inspector in three relating the exploits of a "rival" of Maigret, Inspector Sancette: *Matricule 12, L'homme qui tremble* (both signed Georges Sim) and *Les amants du malheur* (signed Jean du Perry). He's still an inspector in *Les errants* (signed Georges Sim), becomes a sergeant under the command of Chief Inspector Lucas in *L'inconnue* (signed Christian Brulls), and finally he's Chief Inspector in two novels signed Christian Brulls, *La maison des disparus* and *Fièvre.* In this last, the roles are reversed, since it's Lucas who works as inspector for Chief Inspector Torrence. We find Torrence again in the story

La bonne fortune du Hollandais (in the collection *Le petit docteur*), as an inspector working with Chief Inspector Lucas, also Chief in the collection *Les dossiers de l'agence O*, where Torrence runs a private detective agency. Torrence is mentioned in the story *L'invalide à la tête de bois*, as an inspector who'd worked with Chief Inspector Duclos. Finally, Torrence accompanies Maigret in three of the proto-Maigrets, *Train de nuit*, *La femme rousse* (where he is a sergeant and the Chief Inspector's "right arm") and *La maison de l'inquiétude*.

PHYSICAL DESCRIPTION

First described as "*a slightly reduced reproduction of Maigret*" (*Pietr le Letton*, LET: 3), Torrence will find himself bearing the adjective "*fat*" as an automatic description, but also the qualifiers *massive, broad and powerful, a heavyweight*. He has also a "*big thunderous voice*," which takes on over the phone "*the sonority of a bugle*," the hands of a butcher's boy, and a ruddy face. In *Les dossiers de l'agence O*, his portrait is completed, and Simenon multiplies these qualifying adjectives: *solid, tall* (over 6 feet!), *thick, fat, powerful, bulky, imposing, fiery*, he's *an easy-going colossus about 40, well-groomed and well-fed*, with the look of a *good giant*, with *the broad nostrils of a bon vivant*, a brick complexion which turns crimson when he becomes emotional, with *heavy shoulders*, a *protruding belly* (Torrence, like his old boss, Maigret, is far from scorning good food!).

As for dress, we note that Torrence wears black leather shoes, a soft hat, an overcoat, over his gray suit, and shirts with false collars.

We add also that if in *Pietr le Letton*, Torrence smokes a pipe (obligatory resemblance to Maigret!), and that that's always the case in *Les dossiers de l'agence O* (cf. this extract: "*Torrence, pipe in his jaw, for he happily aped his old chief Maigret and took up a pipe even bigger than his*"), and in the story *La bonne fortune du Hollandais*, the rare occasions when this aspect is noted after his "resurrection" in the Maigret saga, usually say that he smokes cigarettes.

CHARACTER PORTRAIT

Lover of good food and drink (see *Signé Picpus* (SIG: 3), when Torrence telephones his report to Maigret from a bar, "*I had the luck to unearth here a splendid Vouvray…*"), Torrence under his appearance as a colossus, hides a kind soul. In reality, he's a *softy, tender-hearted*, who has kept a slightly childish spirit and amuses himself by carving his initials into his desk at the

PJ. He is also happily sentimental (*Les dossiers de l'agence O*). And he's also *the most talkative inspector in the PJ*.

As for his professional side, while he's a *resourceful* and tenacious man who will not quickly abandon the game, who follows a trail with *the obstinacy of a hunting dog*, he's nonetheless lacking the requisite qualities for ascending in rank, and his "*terrific appetite for life at the same time as a business sense hardly compatible with the life of a functionary*" (*Les mémoires de Maigret*, MEM: 8) are the grounds for his decision to quit the police and found a private detective agency.

RELATIONSHIP WITH MAIGRET

In *Pietr le Letton*, the relationship between the two men had been very close, and foreshadowed what would later unite Lucas to his boss. As Torrence "*virtually always worked with the Chief Inspector*," they understood each other "*without pronouncing an unnecessary word*," "*Torrence to whom he had to say but a single word, or just a sign, to have him understand.*" This very strong relationship, could it be said to be too strong to last? Were there perhaps unconscious reasons for the "murder" of Sergeant Torrence by the author, permitting the Chief Inspector to find later, in place of a single man at this side, a team of faithfuls whose characteristics offered Maigret the chance to be surrounded by a number of "children," a family, rather than a single friend.

After Torrence's "return" in the second period of the saga, his relationship with Maigret had changed—he became a member of a team, in the same way as the other three faithfuls. Maigret calls Torrence the classic *vieux* or *mon vieux*, exchanges understanding winks with him. And if he too is a "*true follower*" of the Chief Inspector, he is clearly not as close as he was in *Pietr le Letton*. Perhaps he wasn't forgiven his move to the Agency O (we recall that the collection in question dates from 1938). Maigret employs Torrence above all for "subordinate" tasks, never, for example, giving him the responsibility of replacing him in the office. (Consider this, for instance from *La folle de Maigret* (FOL: 8), "*It shocked the Chief Inspector a little to see Torrence sitting at his desk, in his own armchair,*" where Maigret had more than once allowed Lucas, Janvier, and even young Lapointe). And he rarely takes him into the confidence of his thoughts, which he does freely with Lucas, Janvier, and Lapointe.

PERSONAL INFORMATION

Like Lucas, Torrence has no first name in the Maigret saga, but we can find it in *Les dossiers de l'agence O*, Joseph. Torrence is 15 years younger than Maigret. Unmarried, but he collects feminine conquests… "*He owned a great big American car which stopped from time to time in front of our door, and each time, he was accompanied by a pretty girl, always different, whom he introduced to us with the same sincerity, as his fiancée."* (*Les mémoires de Maigret,* MEM: 8).

Notable Actions

Torrence has to his credit the tailing of Le Cloaguen (*Signé Picpus*), Adrienne Laur (*Maigret, Lognon et les gangsters*), and Jean-Charles Gaillard (*La colère de Maigret*). He was in charge of gathering the information on Oswald Clark and Edgar Fagonet (*Les caves du Majestic*), Ernest Malik (*Maigret se fâche*), Françoise Boursicault (*Maigret en meublé*), the Lachaumes (*Maigret et les témoins récalcitrants*), the residents at Josselin's (*Maigret et les braves gens*), and Guillot's dog (*Maigret et le clochard*). He investigated the telegram from Concarneau (*L'amie de Madame Maigret*) and the taxis taken by Loraine Martin (*Un Noël de Maigret*). A number of stake-outs, notably at the Majestic (*Pietr le Letton*) and Serre's house (*Maigret et la Grande Perche*). He interrogated Philippe Mortemart (*Maigret au Picratt's*) and Carlotta (*Une confidence de Maigret*). He took part in the eventful arrest of the gangsters (*Maigret, Lognon et les gangsters*). He was the one who searched Mme Fumal's apartment (*Un échec de Maigret*). And finally, he was Maigret's driver throughout the Vivien case (*Maigret et l'homme tout seul*).

Portrait of Musketeer Young Lapointe

The "little newcomer" of the Faithful Four appears relatively late in the saga, in *L'amie de Madame Maigret*, the ninth novel of the Presses de la Cité period. In creating this character, did Simenon—and Maigret himself—imagine the importance that he would take on in the Maigret saga? To what unconscious motivation was the author responding when he assigned to the Chief Inspector this young neophyte in the police, awkward in his first steps, but to whom Maigret would quickly attach himself, and for whom he would develop a completely paternal affection? Why wasn't the character of Janvier sufficient to fill the filial role? After becoming the father of his own (large) family, did Janvier become a little distanced, even in spite of himself, from the Chief Inspector, as he had himself founded a new generation? Or simply, to the extent that Janvier gained age and experience, did Maigret feel an increasing desire to have near to him an inexperienced inspector to whom he could transmit, as from father to son, his own experiences as a policeman and "seeker of men"?

We note, moreover, this significant little fact—sometimes Simenon himself makes a mistake in the novels, reversing the characters of Janvier and Lapointe. For example, Maigret sends Janvier to a place, and it's Lapointe whom we find there a few pages later. There are at least four such occasions in the saga, in *Maigret et l'homme du banc*, *Maigret se trompe*, *Maigret tend un piège* and *Maigret et les témoins récalcitrants*.

Present in almost all the following novels, Lapointe will occupy a more and more important place in the investigations, and in particular in the affections of the Chief Inspector, no doubt also because, with the passing of the years, Maigret felt more and more that "nostalgia for paternity," which only the presence of young Lapointe would to some degree fulfill, at least partially...

Other Appearances

Outside of the Maigret saga, Lapointe appears but twice from Simenon's pen, in the two stories *La chanteuse de Pigalle* and *L'invalide à la tête de bois*. We recall that these two stories, written in 1952, were unpublished until their appearance in Volume 12 of *Tout Simenon* from Presses de la Cité in 1990. In these two texts, Lapointe is an inspector under the command of the Chief of the Special Squad, Emile Berna, who also called him "little Lapointe."

Physical Description

Brown-haired "*with lots of hair*," tall and thin, his youth gives him "*more the look of a young student than a police inspector*" (*Maigret et les braves gens*, BRA: 3).

He wears, like his colleagues, a hat and an overcoat, which can be black, a jacket, and in the springtime he sometimes wears a suit "*of a pale gray flecked with tiny red threads*"

He smokes cigarettes.

Character Portrait

While presented as inexperienced in his debuts in the saga (which goes without saying), he already possessed undeniable qualities; he was serious, zealous, and patient, all qualities which will lead him to surprising progress in very little time. Perhaps because of his youth, he sometimes blushes easily.

Relationship with Maigret

This character is even more interesting in that we discover him at the same time as Maigret does, that we experience with him his debuts in the PJ, and observe the progression and deepening of his relationship with the Chief Inspector. In *L'amie de Madame Maigret*, we discover a Lapointe not yet self-assured, awkward and self-conscious before his boss, whom he doesn't call that at first... *"'Are you disappointed, Monsieur Maigret?' Young Lapointe would have liked to call him 'boss,' like Lucas, Torrence and most of those on the team, but he felt too new for that; it seemed to him that it was a privilege that he would acquire like earning his stripes"* (MME: 8). Which he didn't delay doing, however, the occasion presenting itself shortly afterwards... *"Well, Boss, are you pleased? Carried away by his enthusiasm and pride, he allows himself 'the word' for the first time ... not too self-assuredly..."* (MME: 8). But he had nothing to fear from Maigret—who, on the contrary, took him quickly under his protection, and integrated him into his team. *"Then Maigret intentionally spoke to him like to an old-timer, to a Lucas or a Torrence, for example"* (MME: 4). And Maigret asked for nothing better than to play the mentor for the young inspector. *"He was a good boy, still too nervous, too emotional, but something could probably be made of him"* (MME: 5); *"his youth amused him, his enthusiasm, his confusion when he thought he'd made a blunder"* (*Maigret et le corps sans tête*, COR: 1)

The boss-collaborator relationship will quickly be coupled with a paternal-filial one... *"The two of them, with Maigret drawing small puffs gravely on his pipe, had the look of a father and son in serious discussion"* (*Maigret au Picratt's*, PIC: 3), *"Maigret regarded Lapointe with a slightly paternal benevolence, for he had taken him under his protection when ... the young man had entered the Quai des Orfèvres"* (*Les scrupules de Maigret*, SCR: 4). And even later, he would remain *"Maigret's pet."*

From his side, Lapointe never missed the chance to work with Maigret. *"Maigret looked around and saw Lapointe turn away, reddening. The young man was clearly aching to accompany the boss"* (*L'amie de Madame Maigret*, MME: 7); *"he pushed open the door of the inspectors' office, wondering who to choose to go with him... You, Lapointe... Young Lapointe raised his head, happy as a lark"* (*Maigret voyage*, VOY: 1).

As with the other collaborators, understanding passed with the exchange of looks, and Maigret's affection translated itself into terms like *mon petit, mon petit Lapointe*, and sometimes *mon vieux*. When Maigret speaks of Lapointe, or when he thinks of him, he frequently uses two qualifiers: *"young Lapointe" "which he would no doubt continue to call him when he was 50"* (*Maigret et le tueur*, TUE: 2) and *"little Lapointe," "as they called him at the Quai, not because of his size, but because he was the youngest and the last to appear"* (*Maigret et le corps sans tête*, COR: 3). With the passing of the years, the relationship remained just as strong... *"Some minutes later, Maigret opened the door of the inspectors' office and made a sign to Lapointe ... who leapt up with a certain awkwardness which he couldn't overcome when in Maigret's presence. Maigret was his god."* (*Maigret et Monsieur Charles*, CHA: 1).

PERSONAL INFORMATION

Lapointe's first name is certainly known, since it played an important role in the intrigue of *Maigret au Picratt's*—it's Albert (the same as Janvier's). Lapointe was 24 when he started at Quai des Orfèvres, and Simenon often emphasized his youthfulness, having him resemble more a student than a policeman. Consider this sentence in *La chanteuse de Pigalle*, "*Lapointe, at 25 or 26, had a look so fresh, so candid, that no one would take him for a police inspector.*" Furthermore, he keeps this aspect of a young man even ten years later (see *Maigret et Monsieur Charles*). His youth is also the occasion for Maigret to remember his own beginnings, and his affection for the young inspector is no doubt mixed with a little nostalgia. Lapointe's father is in employed at a bank at Meulan, and Lapointe has two sisters, the youngest, Germaine, working for a publishing house in Paris. He also has an aunt confined to a mental hospital. By the very fact of his youth, we learn much of Lapointe through his love life, which is moreover at the center of the intrigue in *Maigret au Picratt's*. With no "girlfriend" in *L'amie de Madame Maigret*, he falls in love with a stripper, Arlette, in *Maigret au Picratt's*, but the young woman is unfortunately killed. Five novels later, Maigret, inadvertently or by some unconscious desire to help him forget his lost love, puts another "Arlette" under the inspector's care, and "forgets" to relieve him from his shift (*Maigret et l'homme du banc*). At around the same time, Lapointe falls a little in love with young Lili, the adopted daughter of the old Chief Inspector Duclos (*La chanteuse de Pigalle* et *L'invalide à la tête de bois*). Another five novels later, he meets another young girl (nothing prevents us however from thinking it's still Lili herself), and we only learn in *Maigret chez le ministre* that he has a date with her. "Almost engaged" in *Les scrupules de Maigret*, we learn in *Maigret et Monsieur Charles* that he has finally married, will have two children, and that his sister-in-law lives in Saint-Cloud. After having lived with his sister, he lives on Boulevard Saint-Germain, in a modest Left Bank building.

NOTABLE ACTIONS

Lapointe was responsible for tailing Xavier Marton (*Les scrupules de Maigret*), Gaston Meurant (*Maigret aux assises*), M. Louis (*La patience de Maigret*), and Léon Florentin (*L'ami d'enfance de Maigret*). Among others, he was on stake-outs at the Martons' building (*Les scrupules de Maigret*) and at the Parendons' (*Maigret hésite*). He gathered information on Piquemal (*Maigret chez le ministre*), on Jean-Charles Gaillard's car (*La colère de Maigret*), on the paper of the anonymous letter in *Maigret hésite*, Oscar Chabut's acquaintances (*Maigret et le marchand de vin*), and Mme de Caramé (*La folle de Maigret*). He participated in the arrests of Oscar Bonvoisin (*Maigret au Picratt's*), Antoine Cristin (*Maigret et le corps sans tête*), and Le Chanoine (*Maigret et les témoins récalcitrants*). Maigret assigned him to the recovery of the suitcase at Me Liotard's (*L'amie de Madame Maigret*), and he's the one who discovered Thouret's room (*Maigret et l'homme du banc*) and the owner of the vest with the torn button (*Maigret tend un piège*). He assisted Maigret throughout Josset's interrogation (*Une confidence de Maigret*), found the owner of the red Peugeot (*Maigret et le clochard*) and Antoine Batille's friend (*Maigret et le tueur*). He was the best stenographer at the PJ.

The Other Members of the Homicide Squad

Maigret became Chief of this Homicide Squad, the object of his desire since his first investigation (*La première enquête de Maigret*, PRE), the squad in which he began as an Inspector under the command of Chief Inspector Guillaume (*Les mémoires de Maigret*, MEM: 7). This squad, according to Simenon, employs numerous inspectors; there could be as many as 20 tapping on their typewriters in the Inspectors' Office. We find a series of inspectors, of whom some are simply mentioned in one or two novels, either because they are charged with tailing or the surveillance of a house, or because they are on duty in the office. But we also find some others whose portraits are more detailed, above all because some of them are encountered in numerous novels. Among these we can mention **Barnacle, Dufour, Dupeu, Lagrume** and **Santoni,** on whom more information is available in *Part III. The Saga.*

We also find inspectors who appear regularly in the saga, from the time of the Presses de la Cité novels. They arrived, in a way, to "reinforce" Maigret's personal team (made up of the *faithful four*, Lucas, Janvier, Lapointe and Torrence). Each of the characters in this group, which we'll refer to as Maigret's "rear guard," is mentioned, in more or less detail, in between 7 and 12 novels. These are inspectors **Baron, Bonfils, Janin, Lourtie, Neveu** and **Vacher,** whose portraits can also be found in *Part III. The Saga.*

If the six members of this group are not part of Maigret's "personal team," they are still men he appreciates, that he calls "my children" (a term used numerous times by the Chief Inspector), and that he likes to visit when they are in their office, "*working diligently as schoolchildren.*" And there's no way to resist the pleasure of mentioning the beginning of Ch. 7 of *Maigret chez le ministre* (MIN), that perfectly summarizes the familiar relation—almost domestic—that Maigret maintains with his men. "*This was not the first time that he'd made such an entrance, less as a boss than as a comrade. He opened the door of the Inspectors' Office and, pushing back his hat on his head, went to sit on the corner of a table, emptied his pipe on the floor by hitting it against his heel before filling another. He looked at them one by one, occupied in various tasks, with the expression of a family father returned home in the evening, happy to recover his own, and taking account of them.*"

On their side the inspectors feel an affection for their boss, to the extent that they "sense" what's going on in him without even needing to look at him ("*Like college students whose professor is passing, they didn't raise their heads, but each knew if he was serious or worried*" (*Maigret et le fantôme*, FAN: 6), "*The typewriters clattered next door. The inspectors checked the boss's door from time to time, exchanging silent glances*" (*Maigret se défend*, DEF: 3). And they admired him, trying to be like him. They knew his way of working well enough not to need long explanations, and they knew what it meant when Maigret asked them to wait with a suspect in an adjoining room, or when, according to a well-established routine, they took turns taking up an interrogation to wear down the resistance of a suspect.

The Other Parisians: The District Inspectors and Chief Inspectors

These are the officers with whom Maigret is brought to collaborate, especially at the beginning of an investigation, as they are often the first to arrive at the scene of a crime. These are plainclothes detectives, the "*bourgeois,*" as they are called, who have their offices in precinct Town Halls or at the District Station. Maigret sometimes has an ambiguous relationship with them. On the one hand he respects them, perhaps remembering his first case, where he'd been "humiliated," as Secretary of the District Police, when he was withdrawn from his investigation, which was passed on to those of the Quai des Orfèvres, and he'd promised himself that if one day he was part of the Quai, he would never "*show disdain for the poor policemen who manned the District stations*" (*La première enquête de Maigret*, PRE: 8); Nevertheless, while he recognizes their utility and their deepened knowledge of the districts wherein they work, there always arrives a moment when he can't stop himself from taking the investigation in hand—he can't confide to anyone else the task of "sniffing around" in all the corners in search of an atmosphere and a truth that in the end only he can sense.

But Maigret wants an investigation to go by the rules. "*As you know, this is the business of the homicide brigade. Which doesn't stop us from accepting or soliciting the help of precinct Inspectors*" (*Maigret et le voleur paresseux,* PAR: 2). As for these District Inspectors, they envy their colleagues of the "Big House," and try to save the interesting cases for them, which unfortunately doesn't please Maigret. In the texts, we encounter a number of district inspectors, but most of them are simply mentioned, more or less casual appearances. With the District Chief Inspectors, Maigret doesn't always have the best of relationships (is it because of his memory of the problems with his former chief, Maxime Le Bret in *La première enquête de Maigret*?), and they quickly disappear from the story after their early appearance in the novels!

Fumel appears in *Maigret et le voleur paresseux* (PAR). First name Aristide, he's an inspector of the 16th precinct, who also belongs to the "old regime," like Janvier and Lucas. He never rose in rank because of his writing problems, and he started pretty much at the same time as Maigret. After a year of marriage, his wife left him, and he continues to search for her everywhere, which doesn't stop him from accumulating sad love stories. He's 51, awkwardly built, but one of the best inspectors in Paris. In certain respects he reminds us of Lognon (with whom Simenon himself compares him at the beginning of Ch. 7), but a Lognon who, rather than grumbling over his misfortunes, is resigned to his fate. He's the kind of inspector Maigret appreciates, because, unlike others, he doesn't try to compete with the men of the Quai, but rather he collaborates while taking into account Maigret's orders (we discover here a Chief Inspector who, in spite of everything, is anxious to preserve the prerogatives of his brigade!). Besides, Maigret has a weakness for these "low-wagers," these men who, like ants, patiently and painfully push their burdens through life.

Louis. We meet Inspector Louis in *Maigret et l'indicateur* (IND). He works in the 9th precinct, and knows in depth the wildlife (the bad boys and girls) of Pigalle, where he was born, and which he never left. He's about 45, and lost his wife, run over by a bus, when he was 30. He continues to wear mourning, dressing all in black (including his tie!), which gives him the nickname "the Widower." He doesn't smoke (rather rare for an inspector!) and drinks only small bottles of Vichy. He is quietly content (unlike Lognon, angry at the whole world for not being able to enter the Quai!) with his station of District Inspector, and makes his profession his only passion. Maigret had at one time considered him for his brigade, but he is too lugubrious a character for the jolly atmosphere of the Inspectors' Office of the Quai. He speaks and moves slowly, makes his reports carefully, with great attention to accuracy. He has very white skin, red lips, and a thick black mustache. He's rather shy, blushes easily, but he's an intelligent boy, who accomplishes alone in his corner (while dragging his ear in the cafés and bars of Montmartre), a patient work, without soliciting the help of the Quai, and especially without encroaching on the territory of the homicide squad, something appreciated by Maigret! And if Louis sometimes dreams of a promotion to the Quai, he doesn't believe it too strongly, first because he needs to work alone, and second because he's too attached to his district of Pigalle.

Lognon

Inspector Lognon works in Montmartre, assigned to Saint-Georges district, at the Rue La Rochefoucauld (9th precinct) station in the earliest novels of the saga he appears in, and later moved to the town hall station of the 18th. Emblematic of the relationships Maigret maintains with district inspectors, Simenon has furthermore created in Lognon a sort of "anti–Maigret," emphasizing throughout the novels the differences between the two men—their visions of the métier and of life—presenting us with delightful scenes of their confrontations, serving to enrich our portrait of Maigret himself.

LOGNON BEFORE MAIGRET

Lognon, whose first name is Joseph, initially sprang from Simenon's pen in 1937, in a non–Maigret novel, *Monsieur La Souris*. The title of the first chapter immediately gives us one of his characteristics, "*The Silences of Inspector Grouch.*" This is certainly how Lognon is referred to by his colleagues. In fact, it's old Mouse, a *clochard*, who gave him that name. Lognon is a plainclothes inspector on the municipal police force, who works out of the *Opera* station in the 9th district. He's charged with monitoring public roads, and in particular with preventing clandestine prostitution, which is why he deals particularly with registered prostitutes and bar girls. His portrait is well drawn, psychologically as well as physically. "*In front of this door waited the doleful Lognon.*" He's dark and sullen, with an unsociable eye, an obstinate face, a sad demeanor. He doesn't like jokes, always worried about being taken in. But basically he's a shy man, aware of his inferiority. He realizes fully that he's "*wrong to want to do too well, as his wife never stops repeating*" and he risks by his actions—which he never announces to his chiefs—compromising his situation. But all in all he's an "*honest man,*" and "*even, in the end, a good man.*"

Entirely caught up in his job, he works overtime, follows his suspects, "*heroically and obstinately.*" He's stubborn, uncompromising in questions of service, respecting professional secrecy, and one who knows all the rules by heart. But his lack of writing skills prevents him from reaching a higher position than that of inspector, which he's put in more than twelve years to attain. His dream is to be assigned to the Quai des Orfèvres. Sometimes attacked by those he pursues, he gets beaten up or shot, rendering him unavailable, and resulting in his cases being "stolen" by the men of the Quai. He lives in the 18th arrondissement, at 29 Place Constantin-Pecqueur, on the fourth floor, and he's married. His wife is in poor health and often reproaches him ("*It's your fault! Why do you always have to put yourself in front? ... Certainly you're not there when it's time to reap the rewards...*") and he has a son (who's not mentioned at all in the *Maigrets*).

At the end of *Monsieur La Souris*, Chief Inspector Lucas supports Lognon's request to enter the Quai, writing in his report that he "*would make a good inspector of the P.J., assuming that he can resign himself to moderating his initiative, and submitting to his superiors.*" Apparently, this request met with success, for we meet Lognon as Chief Inspector of the PJ in *L'outlaw* (1939). In this novel, Lognon has his office at the Quai des Orfèvres, dresses poorly, but has the medal of the Legion of Honor. His manner is calm, with apparent indifference; he "*doesn't seem to think,*" makes little drawings while listening to suspects. He calls his inspectors "my boys." Good grief, our Lognon has changed! Does he take himself for Maigret, now that he's been posted to the Quai des Orfèvres?!

Lognon in the Maigret Saga

Lognon first appears in the short story, *Maigret et l'inspecteur Malgracieux*. We'll find him in *Maigret au Picratt's, Maigret, Lognon et les gangsters, Maigret et la jeune morte, Maigret tend un piège, Maigret et le voleur paresseux* and *Maigret et le fantôme*: And he also appears in the non–Maigret story, *Le petit restaurant des Ternes*, in which he's working at the Rue de l'Etoile police station, at the border of the 8th and 17th precincts. His portrait, so to speak, is in conformity with himself; always called "Inspector Grouch," he wears a badly cut overcoat, a colorless hat, and appears morose.

Physical Characteristics

Lognon's physical appearance does not work in his favor. He wears old clothes, poorly pressed, his shoes are often wet and muddy, his suits are drab (mouse gray), his sole overcoat is gray, and his hat an unpleasant brown.

He wears dark ties, raised by a celluloid device (except for the one time he wore a red tie and even a straw hat, taking advantage of the absence of his wife, who'd gone off for 'the cure'). All that makes him a gray silhouette, short and thin, his step always tired, eyes teary, red-rimmed, and worried-looking, with a long bulbous nose, red from his perpetual head cold. We learn that he hardly ever drinks, because of a stomach problem. He doesn't smoke (or not anymore) because of his wife, who can't abide the odor of tobacco.

LOGNON AND HIS ENTOURAGE

In the *Maigrets*, Lognon still lives in the Place Constantin-Pecqueur, but this time on the 5th floor, in a cramped apartment in a red brick building. He's been married for 30 years, and, unfortunately for him, his wife is "*the world's worst shrew*," always out of sorts, reducing Lognon to doing the housework when he returns home from work. Furthermore, she passes her time browbeating him, telling him he's "*too conscientious, that he's ruining his health, and that no one appreciates him.*" She calls him "Charles" (was he perhaps, actually Charles Joseph Lognon?).

CHARACTER PORTRAIT

Two aspects are mixed in Lognon: on one side, there's "the gloomiest man in the Paris Police force," always in a bad mood, with a sullen look, his voice sad and gloomy. But Maigret ends up discovering that he was "*the best of men, in the end, the most conscientious of the inspectors, conscientious to the point of insufferability*," nit-picking, form-loving, scrupulous, without genius, but meticulous, honest, "*the officer who had the greatest intuition of Paris, the most obstinate, and the one who wanted most desperately to succeed.*" Dead of fatigue, worn down by his cold, he continues nonetheless his relentless work, and refuses to rest. He must feel "*a bitter pleasure of being a victim of injustice and his own conscience.*" But that's not enough to get him into the Quai, in spite of his ardent desire, for he fails all his examinations (he took the exam four times!), due to a lack of basic education.

Bad luck follows him "*with such insistence that he has developed the anger of a mangy dog.*" He hates all those who work at the Quai, all who hold a rank superior to his. He believes himself the victim of a conspiracy keeping him from rising in rank and gaining entry to the Quai. Every time he becomes involved in an investigation, he can't make an arrest because the criminal is highly connected, he falls ill and someone else finishes for him, the Prosecutor takes the credit for himself, a murder occurs when he's not on duty, or the Crime Squad (and Maigret!) take over the investigation. Lognon is furthermore so used to seeing his initiatives turn against him that he starts to make himself look ridiculous in his precautions (like sending copies of the same report to all his superiors); he portrays himself as *"too humble to be true."* And further, we wonder if he doesn't like it… *"At heart, he would have been unhappy to no longer merit the title 'Inspector Grouch.' He had a need to groan and lament, to feel like the unluckiest man on earth."*

MAIGRET AND LOGNON

While the Chief Inspector *"truly feels sorry"* for *"poor Lognon,"* he never achieves with him the familiar rapport that he has with other inspectors. As an example, while in the heat of the action he sometimes calls Lognon *"tu,"* for the most part he uses *"vous."* In spite of the fact that Maigret offers him *"much ointment to soothe his wounded self-esteem,"* that the Chief Inspector is cautious to a fault about the sensitivity of this inspector, that he shows him degrees of patience he can't always find for his own inspectors, that he emphasizes his merits in official reports; such cordiality has no effect on Inspector Grouch, and Lognon *"is too worthy of his name to respond to the advances of the Chief Inspector."* Basically, Maigret likes him, not resenting his moods and even pitying him, since he knows that his wife doesn't help make his life agreeable. And Maigret prefers to call him "Inspector Unlucky," because he has "a gift for attracting all misfortune." Furthermore, Maigret suspects that he *"has developed a taste for bad luck and bad moods, made of it a personal vice, which he lovingly nurtures."*

So there's Inspector Lognon, a stickler for the rules, but who transgresses them himself when he believes he's on the "big case" which will result in his promotion. His gruff manner hides, in fact, a fierce desire not to be taken for an idiot, and his *"excessive humility is only an excess of pride."* Irritating at first, he ends up being almost sympathetic as a result of being a victim of events, more "unlucky" than "grouchy."

Outside of Paris

Besides the Parisian police, Maigret is also led to rub shoulders with Inspectors and Chief Inspectors when he works outside of Paris, whether in the provinces or foreign countries.

With few exceptions, we realize that Maigret doesn't maintain particularly cordial relationships with the provincial police. No doubt we must consider, from the Chief Inspector's side, that he feels the absence of his regular team, who understand his style of investigation. Some information about these Provincial Inspectors and Chief Inspectors can be found in *Part III. The Saga*.

Maigret is not much of a traveler, and he doesn't leave France except when forced to by circumstances of an investigation. There are a few countries he does visit, however: the USA (required by Simenon, of course), Great Britain, Belgium and the Netherlands (in Simenon's footsteps, again), Switzerland and Germany (this latter only in *Le pendu de Saint-Pholien*). And sometimes he has to place a call from his Paris office to one of these officers he has met on his journeys.

Portraits of a number of these foreign policemen can be found in *Part III. The Saga*.

The Men of the Laboratory

JOSEPH MOERS

Contrary to what you might think, Maigret is not disinterested in material evidence. However, unlike a Hercules Poirot, who uses his "tiny gray cells" with these clues as a basis, the Chief Inspector treats them as one element among others, including them in a totality which encompasses, as much as fingerprints or traces of blood on a carpet, the atmosphere of the scene of the crime, the reactions of suspects, and the victim's past. He doesn't ignore the material evidence, but he sets it in its proper place in the whole. Consider in *Le chien jaune* (JAU: 9), the discussion between Inspector Leroy and Maigret:

"However, I note that now you have arrived at the evidence, after which..."

"Exactly—after! After all! Otherwise said, I've done the investigation backwards, which perhaps won't stop me from doing the next one the other way around.... A question of atmosphere.... A question of faces..."

Moers appears for the first time in *Monsieur Gallet, décédé*. Maigret calls him to Sancerre to decipher a burnt letter, the kind of task that this patient man is able to do best. Right off, and in contrast to other secondary characters, Simenon gives us his precise particulars: his first name is Joseph, he's of Flemish origin, a big, skinny, redheaded boy, with infinite patience in his work. He concentrates so hard on his work that he never smiles, never gets excited—*"the very picture of interior peace."* His calm aspect is often in contrast to a Maigret anxious to know the results of an analysis, who circles around him, hardly containing his impatience.

At first he wears a pince-nez, with thick lenses that protect his blue eyes, always a little astonished and shy from his myopia, then later, thick glasses. He has neither beard nor mustache, always wears a crumpled suit, and lives in student lodgings in the Latin Quarter. He's probably a dozen years younger than Maigret ("young man" in *Monsieur Gallet décédé* and *La tête d'un homme*, where Maigret is 45).

He's knowledgeable in many areas—insurance, graphology, papers and inks, dust analysis, fingerprints, *Identikit* portraits, and paraffin tests. He possesses numerous lists and catalogs about all kinds of objects, and if he remains modest about his capabilities, he nevertheless turns *pink with pleasure*, when he can speak of what he knows well, and a small satisfied flame may dance in his eyes. He has no other passion outside of his laboratory, where he spends nearly all his days and nights, as he has no family. He *rejoices* when he can carry away with him, into his "den"—the laboratory—some material to analyze.

At first Maigret addresses him as "*vous*," but he passes quickly to "*tu*," except for occasional lapses (or are they rather Simenon's?), where the Chief Inspector addresses him as "*vous*" once again.

His relation to Maigret is similar enough to that which binds the Chief Inspector to his other inspectors. Maigret speaks to him in an affectionate tone, calls him *my little Moers*, or *old man*, with the same familiarity with which he addresses his "team." He can even call him *son* in moments of "rumination" And, because they work so long together, with the passing of the time, Maigret will end up considering him an *old friend*, an *old comrade*, and he has difficulty imagining Forensic Identity without him.

Moers, for his part, is *moved* when he sees Maigret struggling against difficulties, and he knows that the Chief Inspector, when he comes to join him in laboratories, in the attic of the Palace of Justice, doesn't come just to learn the results of their research, but also to take refuge in the calmness, and to recover there a certain serenity. Moers, like the Faithful Four, is part of the Maigret *cult*.

DOCTOR PAUL

"The footsteps in the hallway, the knocking at the door, finally the appearance of Dr. Paul, carrying his bag. He shakes Maigret's hand... "Well, old partner?" [*Maigret voyage*, VOY: 2].

We know that this character actually existed, and that he was a friend of Simenon's, with whom he sometimes shared first-class banquets.

In the novels, Dr. Paul is cited by name for the first time in a short story, *La Péniche aux deux pendus*. In the Gallimard period, he appears in *Signé*

Picpus, then he takes on a more important role in the Presses de la Cité novels. Medical Examiner, practicing his art at the Morgue, he plays an important role through the material clues he furnishes Maigret within the framework of an investigation. Thanks to him, Maigret can, for example, learn the time of death of a victim, and sometimes it's the analysis of the body which permits the identification of a corpse, as in *Maigret et son mort* or *Maigret et le corps sans tête*.

Simenon, with no desire to provide detailed analyses of forensic police work in his stories, is satisfied to give us the generalities of the work of Dr. Paul, who explains his discoveries to Maigret "broadly," without entering into too much detail. Maigret, moreover, prefers to phone him to hear his first conclusions, rather than to read the fastidious and complex medical reports.

If we base our portrait of Dr. Paul on what we learn from Maigret, we find that his essential physical characteristic can be summed as his *legendary fine beard, brown* in the beginning, *silky* and *neatly trimmed*, but also symbolic of his psychological aspect, since it is *triumphant* and *joyous*.

We also know that he's a great cigarette smoker, who smokes ceaselessly during his autopsies, blithely claiming that *"tobacco is the best antiseptic."* We learn that off the job he's fond of good food and high society evenings, *"the most Parisian of doctors, friends with the stars,"* and that during these dinner parties he amuses himself by telling stories of his autopsies in their rawest detail.

At work, he makes a specialty of determining the people's professions by examining their hands. He's a man always *cheerful, jovial,* and he maintains his alertness with age, still doing autopsies at 76. However, as he's older than Maigret, he eventually disappears from the saga, and is replaced by other medical examiners, certain of whose names we learn. Drs. Tudelle (*Maigret et les vieillards*), Lamalle (*Maigret et le voleur paresseux*), Ledent (*Maigret et les braves gens*), Morel (*La colère de Maigret*), Colinet (*Maigret et l'affaire Nahour*), Delaplanque (*Le voleur de Maigret*), Desalle (*Maigret et le tueur*), Forniaux (*La folle de Maigret*), Lagodinec (*Maigret et l'homme tout seul*), Bourdet (*Maigret et l'indicateur*) and Grenier (*Maigret et Monsieur Charles*).

The Director of the PJ

This character holds, we must say, a relatively unassuming, secondary role in the saga. We realize that his relative anonymity is due to the fact that a Director of the PJ does not hold a stable position, for they are named as high-level functionaries through a sort of hierarchical path, and not as any function of their years of service as Chief Inspectors, as *first among equals*. Or at least that's the case after a certain period in the saga… "*Maigret remembered the time when the Director of the PJ was chosen from among the Chief Inspectors. His colleagues, at a certain period, had teased him by repeating that he'd finish up in the armchair of the top boss.*" (*Maigret se défend*, DEF: 1). In reality, the only "top boss" who truly merited the title in the eyes of Maigret, who'd seen "*nine Directors of the PJ*", and the only one described in any detail in the novels, is his first boss, Xavier Guichard, who had arranged for his entry into the Quai at the beginning.

In the Fayard novels, references to a "Director of the PJ" are rather vague. In *Pietr le Letton*, we meet a "*Director of the Investigative Service*"—Maigret calls him "*Chief*," and only encounters him at the Majestic after Torrence's death. We find a *Director of the PJ* in *Monsieur Gallet, décédé*, mentioned once as being away from the Quai at a conference in Prague. In *Le fou de Bergerac*, the Director is present in the first pages, only used to send Maigret to make verifications at Bordeaux, a good pretext for the author to set the Chief Inspector in pursuit of the "unknown man on the train." In *L'écluse nº 1*, the conversation between Maigret and his "Chief" is a little longer, marked by a certain melancholy—Maigret is on the point of retirement. Finally, in *Maigret*, their relationship is rather strained, for Maigret, already retired, comes in spite of everything, to mix in an affair which only concerns him because his nephew is involved.

After several incidental appearances in the stories, in which we learn all the same that their relationship is cordial enough ("*the Director of the PJ, who knew as well as anyone the moods of Maigret*" in *L'amoureux de Madame Maigret*, amo: 3; "*So you're waiting for a little fact? murmured the Chief with a smile, for he knew his man*" in *Stan le Tueur*, sta: 2), he takes on more importance in the Gallimard novels. Thus in *Cécile est morte*, for the first time, there's mention of the daily "Report," for which all the section chiefs meet in the Director of the PJ's office. It's also in this novel that the Director of the PJ is described for the first time: "*the Chief had long white hair, and a musketeer's goatee*," a portrait evidently inspired by that of Xavier Guichard. We find the Chief of the PJ again in *Signé Picpus*, particularly in the scene where he reads M. Blaise's telegram. We note that in the story *Menaces de mort*, written in the same period as these novels, two scenes in the office of the Chief frame the action, and it's mentioned that the Chief has a white goatee. Still Xavier Guichard.

In the Presses de la Cité period, the chief of the PJ becomes a character more frequently mentioned. He's spoken of at some length in *La première enquête de Maigret*, with the characteristics of Xavier Guichard; that's where we learn that the young Maigret, as a local station secretary, knew personally the "Chief of Sûreté," who had once been a friend of his father's. Guichard is like a guardian figure, who follows Maigret *"discreetly from afar, or rather, from above,"* periodically changing his area of service with the goal of *"quickly giving him experience of all the machinery of the police."* From his side, Maigret has for him an admiration quasi-filial, having transferred onto him *"a little of the veneration which he'd had for his father."* Les mémoires de Maigret presents us Xavier Guichard anew, and his relationship with Maigret: *"And this big boss, in my eyes, was truly the big boss in all the senses of the word. It was under him that I made my debut at the Police Judiciaire—without protecting me in the true sense of the word, he followed me discreetly from above.... I'm speaking of Xavier Guichard, with the roguish eyes and long white hair of a poet."* (MEM: 1).

We meet a Director of the PJ, for brief scenes in the following novels, but the character becomes more and more anonymous, and we must probably assume, in the internal chronology of the investigations, that Guichard is no longer, at this point, the Director. And after *Maigret voyage*, there's no question about it, since it's written that the Director of the PJ is M. Benoît. We note also, that apart from a few exceptions, in general Maigret only meets his Chief in the Director's office, when he comes to report on the progress of an investigation, as if the Chief were just a symbolic entity who animates his office, a personification of the hierarchy that Maigret must comply with. In *Maigret se défend*, we meet a Director named Blutet, who had only been on the job three years, and who hadn't *"any experience with the police, except, perhaps, through novels. He was a high-level functionary who had served in various ministries."* Which explains the relatively strained relations described between the two men in this novel. Another few appearances, always fairly brief and anonymous, in the last novels of the period, and we learn finally in *Maigret et Monsieur Charles,* that this Director has retired, and that his position had been offered to Maigret, who refused it, for the Chief Inspector is above all a man of action, for whom it would have been *"painful to pass his days in an office, studying files and spending his time with more or less administrative tasks...."*

The Usher at the PJ

A little riddle—do you know who is the first person, besides Maigret, to appear in the saga? Well, it's the usher, a secondary character in the novels, but all the same useful to the action. It's he who has the role of introducing Maigret's visitors, and he is, in a way, "a part of the furniture" of the PJ—the old orderly in his glass booth at the head of the hallway is as necessary a part of the decor as the waiting room or the dusty staircase.

In the saga, this character has gone under various names, and he is sometimes called an "office boy" and sometimes an "usher." If we follow the chronological order of the writing, we find that the office boy is first named *Jean* in the Fayard texts, then there's an *Emile* and a *Jérôme* in two stories, then the usher *Léopold* or *François* in the Gallimard period, and we have to wait for the Presses de la Cité novels to finally encounter *Joseph*, the old orderly, whom we'll meet most often in the saga.

JEAN

The first character to appear at Maigret's side in the saga, this office boy has for an essential function, besides receiving telephone calls, feeding the fire in Maigret's stove, which furthermore he's not very good at, since the Chief Inspector, each time he returns to his office, must refill and stoke his stove himself (see *Pietr le Letton* and *La tête d'un homme*), and perhaps that explains why his name disappears so quickly from the saga. We recognize, however, that after *Pietr le Letton*, a place will be reserved for him henceforth, on the landing serving the anteroom, commanding the long hallway bordered with a multitude of offices.

EMILE

He appears with this name only once, in the story, *La pipe de Maigret*. We learn that he's old, that he occupies "his glass booth," that Maigret rings for him using an electric button, and that unlike Jean, whom Maigret used "*tu*" with, the Chief Inspector uses "*vous*" with him.

JÉRÔME

He makes but a brief and unique appearance in the story *Maigret et l'inspecteur Malgracieux*, in a long descriptive sentence, reminiscent of Balzac— "*At the very end of the hallway, the old night office boy, Jérôme, who'd been in the house for more than 30 years, and who had hair as white as snow, was seated before his little table with its green-shaded lamp, steel-framed glasses on his nose, invariably reading a large treatise on medicine, the same one over the years. He read like a child, moving his lips, sounding out the syllables.*"

LÉOPOLD

He appears in *Cécile est morte*, with the title "usher," with the essential mission of announcing the visit—and then the departure—of Cécile. He is also called "*vous*" by Maigret. Léopold is not his real name, but he's so nick-named because he resembled the king of Belgium.

FRANÇOIS

Encountered in *Signé Picpus*, we only know that he's old, and that Maigret asks him to order demis from the Brasserie Dauphine.

JOSEPH

After these transitory characters, we concern ourselves with old Joseph, to whom Simenon gives indifferently the title of *office boy*, *night boy*, *usher* or even *porter*. His name is mentioned for the first time in the first novel of the Presses de la Cité period in which the action takes place in Paris, *Maigret et son mort*. As he is present in so many of the novels of the period (18 of the 41 which occur in Paris), we can assume that he's the one in the other novels where an orderly is mentioned but not named. We learn of him that Maigret enjoys "*finding his good face*" when he comes to the office, and that he greets him with the traditional "*Bonjour, Joseph.*" The old usher has white hair, very sparse, which haloes his bald pate, and he wears a heavy chain around his neck with an enormous medallion. Maigret, depending on the case, calls him "*vous*" or "*tu*." Joseph walks very quietly, after knocking, always discreetly, at the door, he has the habit of entering Maigret's office without waiting for a response. Maigret summons him with a call button or an electric buzzer (found under his desk). Joseph is *the oldest one in the house*, and "*as he lives in an anteroom without any daylight, he's taken on the color of ivory.*"

8

The Judiciary

Here is one of the essential differences between Maigret and other literary investigators. For Sherlock Holmes or Hercule Poirot, for example, the discovery of the guilty party is basically the solution to the mystery, and when this has been accomplished, the guilty one confesses and accepts his defeat. Therein is the principle of the *whodunit*, where the investigation is a kind of game concerning the detective, the suspect, and the reader. It's different for Maigret, since it's not so much a question of "who did it?" that's of interest, but "why did he do it?." Rather than questions about the crime, Maigret asks about the motives of the murderer. That's why he ends up "putting himself in the murderer's shoes," and the links he forges with him mean that true to his motto, "*to understand and judge not*," he always experiences a certain difficulty delivering the guilty party to justice. While the culprit in the novels of Conan Doyle or Agatha Christie, "disappears from the scene" once the mystery is solved, giving up his place to the triumphant detective, in Simenon's novels, things work differently. Maigret, following the arrest, ponders over what will become of the man once he's convicted. It's a different man who will leave the prison, another destiny which will continue. Which is also why, more than once in the saga, the Chief Inspector deliberates over whether to make an arrest or not, sometimes choosing to let someone go free. This view of human responsibility, so characteristic of Maigret, explains why he has so many problems in this relationships with "justice," personified by the judges and magistrates of the judicial system, in this "*open battle, the old struggle never admitted but always latent, between the Prosecutors and the Quai des Orfèvres*" (*Maigret et les témoins récalcitrants*, TEM: 7).

The Examining Magistrates

In the beginning of the saga, particularly in the Fayard novels, the Examining Magistrate is content to make a brief appearance in the novel, not even receiving a name, as anonymous as functional, "leaving the way free" for Maigret to tranquilly lead his investigation. Thus, in *L'ombre chinoise*, "*The Examining Magistrate had a short meeting with Maigret. 'I'll leave you to your work.... Naturally, you'll keep me up to date'*" (OMB: 2). From the Gallimard period, and then in the Presses de la Cité period, Examining Magistrates get the right to a name, as well as some description. So we find the "minuscule Examining Magistrate, Mabille" in *Cécile est morte*, Judge Cajou, "*brown hair, in his forties*" in *Maigret et le voleur paresseux*; Judge Dantziger, "*small and round, ... dressed carelessly*" in *Maigret et le clochard*; or Judge Bonneau in *Les caves du Majestic*, "*an honest man, even a good man, father of a family, a collector of rare bindings. He had a fine gray squared beard*" (MAJ: 5).

We also note that Examining Magistrates, as the years pass, are more and more often young judges, of an "*insulting youth*" for Maigret. Thus, in *Maigret et les témoins récalcitrants*, Judge Angelot, archetype of the young judges for whom Maigret has a particular aversion... "*The young magistrate, who had just been appointed, offered a firm and well-kept hand, a tennis player's hand, and Maigret thought once more that a new generation was taking over*" (TEM: 1). The same thoughts in *Maigret et le tueur*, where Maigret has to work with Judge Poiret: "*Another young one. It seemed to the Chief Inspector that the judicial personnel, for some years, renewed itself with disconcerting rapidity*" (TUE: 2). If certain judges "*prudently leave the police the time to do their job*," like Judge Cayotte in *Maigret et l'affaire Nahour*, who has "*a policy of letting the police work alone for two or three days before getting involved with a case*," others are classified by Maigret in the "*pain-in-the-neck*" group, adding to their interference an extremely offensive haughtiness. Consider the Examining Magistrate in *Signé Picpus*, "*Another one who would grow impatient, feel that the case was taking too long, talk about the press, critics, insist that measures be taken....*" The judges, because of their social position, are often connected to the same milieu as certain suspects, and their "*bowing and scraping*" irritates Maigret, whose job is not simplified by these social relationships. Judge Alain de Folletier, in *Les vacances de Maigret*, "*big, fat, a ruddy complexion*," with a fine brown mustache, smoking a cigar and adopting with Maigret a tone "*amiable to the point of condescension, a gentleman of old stock conversing with a man who was interesting, but a little common*" (VAC: 6).

There are a few exceptions among the string of unpleasant judges: Judge Bréjon in *L'inspecteur Cadavre*, "*a fine, delightful, shy fellow, with the manners of another century*"; the shy Judge Dossin in *L'amie de Madame Maigret*, with the "*aristocratic silhouette of a Russian wolfhound*"; Judge Urbain de Chézaud in *Maigret et les vieillards*, with "*an intelligent air*" who Maigret liked, and besides, a pipe smoker!; Judge Bouteille (whose name itself, "Bottle," should be pleasing to Maigret's ears) in *Maigret et l'indicateur*; and in *Maigret et Monsieur Charles*, Judge Coindet, "*an old judge, friendly and smiling*," and he too a pipe smoker! And finally Judge Ancelin in *La patience de Maigret*, "*a plump little man, very blond, his hair ruffled, with the white skin of a baby, and candid blue eyes*," with whom a sort of "complicity" developed. And he's the only judge with whom Maigret will go so far as to share a meal—a judge who loves a good meal, and shares Maigret's taste for "country" food, which you don't find everyday!

And finally we have the special case of Julien Chabot, Examining Magistrate of Fontenay, a friend of Maigret's from his school days, whom we meet in *Maigret a peur* and *Maigret chez le ministre*. His special relationship with Maigret makes him a special character, outside the list of judges, and if Maigret meets him during the exercise of his functions, it's as much as Chief Inspector as friend that Maigret both opposes him and allies himself with him in his investigation.

Judge Coméliau

This character personifies the difficulties of Maigret relationship with the judiciary. The "personal enemy" of the Chief Inspector, the confrontation between the two men often takes a more or less dramatic turn in the novels, almost comic on occasion.

Coméliau Before Maigret

The character Coméliau had already appeared, in his function as judge, in novels preceding the Maigret saga, and thus before Simenon's work signed "Simenon." We find him mentioned for the first time in *Mademoiselle X*, a novel signed Christian Brulls. Coméliau plays a part in four novels signed Georges Sim, *La femme qui tue*, *En robe de mariée*, *L'homme qui tremble*, and *L'épave*. We also note that Coméliau is present in the last of the "proto-Maigrets," *La maison de l'inquiétude*. He's not yet the "personal enemy" of Maigret that he will become later. On the contrary, he seems rather amiable toward the Chief Inspector; the only words he addresses to him at the beginning of the investigation are, "*Of course, you'll take charge of the case.... I'll make the first reports and leave you free rein.... What do you think?*" and "*Just let me know if there's anything new.... With you on the case, I can relax!*" Not yet any rivalry at all between the two men, the judge lets Maigret work as he pleases; even if this polite withdrawal of the judge doesn't seem to be appreciated at face value by the Chief Inspector, who "*welcomes flattery with the amenity of a porcupine."* Hmm! If Maigret had known what was coming in his future relations with the judge, perhaps he would have had a greater appreciation of Coméliau's amiability.

COMÉLIAU IN THE FAYARD PERIOD

Coméliau is present from the beginning of the saga. In *Pietr le Letton*, it's to him that Maigret tells his reconstruction of Pietr's origins. Coméliau, in this novel, plays in a way "without intending to" the role of Maigret's confidant. Not yet a trace of any particular animosity between the two men, and Maigret not only smokes his pipe in the judge's chambers (which the judge would hardly have tolerated later on), but the Chief Inspector even feels "at home there." It must be mentioned that the judge's chambers included a stove, a more than attractive object for Maigret. We note further that we learn in this novel that Coméliau wears gold-rimmed glasses, whose lenses he has a habit of endlessly polishing. He returns in *La tête d'un homme*, a novel in which little touches are added to his portrait. He has a carefully trimmed narrow mustache, smokes cigarettes, and he's thin, nervous. His relationship with Maigret becomes more complex, oscillating from the trust he first shows the Chief Inspector, his irritation when he sees that the experiment of Heurtin's escape fails, and finally a certain contrition in the face of the "success" of Maigret, who has in spite of everything discovered the truth. We also note that Coméliau's chambers have already lost the stove, replaced by the central heating that Maigret hates, which does not improve the relationship between the two men. We briefly meet Coméliau again in *La nuit du carrefour*, then, for the remainder of the Fayard novels, Coméliau is—for the moment— shelved. And there's no further trace of him in the Gallimards, so we must await the first volumes from Presses de la Cité for the reappearance of the nervous little mustachioed judge.

COMÉLIAU IN THE PRESSES DE LA CITÉ PERIOD

The first appearance of Coméliau in this period occurs in two stories, first in *La pipe de Maigret*, where only his name is mentioned, and then in *On ne tue pas les pauvres types*, where Coméliau "returns by the back door" in the saga, merely telephoning Maigret to assign him the case of Tremblet's murder. Thus the judge gives the Chief Inspector time to "reacquaint himself" with him. In the first "Parisian" novel which follows this story, *Maigret et son mort*, Coméliau will play an important role. Indeed, it's in this novel that we find the famous telephone scene between Maigret and the judge, where the Chief Inspector is at home with a sham cold. Here the rapport between the two men already appears strained. The Director of the PJ tells Maigret, "*You ought to see Coméliau though, or telephone him…. He's pretty touchy…. Maigret already knew that.*" And further, "*Let's go see the old monkey! sighed Maigret, who'd never been able to stand Judge Coméliau.*" We'll learn, in subsequent novels in which Coméliau appears, some supplementary details. The judge is small, with brown hair, and a toothbrush mustache, which *quivers* when he gets angry. In *Maigret et le corps sans tête*, Coméliau is present from start to finish, and his relationship with Maigret is filled out in detail. It's there too that he receives for the first time the qualifier 'personal enemy of Maigret,' who describes him in a stroke as "*the most conformist and complaining magistrate in the Prosecutor's Office.*" In Maigret's classification of judges, he is certainly in the "*pain-in-the-neck*" group… "*Most of the Examining Magistrates were happy to leave matters in the hands of the police until they had finished their investigation. Coméliau, however, wanted to direct operations from the beginning of a case.*" He was an intelligent man, but "*his intelligence was incapable of handling certain realities,*" as a result of his being a part of "*the Establishment, with rigid principles.*" He is also "*nit-picking, concerned with appearances, nervous about public opinion.*" The judge has a fear of complications, all the more so because his brother-in-law in politics is in the public eye. Furthermore, he mistrusts the less than "orthodox" methods of Maigret. And it's in this novel as well that we find the scene in Coméliau's office where Maigret skillfully maneuvers being able to smoke his pipe, since Coméliau has developed a phobia against tobacco (and maybe particularly Maigret's tobacco). In *Maigret tend un piège*, the Chief Inspector allows himself to smoke in the judge's chambers. In *Maigret s'amuse*, it's Janvier, in the absence of Maigret, who will do battle with Coméliau, and the magistrate does not show himself to be any more accommodating than ever. "*Janvier had been landed with Judge Coméliau, who was certainly the most disagreeable magistrate to handle. Fifty times, a hundred times in his career, Maigret had held out against him, sometimes risking his position. Janvier didn't have Maigret's patience, his stubborn or absent air when Coméliau flew into a rage*" (AMU: 2).

After *Maigret et les témoins récalcitrants*, Coméliau will only be invoked as a memory, for the changeover to the young judges had occurred… "*His personal enemy, as he chose to call him, Judge Coméliau, had retired and was now no more than an elderly gentleman who walked his dog in the morning, on the arm of a lady with bluish hair.*" And in *Maigret et l'affaire Nahour* as well, the name of the judge is mentioned in one sentence, "*others also had disappeared with time, like Judge Coméliau, that the Chief Inspector had always called his personal enemy, and whom he sometimes missed.*" What! If Maigret is sorry to have lost the chance to do battle with his personal enemy—Well!

Finally, in *Une confidence de Maigret,* Maigret has another lengthy reflection about the judge: "*The judge did not act so out of personal animosity, and if Coméliau was always mistrustful of the Chief Inspector and his methods, it was more a result of the gap separating their points of view. And didn't that, in the end, come down to a question of social class? The magistrate remained, in an evolving world, a man in a fixed space.... He was a man of his world, a slave of its ways, its rules of life, its language*" (CON: 6).

We can clearly see what separates the two men, antagonists physically (Coméliau, the nervous little judge, wasn't he the exact opposite of Maigret, the calm man with the imposing stature?), as well as psychologically … while Coméliau remained a slave to his class prejudices Maigret, for his part, plunged into each new case in what was for him a new world, crossing social barriers to search behind appearances for the "naked man," stripped of his artifices.

We find among the personnel of the judiciary, other officials, *substituts,* prosecutors, lawyers and notaries. More details are given about these characters in *Part III. The Saga.*

9

Maigret's Paris

The character Maigret is anchored, planted, embedded in a particular setting, this Paris, object of so many fantasies. The streets of Paris in which Maigret wanders in search of a truth, are an integral part of the saga, as much as a backdrop as to give special color to the atmosphere in which the character evolves. And Simenon has the power to successfully evoke these streets by simply mentioning a name, with no detailed description, so that it's enough for readers to see "Rue Rambuteau," "Rue du Chemin-Vert" or "Place Blanche," for their imagination to do the work of setting the Chief Inspector in the middle of the scene. Here Michel Carly, in his *"Maigret, traversées de Paris."* *"Simenon's Paris is not a decoration, it's a breathing presence, familiar and tamed.... The Paris of the Chief Inspector is the geography of the writer, private, emotive, subjective, sensory. Poetics of space, emotional relationships. A Paris at once reinvented and simplified.... Rarely have a city and a literary character merged to this extent. The one identifies the other."*

The Streets of Paris

If you were to ask a knowledgeable Maigret fan which street is most often mentioned in the novels, as a rule, he'd probably answer with a typical street in Montmartre.

We've done an analysis of the frequency of the mentions of the streets of Paris in the saga, counting, not the number of times the name of the street appears, but rather the number of novels in which it appears at least once, whether simply mentioned, or one of the sites of the action. For this analysis we've ignored the Boulevard Richard-Lenoir and the Quai des Orfèvres, for these two names can be considered more as symbols (of Maigret's home and office) than true streets. We've found 317 street names, of which 154, about half, are mentioned in but a single novel, but in which they may still be an important part of the action. (Thus, Rue Saint-Dominique where the Count de Saint-Hilaire lives in *Maigret et les vieillards*, Rue Lhomond, the location of Mlle Clément's boarding house in *Maigret en meublé*, or Rue Fortuny where we find Madame Blanche's house "for surreptitious meetings" in *Maigret et le marchand de vin*.)

And here's the surprise we've been waiting for: the street mentioned in the largest number of novels is.... Avenue des Champs-Elysées! Mentioned in 34 novels, the mythical symbol of Paris, leading from the Place de la Concorde to the Arc de Triomphe. It's sometimes the location of an investigation (especially in one of the grand luxury hotels which line it, including the legendary Majestic), but it's also a place of passage for getting to the "upper class neighborhoods."

The second most often mentioned street (in 26 novels) is Boulevard Voltaire. In fact, this one is most often mentioned as the street which leads from Maigret's home to his office; it's more a path than a place where something happens. We further note that it isn't mentioned until the Gallimard period, and it's above all in the Presses de la Cité novels that it's found, at the point in the saga where Maigret's home takes on more importance. We also note that it's where Dr. Pardon's house is, at least in certain novels.

The third most mentioned street (in 21 novels) is Boulevard Saint-Michel. Here too, it's more a place of passage, permitting Maigret to go from the Quai des Orfèvres to the districts of the Left Bank. Boulevard Saint-Michel opens onto Pont Saint-Michel, the bridge Maigret sees from his office. How often has he contemplated the movements of those crossing the bridge, the Seine flowing below.

The next two streets are each mentioned in 19 novels, Rue Lepic and Rue Notre-Dame-de-Lorette. This time we truly are in Montmartre, one of the favorite quarters for Maigret's investigations. Rue Saint-Antoine, bordering Place des Vosges, is mentioned in 18 novels. We find here another district in which Maigret often investigates, whether in one of the apartments of the Place des Vosges, or on one of the neighboring streets (the Steuvels affair, Rue de Turenne in *L'amie de Madame Maigret*, or the Poles of Rue de Birague, for example). Two streets are mentioned in 17 novels. One, Boulevard Saint-Germain, emblematic street of the Left Bank, and the other, Rue Saint-Honoré, a street of deluxe shops which runs near Place Vendôme and leads to the Louvre. We return to Montmartre with Rue Caulaincourt (mentioned in 16 novels), home to many of the young women encountered by Maigret (for example, Mlle Berthe in *Mademoiselle Berthe et son amant*, Annette Duché in *Une confidence de Maigret*, Mlle Vague in *Maigret hésite*), and the street which leads to Place Constantin-Pecqueur, home of Inspector Lognon. Mentioned in 15 novels, we have on the one hand Rue Fontaine (still Montmartre), and on the other, Rue de Ponthieu, parallel to the Champs-Elysées, forming a sort of "back-stage" of the grand Parisian avenue. We find next two streets mentioned in 14 novels, both leading to Pigalle, Boulevard des Batignolles and Boulevard de Rochechouart. Next the historic center, with Rue de Rivoli (13), bordering the Tuileries; then nearby, the intersection of Place de l'Etoile with Avenue de Wagram (12); then back to Montmartre with Rue de Douai (11), and Rue Montmartre (10). Lastly, the district of Maigret's home, crossed by three streets mentioned in 10 novels, Boulevard Beaumarchais, Rue du Chemin-Vert and Rue Picpus.

To sum up, we can say that the streets most often cited in the Maigret novels group themselves into five main zones—Montmartre; the neighborhoods of Champs-Elysées and Place de l'Etoile; the Left Bank and Montparnasse; the "historic center" of Paris, between the 1st and 4th *arrondissements*; and the Bastille district, with the neighboring Boulevard Richard-Lenoir.

This observation is confirmed when we do an analysis of names of Places (squares) mentioned in the novels. Of the 34 Places cited, we find Place de la République (which forms one of the corner streets of Maigret's home area) in 19 novels, Place de Clichy (Montmartre) in 17, Place de la Bastille (another corner of the Boulevard Richard-Lenoir quarter) in 16 novels, Place Blanche (another "beacon" of Pigalle location), and Place des Vosges in 14, then Place de l'Etoile (at the end of the Champs-Elysées) in 13, and Place Pigalle, and Place Vendôme, in the heart of historic Paris and symbol of wealth with deluxe shops, in 11 each.

Thus, Paris, symbolic, mythical and Maigret-like, is evoked by a few street names, whose mere mention is enough for a reader, even one never having been to this city, to visualize a representation which should correspond to Maigret's image of "his" city, divided into quarters whose specifics match those of their inhabitants.

Primacy of Paris

Where has Maigret spent the most time in his investigations? It seems obvious to answer, "Paris, of course!" To confirm this impression, and to clarify it, we've done still another analysis, tabulating, for each novel, the number of chapters in which the action is situated in Paris, elsewhere in France, or in a foreign country. In adding up the chapters of all the novels in each of these three location categories, we obtain the following results ... two-thirds of the chapters are situated in Paris, the other third primarily elsewhere in France, with a few chapters in foreign lands.

We can thus say that Maigret not only travels infrequently outside of France (as we knew), but that his author even avoids having him lead his investigations outside his city of choice. Or, to be more exact, if he had his Chief Inspector travel frequently at the time of the Fayard period, a third of the chapters in Paris against two-thirds elsewhere in France (Fécamp in *Pietr le Letton*, the banks of the Loire in *Monsieur Gallet, décédé*, the canals on the Marne in *Le charretier de La Providence*, Concarneau in *Le chien jaune*, Arpajon in *La nuit du carrefour*, Fécamp in *Au rendez-vous des Terre-Neuvas*, Ouistreham in *Le port des Brumes*, the Allier in *L'affaire Saint-Fiacre*, Givet in *Chez les Flamands*, the Dordogne in *Le fou de Bergerac*, the Côte d'Azur in *Liberty Bar*), and some outside of France (Belgium in *Le pendu de Saint-Pholien* and *La danseuse du Gai-Moulin*, the Netherlands in *Un crime en Hollande*); in the Gallimard texts the proportion is equal ... we find about half the chapters in Paris and the other half elsewhere in France (Vendée in *La maison du juge* and *L'inspecteur Cadavre*); while in the Presses de la Cité period, Maigret is clearly established in *his* capital; four-fifths of the chapters in Paris, a fifth elsewhere in France and a few outside. And again, let's be precise—at the beginning of the Presses de la Cité period, the Chief Inspector is "taken" overseas (to the United States in *Maigret à New York* and *Maigret chez le coroner*, Great Britain in *Le revolver de Maigret*), and occasionally to the provinces (Les Sables-d'Olonne in *Les vacances de Maigret*, Porquerolles in *Mon ami Maigret*, Etretat in *Maigret et la vieille dame*, Fontenay-le-Comte in *Maigret a peur*, Charente in *Maigret à l'école*), before leading the majority of his investigations in the capital. And in the last part of the saga, the chapters "outside Paris" are concerned above all with the Maigret couple's weekends, whether at Morsang, or Meung-sur-Loire, with a few rare excursions in the provinces (the Côte d'Azur in *Maigret voyage*, *La folle de Maigret* and *Maigret et l'indicateur*, the Atlantic coast in *Maigret et l'homme tout seul*) and outside France (Lausanne in *Maigret voyage*). With the exception of *Maigret à Vichy*, which takes place entirely outside of Paris. Moreover, the "completely Parisian" novels, where Maigret never goes out of the city, number 26, with a significant increase towards the end of the saga.

A Microcosm in an Apartment

STAIRS

In his Parisian investigations, Maigret is frequently brought to climb the stairs of a building, and, before meeting the tenants, the condition of these stairs often gives him an indication of their social status. In the novels, the descriptions of stairways generally concern two or three elements, of which the variation provides a clue to the "type of house," the steps, the walls, doors and elevator (the presence of which being a good indicator of the status of the building). For example, in the apartments of the Place de Vosges, the height of the floor is in inverse proportion to social status. Thus, in *L'ombre chinoise*, *"Up to the second floor, the building had been redone, the walls repainted and the steps varnished. From the third floor on, it was another world, dirty walls, a rough floor* (OMB: 4). *"The stairway of the building ... at that point stopped rising majestically with wrought iron banisters and walls of false marble ... it became narrow and steep"* (*L'amoureux de Madame Maigret*, amo: 1).

We find a contrast of the same sort between buildings in the center of the city and those in the suburbs. On Boulevard des Batignolles, at the home of Le Cloaguen (*Signé Picpus*), *"The stairway was dark, varnished, covered with crimson carpet, held in place by brass rods.... A single door on each floor, great doors in dark oak, with well-polished brass"* (SIG: 2); in Bourg-la-Reine, where Cécile and her aunt lived (*Cécile est morte*), *"Six floors. Maigret hated stairways. These were dark, garnished with a rug the color of tobacco juice. The walls were worn"* (CEC: 1st part: 1).

The contrast also appears among the districts of Paris. At the Quai de la Mégisserie, we find an older building, where Saimbron lives (*Maigret et l'homme du banc*), and here *"it was in vain that Maigret sought the elevator. There wasn't one, and he had to climb the six flights on foot. The building was old, the walls dark and dirty"* (BAN: 3), while on Avenue Carnot, in the building where Dr. Gouin lives (*Maigret se trompe*), *"the elevator functioned noiselessly, like in all well-maintained buildings. The carpet, on the waxed oak stairway, was a beautiful red"* (TRO: 1). On Rue Mouffetard, at Cuendet's mother's house (*Maigret et le voleur paresseux*): no elevator, but a stairway *"with worn steps," "held by a cord instead of a bar."* Quai d'Anjou, on the Île Saint-Louis, at the Batilles' (*Maigret et le tueur*), *"the walls were of white stone, light provided by engraved bronze candelabras. On the marble landing, the doormat had a great red letter "B"* (TUE: 1). At the Quai de la Mégisserie, at Mᵐᵉ de Caramé's (*La folle de Maigret*), Maigret *"descended the dark stairs, with its worn steps, the banister polished by two or three centuries of use,"* while at the Parendons (*Maigret hésite*), on Avenue Marigny, the stairway is marble, a *"wide stairway with a wrought-iron banister."*

From stairs without carpets, polished by use, buildings in populous neighborhoods, to the comfortable elevators of the luxurious buildings in the high-class neighborhoods, it's all a social geography of the capital that Maigret travels tirelessly, from the top to the bottom of the scale.

TENANTS

As Simenon can well present the many-faceted world of Paris, he enjoys creating a "condensed version" of this world in describing the residents of an apartment. More than once Maigret is led to traverse from cellar to attic a Parisian apartment, whose inhabitants comprise a complete universe. Consider, for example, the apartment where Couchet had his laboratories in *L'ombre chinoise*. 61 Place des Vosges accommodates, besides the inescapable concierge, on the second floor, an aristocrat whose wife is in the process of giving birth, on the third, two young girls who love music, a couple where the husband is a civil servant, and two spinsters. Still at Place des Vosges, but this time 17-*bis* (*L'amoureux de Madame Maigret*), the second floor is occupied by a couple where the husband is—ostensibly—in import-export. We don't know about the third, but on the other hand the fourth, in the roof, is that of maids' rooms, occupied by a beautiful blonde spy, a composer of music, and an elderly fashion designer.

Let's leave the center of Paris and head for the suburbs, to Bourg-la-Reine, and a large six-story apartment building (*Cécile est morte*). On the ground floor we find a bicycle shop and a grocery store. On the second, a family where the husband is a traveling salesman and the wife is awaiting her fifth child. On the third, a bus conductor and a spinster piano teacher. The fourth is empty. On the fifth, an elderly attorney, disbarred because of a sex scandal. On the sixth, an elderly invalid and her niece, and on the other side, a Hungarian family whose two provocative-looking daughters are always on the stairs.

We return to Paris, more precisely, to Montmartre. At 42-B, Rue Notre-Dame-de-Lorette (*Maigret au Picratt's*), the building is guarded by a concierge married to a policeman. A women's hairdresser lives on the mezzanine floor, a masseuse on the second, and on the third we find an artificial flower business, a litigator, and a fortune-teller. The fourth floor is inhabited by a young strip-tease artist, a fat blonde woman who runs a checkroom in a theater, and a girl working in a brasserie. On Rue Caulaincourt (*Maigret et le voleur paresseux*), we find a dentist on the third floor, a midwife on the fourth and a milliner on the sixth. On Rue Notre-Dame-de-Lorette, 17-*bis* (*L'ami d'enfance de Maigret*), on the first floor, next to the lodge of a "monumental" concierge, we find a lingerie shop and a shoe store. On the second, a dentist, a retired couple, and another couple who work as caterers. On the third, a corset-maker and a woman with three children. On the fourth, a young kept woman, and next door, a middle-aged woman. On the fifth, a couple with two children, a retired trainman who lives with his grandson, and an elderly woman, half deaf.

Next, in Montparnasse, we find, on Rue Lhomond, Mlle Clément's building (*Maigret en meublé*). On the ground floor, the owner's room, and that of an elderly operetta singer. On the second floor, the room of a young woman kept by an elderly gentleman, that of a couple with their infant, where the husband works in insurance, the room of an accountant and that of a student. On the third, another couple, the husband Polish, the wife caring for their child, a young secretary, a Yugoslav male nurse at a mental asylum, and a young man who, from peddling encyclopedias, moved to armed robbery. Opposite the building, another apartment, with a couple on the second floor; the husband is a ship's purser, and the wife an invalid. On the third, a bearded man who works at Bon Marché. On the fourth, a widow in curlers who does housekeeping, and on the top floor, a maid who has male company every night. At 37-*bis*, Rue Notre-Dame-des-Champs (*Maigret et les braves gens*), the ground floor has the concierge's lodge, the rooms of an elderly woman, rich and greedy, and those of a widower, assistant manager in an insurance company. The second floor is occupied by a South American family and an art critic, the third by some Americans. On the fourth floor, a couple of good people, with the husband the retired owner of a box company, and another middle-aged couple. On the fifth, a couple and their young daughter, the husband an architect, and another couple where the husband is a manufacturer. On the sixth, a single woman and a young couple. On the seventh, the maids' rooms, one of which sheltered the murderer.

On the Rue des Acacias (*La patience de Maigret*), a six-story building. On the first floor, the concierge's lodge, the apartment of a young man who works in television, and that of a podiatrist. On the second, a family where the father is a ticket collector for the *métro* and the daughter is a student in an art academy, and another family where the father works in insurance. On the third, an American journalist and a well-to-do couple. On the fourth, a physical training instructor and an Italian couple. On the fifth, an old gangster, more or less "gone straight" and his companion, an old "girl of the streets," and incidentally, owner of the building, then a couple where the husband is a traveling salesman, his wife Belgian, and on the fifth, a family where the father is a bartender, and an Englishman. And finally, in the attic rooms, four maids, an elderly spinster, and an elderly deaf-mute.

At the Quai de la Mégisserie (*La folle de Maigret*), we find on the ground floor a bird-seller's, on the second a charming old lady, and a young girl with her mother. On the third, a curious old lady, a bachelor historian, and a young couple who work for the cinema. On the fourth floor, a couple where the wife works in a men's shop, and the husband in insurance, their infant tended to by the devout grandmother on the same floor. On the fifth, a couple with their two children. And on the sixth, and elderly invalid and a brasserie cashier.

Concierges

It's the same with concierges as with maids ... all good or all bad. He'd met charming ones, neat and cheerful, whose lodges were a model of order and propriety ... and the other category, the grouches, unhappy, always ready to complain about everything and how badly the world treated them [La patience de Maigret, PAT: 3].

It's impossible, when speaking of Parisian buildings, to pass over a character who is its essential symbol, that is to say, the concierge. Appearing in just over half the novels, she's a relatively indispensible figure in Maigret's Parisian universe. Examining the texts, we can divide concierges according to two criteria. One is more or less psychological: those concierges Maigret liked, and those he didn't; and this psychological notion is further augmented by physical characteristics. For example, in *Maigret au Picratt's*, Mme Aubin, the concierge at Countess von Farnheim's, speaks with an acid voice, her lips pinched, while Mme Boué, Arlette's concierge, speaks in a calm voice, with an intelligent air. The likable concierges are often referred to as "good women," while unsympathetic concierges are slovenly, with vulgar voices, distrustful eyes or suspicious looks. The second criterion categorizing the concierges is their age—the author almost always gives an indication regarding the age of this character, and it's always an important element in determining her personality. We can divide them into two groups, the first comprising women fairly old (described by the terms "old," "aged," "middle-aged," "ageless"), and the second that of the young concierges (described as "pleasant," "comely," or "appetizing"). We find a fairly significant correlation between the age and the degree of likability. Clearly, the older concierges are, for Simenon–Maigret, generally unpleasant, while for the young ones, the great majority are pleasant women. Further, psychological and physical aspects seem to go together; an unpleasant concierge has an ungainly body, "small, thin, completely flat, an ageless and more or less sexless woman," "colorless, shapeless"; while an attractive concierge has "delectable skin," a "mellow" shape. We note in closing that the "archetype" of the disagreeable concierge is the "monumental" Mme Blanc of *L'ami d'enfance de Maigret*, the character of a concierge doubtless the strongest portrayed in the entire saga.

Bars, Bistros, Cafés and Restaurants, Maigret's Favorite Places

It was good to see once more a real zinc countertop, sawdust on the floor, a waiter in a blue apron... [Maigret et l'affaire Nahour, NAH: 5].

The Places

During his lengthy Parisian wanderings, Maigret makes almost "obligatory" stops in cafés, restaurants, bistros and other bars. Indeed, whenever Maigret is looking for something to eat or drink (or even to make a phone call, since there were no cell phones in his day, and telephone booths were not yet widespread), he'd go into one of these public places. And if restaurants are expressly reserved for culinary pleasures, the others serve particularly as places for relieving one's thirst, though if they happen to serve food as well, Maigret can't be blamed for giving it a taste.

Out of the 350 mentions of these establishments that we've located in the texts of the saga, about a third of them refer to bars, a third to restaurants and brasseries, then about a fifth to bistros. Citations of cafés are slightly less numerous, but sometimes these designations are actually interchangeable, the author describing the same location as here a bistro, there a café or a bar.

Another element we've considered is their locations. The largest share (over a fifth) is found in the 9th arrondissement, one of those in which Maigret investigates most often (which probably explains it). This is where we find Pigalle, with its mythical Simenonean locales—Place Clichy, Place Blanche, and the Rue Fontaine. But it also encompasses all of Montmartre and the Grand Boulevards, other favorite sites of the Chief Inspector. Next comes the 8th, the district with the Champs-Elysées, but also of those little streets "behind the scenes" of the major arteries, and the Place des Ternes. And then the 13th, 1st, 6th, 3rd and 4th arrondissements. Among them they encompass almost three-quarters of all the establishments mentioned.

The décor of these establishments, to the extent the author sketches them with strokes of his pen, evokes for us the black and white photographs by Doisneau or Brassaï ... murky gray light around the light bulb; in a corner, a phone booth enclosed by a frosted glass door; sometimes a billiard table or a slot machine; smoke rising from pipes and cigarettes; the walls plastered with mirrors and advertising calendars; the waiters polishing the counter, spreading sawdust on the floor; the *patron*, from Auvergne, with a black mustache, shirtsleeves rolled up, a blue apron; a fat, blonde cashier; two masons in white jackets leaning on the tin counter; card-players; and, sometimes, a lady of the night, relying on a hypothetical client; without forgetting the terrace, where one can settle down in front of a marble pedestal table, *"to drink a cold beer or some aperitifs, looking admiringly at the pretty women passing by"* (*Félicie est là*, FEL: 6).

CONSUMPTION

We should note that these 350 notations concern not only places frequented by Maigret, but also those simply mentioned in the text. For now we'll focus on the establishments actually visited by Maigret, and examine what he drinks and what he chooses to eat, and thereby create a list of the Chief Inspector's "favorite places."

DRINKS

The first point we'll consider is the drinks Maigret consumes in bars, cafés and bistros. And we find that when the Chief Inspector visits one of these establishments, the author doesn't always tell us what he has there. However, we find a good hundred of them specified. And when we examine these, over a third are—no surprise—beer, the famous *"demis"* our hero imbibes, leaning on the zinc counter. We then find almost a fifth are glasses of white wine, and almost a tenth, Calvados. And then, in lesser quantities, rum grog, coffee, marc brandy, anise aperitifs (Pernod, Pastis), Cognac, and various others. *(For more, see* Drinks—an array of beverages, *in Part I. Maigret the Man.)*

FOOD

Now let's consider the varieties of more substantial food that Maigret consumes in these places. Of course, cafés, bars and bistros generally serve only drinks, but it happens, from time to time, that Maigret might pick up a sandwich or a croissant. And in even rarer cases, the Chief Inspector might even have a complete meal. Thus, down a few steps in a little Norman bar on the Quai des Grands-Augustins, smelling strongly of Calvados (*Maigret s'amuse*), Maigret, awaiting the results of the interrogation of Dr Jave, accompanied by Martine Chapuis, will eat a *sole normande, rôti de veau*, some cheese, and finish with a coffee and a Calvados. In the Auvergnat's bistro, Rue Lhomond (*Maigret en meublé*), he enjoys the mutton stew, even if it causes him an unquenchable thirst. Another Auvergnat's, Rue des Acacias this time (*La patience de Maigret*), offers *rillettes du Morvan*, calf's leg with lentils, cheese, and plum pie with cinnamon, a tempting menu the Chief Inspector savors in the company of Judge Ancelin.

In brasseries, Maigret is often satisfied with beer, but he'll sometimes order the specialty of the house, *choucroute*, sauerkraut, served with beer as well. Perhaps at the *Cadran*, Rue de Maubeuge ("*A fine brasserie, to Maigret's taste, still not modernized, with its classic belt of mirrors on the walls, its dark red moleskin seats, white marble tables, and, here and there, a nickel bowl for used dishcloths.*" *Maigret et son mort*, MOR: 5), or an Alsatian brasserie, situated in an (unfortunately) unknown location, between the *Quai de la gare* and Maigret's office, but where they served a *choucroute* "*lavish and plentifully garnished with shiny sausages and fresh pink pickled pork*" (*Maigret et les témoins récalcitrants*, TEM: 5). And let's not forget the two famous brasseries, *Chez Manière*, on Rue Caulaincourt, where Maigret ordered the *andouillette* sausage, while Madame had the cold lobster *à la mayonnaise* (*Maigret et le fantôme*), and *La Coupole*, Boulevard du Montparnasse, the setting for the memorable dinner at the end of *Les caves du Majestic*. "*What do I owe you, waiter? ... I had a steak, something from the trolley, prime rib, and let's see ... three portions of chips, and three demis...*" (MAJ: 10).

Besides the bistros of Les Halles, where Maigret had M. Pyke try *tripes à la mode de Caen* and *crêpes Suzette* (*Mon ami Maigret*), we find a list of restaurants with diverse and varied menus. Sometimes Maigret eats there alone, as at the *Filet de Sole*, Place des Victoires (*Maigret chez le ministre*), where he orders a Dieppe sole, and drinks Pouilly; for *andouillette*, Maigret goes to a restaurant on Rue Neuve-Saint-Pierre (*Maigret et le voleur paresseux*) or Rue de Miromesnil, *Au Petit Chaudron*, where, if you're on the *patron's* "good" list, you also have the right to the "*baba au rhum smothered in whipped cream*" (*Maigret hésite*); on Rue Caulaincourt, Maigret unearths a little drivers' restaurant, where he savors the veal with sorrel and a Beaujolais (*Mademoiselle Berthe et son amant*).

But the Chief Inspector often prefers to share these feasts. At the *Chope Montmartre*, Rue du Faubourg-Montmartre, Maigret, in the company of Chief Inspector Colombani of the Sûreté, and the Director of the Folies-Bergères (*Maigret et son mort*), does honor to the menu: blue trout, partridge with cabbage, washed down with Châteauneuf; at Pozzo's Italian restaurant, Rue des Acacias (*Maigret, Lognon et les gangsters*), Maigret has Lognon to dinner of spaghetti and scallops *à la florentine*, with Chianti; in a restaurant on Rue de Bourgogne, Maigret, with Janvier, enjoys skate with black butter and asparagus (*Maigret et les vieillards*); at *La Sardine*, Rue Fontaine (*Maigret et l'indicateur*), the Chief Inspector, again accompanied by Janvier, is served *coquilles Saint-Jacques*, braised beef ribs, and Beaujolais; at the *Clou Doré*, Rue Fontaine, Maigret dines with Lapointe, on paella, with Tavel (*La patience de Maigret*); at the *Vieux Pressoir*, Boulevard de Grenelle (*Le voleur de Maigret*), the Chief Inspector finds a good table, and then he eats twice: the first time, with Lapointe, a chowder *fourasienne*, with a little white wine from Charentes, salt-marsh lamb with a red Bordeaux, and to finish it off, an old Armagnac. The second time, Maigret is alone, and he has the scallops, then the duckling *à l'orange*; Maigret invites an American criminologist to dinner on a little street near the Porte d'Orléans, (*Cécile est morte*)— they feast on ceps *à la bordelaise* and *coq au vin*, served with a Beaujolais, then a creamy mocha cake, and to finish in style, an old Armagnac; in another Italian restaurant, *Chez Gino*, near the Rue de l'Etoile (*Un échec de Maigret*), Maigret, accompanied by Martine Gilloux, has hors-d'œuvres and a spaghetti Milanaise.

And there are also restaurants where Maigret brings his wife: the Alsatian restaurant on Rue d'Enghien, where Maigret savors a "*choucroute as he likes it*," while his wife prefers the hot pot Lorraine (*L'amie de Madame Maigret*); sometimes Maigret chooses a restaurant for its specialties of fish and seafood on the Champs-Elysées (*Maigret s'amuse*); on Rue de la Grande-Armée, the Maigrets go to eat vichyssoise, duck *à l'orange* and brie, while drinking Saint-Emilion *(Maigret se défend)*; on the Place des Victoires, the Maigrets savor delicious sweetbreads, lamb chops, and strawberry cake *(La folle de Maigret)*; in a little restaurant on Boulevard du Montparnasse, the Maigrets, this time accompanied by the Pardons, once more enjoy the menu of their first meal together, mutton stew with a carafe of Chavignol *(Maigret et les vieillards)*.

Lastly, to finish up, let's make a little getaway "outside the walls" of Paris, shall we say to the banks of the Seine, at Bougival, where Maigret sits down to dine in a little inn in the company of Dédé (*La première enquête de Maigret*), to savor fried gudgeon and a *coq au vin rosé de beaujolais;* or on the banks of the Marne, at Joinville where the Maigrets and the Pardons return to *Chez le Pères Jules (Maigret s'amuse)*, again for fried gudgeon!, then a grilled *andouillette* and French fries, finishing with Calvados.

And so we conclude our tour of public places dear to Maigret, necessary stops on the route of an investigation: "*He needed to escape from his office, to breathe the air outside, to discover, with each new case, new worlds. He needed the bistros where he wound up waiting so often at the zinc counter, drinking a demi or a Calvados depending on the circumstances.*" (*Maigret et Monsieur Charles*, CHA: 1)

(For more on this theme, *see Maigret's favorite meals* in *Part I. Maigret the Man*)

The Brasserie Dauphine

The Brasserie Dauphine is more than just a place to eat, for it has become a sort of annex, an extension of Maigret's office. Between the two "affective poles" which are his home on Boulevard Richard-Lenoir and his office at the Quai des Orfèvres, the Brasserie Dauphine represents a resting place, an obligatory stop at the close of an investigation, time for a well-earned *demi* or an aperitif, to shake off the weight pressing down on Maigret's shoulders over the course of an exhausting interrogation, before returning to the haven where delicious dishes and the tenderness of Louise await him. It's sometimes also a refuge where the Chief Inspector can "ruminate" at his ease, or exchange impressions with close collaborators, over the course of a savory meal. And finally, the third function of the Brasserie Dauphine, the "official purveyor" of the indispensible sandwiches and *demis* in the course of interrogations in Maigret's office.

Mentioned from the beginning of the saga, in *Pietr le Letton* (where the waiter from the brasserie brings his tray "*holding six demis and four fat sandwiches*"), it will be frequented by Maigret throughout the course of his investigations, all the way through to the final novel (*Maigret et Monsieur Charles*).

At the Brasserie Dauphine, Maigret has *his* table, *his* corner, "*near the window, from which he can see the Seine and the passing boats*" (*Maigret et l'indicateur*, IND: 4). It's a place charged with olfactory memories, a "*beneficial concentrate of all the bistros of Paris*" (as said Michel Carly, in *Maigret, traversées de Paris*); "*against a background of aperitifs and alcohol, a connoisseur would discern the slightly sharp aroma of the local wines of the Loire. In the kitchen, it was the scent of tarragon and chives that dominated*" (*La colère de Maigret*, COL: 1).

Besides its substantial sandwiches it offers a well-stocked menu, where veal seems to occupy the place of honor; various appetizers, small Brittany whiting or herring fillets to begin, then, for the main dish, veal marengo, veal stew "*with the good scent of a family kitchen*," calf's head, veal liver *en papillotes*, sweetbreads with mushrooms, and above all smooth, creamy *blanquette de veau*, "*with a golden yellow sauce, very fragrant*," or, for a bit of a change, *andouillette* with mashed potatoes or French fries, or *tripes à la mode de Caen*, and for dessert, almond cake.

And we note that the brasserie is run "as a family," "*the mother at her oven, the father behind the zinc counter, the daughter helping the waiter with the serving*," and that the *patron*, Leon, was already there when the Chief Inspector began at the Quai, and that his son also works in the kitchen.

10

Transportation

The Métro, the Bus, or a Stroll...

Maigret sometimes takes the métro in the course of his investigations, but when he does, it's "under duress," he's resigned to it. Each time he does so, it's for some unavoidable reason; either there's no car available at the PJ, he has to save time, or it's a case of just getting from one place to another, without any pleasure of the trip. The métro, it's true, is the fastest method of locomotion, but Maigret is not a man of speed, he has need of all his ponderousness, all his slow rumination, to lead his investigations well. And so he prefers taxis or the bus, first, because he enjoys the spectacle of the streets, which he can find through the windows of a taxi, or from the platform of a bus. "*He was lucky. An old platform bus stopped by the sidewalk, and he could continue to smoke his pipe while watching the scenery and the silhouettes of the people in the streets slide by*" (*La patience de Maigret*, PAT: 1).

This spectacle Maigret savors even more if he's on foot, for Maigret is a stroller, as is also his creator, and as was Désiré, Simenon's father, one of the sources of inspiration for the character of the Chief Inspector. That's why Maigret so often made the walk from his house to his office, "*he loved to travel on foot the fairly long way from his home on the Boulevard Richard-Lenoir to the Quai des Orfèvres. Basically, in spite of his activity, he'd always been a stroller*" (*Maigret à New York*, NEW: 4); "*Like him, others walked along the sidewalks for the pleasure of blinking their eyes in the sun and breathing the occasional warm puffs of air*" (*Maigret hésite*, HES: 3); "*It was so clearly spring that he'd walked the whole way from the Boulevard Richard-Lenoir, sniffing the air, the odor of the shops, sometimes turning at the bright, gay dresses of the women*" (*Maigret et le tueur*, TUE: 7).

If Maigret prefers the platform bus, it's because he doesn't like to be closed in—witness his propensity for camping himself in front of windows, or his need to often leave his office to roam the streets of Paris.

And besides, the métro is an unpleasant place for Maigret, it's too hot, everyone piled on top of each other. "*He took the métro, which was jammed, permitting him to maintain his bad mood*" (*Le revolver de Maigret*, REV: 2); "*As for himself, he never took the métro except when he had to, as he found it suffocating*" (*Le voleur de Maigret*, VOL: 6). And besides, in the métro he had to put out his pipe (which was already hard enough to have to do on a bus without a platform!). "*Soon he would have to empty his pipe before shutting himself up in one of these enormous vehicles of today where you felt like a prisoner*" [*Le voleur de Maigret*, VOL: 1]), and in addition, there were none of the good odors of the street, those of the shops, the little handcarts of the Rue Lepic and the markets, "*the flavorsome odor of morning Paris,*" nor the lights and colors of the Parisian streets; just the opposite: "*And, as usual, the little car of the homicide squad wasn't available. The two men took the métro, which smelled of bleach and where Maigret had to put out his pipe.*" (*On ne tue pas les pauvres types*, pau: 1); "*The métro smelled of detergent. The advertising posters in the stations, always the same, sickened him*" (*Le revolver de Maigret*, REV: 2).

And so we can conclude from all this that when Maigret does take the métro, it's always for a practical purpose, never for the pleasure of the voyage, a pleasure he can find in slumping in the seat of a taxi, or in smoking his pipe on the platform of a bus, while regarding the spectacle of the teeming streets of "his" city ("*colored images which he let slide voluptuously over his eyes*" (*La patience de Maigret*, PAT: 5).

Taxis

As we know, Maigret never drives a car. He has certainly tried to learn, but "*it sometimes happened that, plunged into his reflections, he'd forget he was behind the wheel. Two or three times, he hadn't thought of using the brakes until the last minute, so he didn't persist*" (*Maigret chez le ministre*, MIN: 7). And as he "*would risk remaining, nose in the air regarding the sky playing through the leaves of the trees, watching the passers-by, or else, in the course of an investigation, losing himself in one of his gloomy reveries*" (*Maigret se défend*, DEF: 5), it was better to be reasonable, and let himself be driven by one of his inspectors, or to take a taxi.

When the black cars of the PJ are not available, or when Maigret wants to "ruminate" in his corner, he prefers a taxi. "*And Maigret, wedged into the corner of the car, whose windows were fogged up on the inside while the outside was beaded with rain, passed the kind of hour he liked*" (*La tête d'un homme*, TET: 7); "*Maigret chose an open taxi, a beautiful car, almost new, and settled himself into the cushions.... And he dozed voluptuously throughout the journey, his eyes half-closed, a thread of smoke leaving his lips around the stem of his pipe" (Le client le plus obstiné du monde*, obs: 2). It's rendered even more enjoyable by the fact that almost all the taxi drivers recognize the Chief Inspector... *"'Quai des Orfèvres...' 'Certainly, Monsieur Maigret!' It was childish, but human—it pleased him that the driver had recognized him and given him a friendly greeting" (Signé Picpus*, SIG: 2); *"He took the first taxi. 'Boulevard Richard Lenoir.' 'I know, Monsieur Maigret'" (Maigret se trompe*, TRO: 4); *"a taxi stopped in front of the house. He was giving the address where he wanted to go when the driver, mischievously, asked: 'Quai des Orfèvres?'" (Maigret et Monsieur Charles*, CHA: 6).

The Black Cars of the PJ

During the Fayard period, Maigret only takes taxis. The first—and only—mention in the Gallimard novels, of a *"police car"* appears in *Signé Picpus*. We have to then wait until the Presses de la Cité texts, and the story *Maigret et l'inspecteur Malgracieux*, to find mention of a *"fast little car reserved for police officers,"* and it's in *Maigret en meublé* that we meet for the first time the term *"little black car,"* sometimes referred to as the *"little black car of the PJ,"* *"little black auto,"* or *"little black auto of the PJ."* We note, anecdotally, that mention is made of a "blue Peugeot" in *L'amie de Madame Maigret*, and of a "black-and-white [patrol car]" in *Maigret et le voleur paresseux*.

The Chief Inspector's Car

Maigret discovered another means of transport, very useful for getting him to the country on weekends. In the beginning, the Maigrets went to Morsang or Meung by train, but little by little, another idea came to them: what if they bought a car? Yes, but then, Maigret doesn't drive. So, what to do? And if Mme Maigret were to learn to drive? Mentioned for the first time in *Maigret se défend*, *"Mme Maigret could drive it... 'Can you see me, me, responsible for a ton of steel speeding along at 100 km per hour?'"* (DEF: 5), the idea, at first rejected by Louise, eventually came to pass... *"It would be nice, on a Sunday, to go by car to Meung-sur-Loire, their little house.... They wound up deciding, all at once. His wife couldn't help laughing. 'You can imagine it.... Learning to drive, at my age?...' 'I'm sure you'll be a good driver...'"* (*Le voleur de Maigret*, VOL: 1). The proof: Mme Maigret got her license, and the Maigrets bought a [Renault] 4CV!

At the Station

Stations are symbolic places in the Maigret saga, as in Simenon's other novels. Maigret more than once leads investigations beginning in a station, since he often has occasion to take a train, especially at the beginning of the saga. (*see* below, *Maigret takes the train*).

GARE DU NORD

Symbol of cold, the flight to Belgium for criminals seeking to escape justice, the station most frequently mentioned in the saga. It's there that Simenon disembarked in Paris in 1922, "*on a December morning, rainy and cold. Because of that image, I hate the Gare du Nord. Nothing depresses me more than seeing it in the distance*" (in *Un homme comme un autre*). As Michel Carly writes in *Maigret, traversées de Paris*: "*the novelist doesn't hesitate to transfer this lack of esteem*," and in fact, he gives his Chief Inspector the same dislike for this station. It's in the Gare du Nord, under "*the monumental sky-light*," on "*the platforms … swept by windy gusts*" that Maigret awaits the arrival of the train bringing *Pietr le Letton* to Paris. First image of an inhospitable station, first image also, of a Chief Inspector leading an investigation in the cold of November, and what better place to represent the desolate atmosphere of late fall than this station! It becomes a symbol in itself, and its very name evokes the cold of the wind: "*I was assigned to a certain building, somber and sinister, called the Gare du Nord.… It had the advantage of being a shelter from the rain. Not from the cold and wind, for there's probably nowhere in the world with such currents of air as in a station, as in the Gare du Nord*" (*Les mémoires de Maigret*, MEM: 5). But this station is also the symbol of daily life, in which it's the hardest and gloomiest… "*The Gare du Nord, the coldest, the most bustling of all, evoked to my eyes a harsh and bitter battle for one's daily bread. Was it because it led to the regions of mines and factories?*" and further, "*I always had a grim memory of the Gare du Nord.… I always see it filled with the damp and sticky fog of early morning, with a half-awake crowd, trooping towards the streets or Rue de Maubeuge*" (*Les mémoires de Maigret*, MEM: 5)

Maigret also goes to this station in *Le pendu de Saint-Pholien*, when he takes a train for Germany, and he disembarks there on his return from Belgium. And that's where he leaves from to follow Graphopoulos in *La danseuse du Gai-Moulin*, and when he follows Martin to Jeumont in *L'ombre chinoise*, and Jehan d'Oulmont in *Peine de mort*. It's near the Gare du Nord, at the Brasserie du Cadran on Rue de Maubeuge, that Little Albert worked (*Maigret et son mort*), where Loraine Martin had bought a suitcase (*Un Noël de Maigret*), where Maigret investigated at the hotel Etoile-du-Nord (*L'Etoile du Nord*), where Lognon "retrieved" Philippe Mortemart (*Maigret au Picratt's*), where Sad Alfred telephoned to Ernestine (*Maigret et la Grande Perche*). And it's in the checkroom of this station that Lagrange checked his trunk, on Rue de Maubeuge that Alain attacks a passer-by and from this station that Jeanne Debul embarks (*Le revolver de Maigret*). And it's also in this station that Maigret finds Gérard (*Cécile est morte*), and where Stiernet is discovered sleeping on a bench (*Maigret et le marchand de vin*).

GARE DE LYON

As opposed to the preceding one, this station has a rather cheerful image. "*The Gare de Lyon ... just like the Gare Montparnasse, makes me think of vacations.*" (*Les mémoires de Maigret*, MEM: 5). It's a station Maigret uses when he goes to the south of France, to warm places, and the station itself makes you think of spring or summer. And so it's via the Gare de Lyon that he goes to Saint-Fargeau (*Monsieur Gallet, décédé*), Cannes (*Les caves du Majestic*), or Porquerolles (*Mon ami Maigret*); it's from there that Meurant leaves for Toulon (*Maigret aux assises*). And if the Gare du Nord is, in Simenon's descriptions, always swept with a cold wind, the Gare de Lyon is just the opposite, it makes him think of throngs leaving on vacation ... "*at the Gare de Lyon, the trains—double and triple added for the holidays—whistled frantically.*," "*They announced eight supplementary trains, and the crowd, in the main hall of the station, on the platforms, everywhere, with their suitcases, trunks, bundles, children, dogs and fishing poles, looked like an exodus. They were all headed for the countryside, or the sea*" (*Maigret s'amuse*, AMU: 1).

GARE SAINT-LAZARE

Used for trips to Normandy and Great Britain via Dieppe, it's to this station that Maigret returns from Fécamp (*Pietr le Letton*), that he gets the train for Dieppe (*Tempête sur la Manche*) and Etretat (*Maigret et la vieille dame*), that Pétillon leaves from for Rouen (*Félicie est là*), and Campois for Le Havre (*Maigret se fâche*), and from which Jeanine Armenieu departs for Deauville (*Maigret et la jeune morte*).

GARE MONTPARNASSE

The station of departure for the west and southwest of France, it's from there that Boursicault leaves for Bordeaux (*Maigret en meublé*), that the lawyer Chapuis leaves for Concarneau (*Maigret s'amuse*), where Nicole Prieur says she arrived from La Rochelle (*Maigret se défend*) and where Calas would have left from for Poitiers (*Maigret et le corps sans tête*).

GARE DE L'EST

This station is more ambiguous in the saga, both sad, "*Seeing the Gare de l'Est, for example, I can't stop myself from feeling gloomy, because it always reminds me of the mobilizations*" (*Les mémoires de Maigret*, MEM: 5), as its role in *Maigret et le corps sans tête*, since it's there that Calas's suitcase was consigned; and cheerful, for it's from there that the Maigrets take the train for vacations in Alsace with Mme Maigret's family. And it's also where Mme Maigret's sister disembarks when she comes to visit (*Mon ami Maigret*).

GARE D'ORSAY AND GARE D'AUSTERLITZ

Serving the Central lines, it's from the Gare d'Orsay that Maigret leaves for Dordogne (*Le fou de Bergerac*), and where Mme Maigret departs for Meung (*L'écluse n° 1*). It's from the Gare d'Austerlitz that Martin Duché leaves for Fontenay-le-Comte (*Une confidence de Maigret*) and where the lawyer Canonge arrives from Boissancourt (*Maigret et le corps sans tête*).

Maigret Takes the Train

"Railway atmosphere" is frequently encountered in the Maigret saga. More than once, Maigret takes the train to investigate in the provinces, providing an opportunity for the author to paint "a landscape seen from a train," often a rainy, nocturnal atmosphere.

From the beginning of the saga, Maigret splashes about in the rain of poorly lit quays. That's the case in *Pietr le Letton*, when he goes to Fécamp, on a "*nasty little train, made up of cast-off cars,*" "*in compartments filled with bursts of air,*" by windows through which he sees "*badly drawn farms in the early light, pale, half-obscured by the streaks of rain*" (LET: 4). The novel *Le port des brumes* opens with a scene from a train where we trace a nocturnal landscape... "*Then, towards Mantes, the compartment lamps were lit. After Evreux, it was completely black outside. And now, through the glass where drops of mist streamed, you could see a thick fog which muffled the lights of the route in halos*" (POR: 1). It's the same at the beginning of *L'inspecteur Cadavre*, where, once more, we find Maigret travelling on the night train. "*The window was streaked horizontally with great drops of rain. Through this transparent* water, the Chief Inspector first saw the light of a signal box burst into a thousand rays, for it was now night" (CAD: 1). This is also the case at the beginning of *Maigret a peur*: "*Suddenly, between two little stations whose names he hadn't heard and of which he could see almost nothing in the darkness, except for lines of rain before a large lamp ... every now and then, across the dark expanse of the fields, the lighted windows of an isolated farm*" (PEU: 1).

Sometimes the landscape is more humorous: "*The grass of the embankments was yellow, the little stations with their flowers streamed by.... A man, in the steam of the sun, agitated ridiculously his little red flag and blew a whistle, like a child*" (*Maigret se fâche*, FAC: 1), or the landscape of the Midi: "*the houses of pale pink or a lavender blue with roof tiles cooked and re-cooked by the sun, villages planted with sycamores*" (*La folle de Maigret*, FOL: 5).

Sometimes Maigret rides in a car "*of an old model, with an unfamiliar green, resembling a toy, a child's drawing, difficult to take seriously*" (*Maigret et la vieille dame*, DAM: 1). The contrast between the heat of a compartment "*white hot*" and the cold air outside created a mist which "*transformed itself into great drops blurring the windows.*" If Maigret wipes away this mist, he sees "*a tiny construction, a single lamp, the end of a quay,*" then, a little further, "*a farm, here and there, near and far, always below, and when you saw a light, it was invariably reflected on a surface of water, as if the train were running alongside a lake*" (*L'inspecteur Cadavre*, CAD: 1).

Alas! The heat of the car is suffocating. "*The curtains were closed, the windows lowered, but it was only occasionally that you received a little spurt of cool air*" (*Monsieur Gallet, décédé*, GAL: 1). "*A muggy heat reigned,*" and "*it was Maigret who tried to adjust the radiator! The device was out of order!*" (*Le fou de Bergerac*, FOU: 1); "*the compartment, once more, was overheated, or rather you had the impression of a special heat, the smell of the train, sweating from everywhere, the walls, the floor, the benches*" (*Les caves du Majestic*, MAJ: 5). And if Maigret finally finds sleep, he awakes "*at every stop, confusing the noises of the train and the jolts with his nightmares.*" (MAJ: 5). So then it's better to stay in the corridor, "*regarding the confused landscape that the night erodes little by little*" (*Pietr le Letton*, LET: 6).

And when he gets back to his compartment, after having drawn some puffs on his pipe in the corridor, or paid a visit to the dining car to soothe his thirst, the Chief Inspector makes all sorts of acquaintances—"*a livestock salesman from Yvetot undertook to tell Maigret his stories in a Normandy patois*" (*Pietr le Letton*, LET: 5), "*two NCOs who, along the route, had recounted racy stories*" (*L'ombre chinoise*, OMB: 10), and "*a woman who kept a horrible Pekinese on her lap*" (*Les caves du Majestic*, MAJ: 3).

Maigret Takes a Plane

The airplane is the least preferred means of transportation used by the Chief Inspector, who, when traveling outside the capital, most often takes the train, or rarely, a ship (*Maigret à New York*). Even if he sometimes claims to want to take a plane (he only does so humorously, in *La danseuse du Gai-Moulin*: "*the idea of taking a trip to London, above all by plane, made me smile*," he said to Delvigne when he told him how he'd tailed Graphopoulos), it's more often because he's forced to use this mode of transportation, "*because he didn't particularly care for planes, where he always felt a sense of confinement*" (*Maigret et l'homme tout seul*, SEU: 5).

And so he'll take a plane to cross America (*Maigret chez le coroner*), or to set off to England in pursuit of a young man armed with a revolver (*Le revolver de Maigret*), or to the Côte d'Azur and Switzerland, after a panic-stricken little countess (*Maigret voyage*), or for a quick stop during the course of an investigation, to Bandol, for Marcia's funeral, in *Maigret et l'indicateur*, or La Baule, investigating Mahossier, in *Maigret et l'homme tout seul*. But an airplane voyage offers, all the same, some compensations: "*a stewardess, as pretty as a magazine cover girl, kindly adjusted his seat belt*" (*Maigret chez le coroner*, CHE: 9); "*Maigret had the luck to see the ocean sparkling like fish scales, and fishing boats trailing behind them a frothy wake*" (*Le revolver de Maigret*, REV: 6).

Maigret Rides a Bike

Did you know that Maigret sometimes travels by bicycle? Actually, it's a pretty rare occurrence, but sufficiently unusual to bring it up.

In fact, we only find Maigret on a bicycle at the beginning of the saga, and his "cyclistic acrobatics" are reserved for novels of the Fayard and Gallimard periods, when the author describes to us his character in attitudes much less sober and serene than they'll be in the Presses de la Cité period. Paradoxically, even if he's described as much more "elephantine" in the Fayard and Gallimard novels, at the same time it's also in these two periods that Maigret has occasion to display much more "athletic" attitudes. For example, falling with all his weight on an adversary menacing him with a gun (Radek in *La tête d'un homme*), or jumping from a moving train (*Le fou de Bergerac*). In the Presses de la Cité period, Maigret leads his investigations in a much more "suppressed" and "muted" fashion, and his corporal mass becomes, in a way, a more mental than physical weight.

This is no doubt why we never find Maigret perched on a bicycle in the Presses de la Cité novels, with one exception. It's in fact in *Les mémoires de Maigret* that the Chief Inspector, returning to the beginning of his career, tells us how he began his police activities wearing a uniform and riding a bicycle. *"As I had long legs and was very skinny, very fast, strange as it may seem today, they gave me a bicycle, and so that I'd learn my way around Paris, where I was constantly getting lost, they assigned me to delivering envelopes to all the various government offices"* (MEM: 3). But those days wouldn't last, and the uniform and bicycle soon disappeared, when Maigret was appointed to the post of Secretary to the District Chief Inspector.

And so it's much later, when he's already a seasoned Chief Inspector, that Maigret will have occasion to mount a bicycle once more, on rare occasions at that, and often pushed by circumstances, for at a given moment in an investigation, this means of locomotion will sometimes prove most convenient, or most quickly "at hand."

In *Monsieur Gallet, décédé*, the Chief Inspector borrows a bike he finds in front of M. Tardivon's inn, to go and fetch a doctor for Moers. *"Maigret straddled the bicycle, much too small for him, making the springs in the seat groan."* Then, he keeps it to go to interrogate Eléonore Boursang, who's spending her afternoon reading on a hill; then he comes back down the hill, heading for the post office, to send a telegram to Paris. Useful, then, this bicycle, which lets him move quickly from one part of the area to another.

It's the same use we find in *Le charretier de La Providence*, where Maigret rents a bike so that he can go back and forth along the canal where the barges are hauling, and that's how he does the 20-mile (!) route from Dizy to Saint-Martin the first time, in the rain, to interrogate the carter. Then he returns to Dizy by the same method, and later returns to Aigny, first to interrogate Vladimir about the beret, and then, continuing all the way to Vitry (42 miles, this time!) to interrogate the carter once more, the rhythm of pedaling modulating his thoughts. *"The Chief Inspector sat once more, his head heavy with confused hypotheses ... while rolling in the monotonous décor of the canal, pressing with greater and greater effort on the pedals.... Maigret sketched out his reasoning.... The Chief Inspector remounted his machine more slowly each time, obstinately taking up, in the solitude of a long stretch of the canal, one of the threads of his reasoning.... Maigret began to adopt the right-to-left and left-to-right movement of the tired cyclist. He thought without thinking. He put ideas end to end that he couldn't yet group into anything solid..."* (PRO: 7).

In *Un crime en Hollande*, it's for the reconstruction of the crime that the Chief Inspector uses a bicycle. To interrogate Beetje about the circumstances of the evening of the murder, he has her retake the same route she took with Popinga, and since they'd returned by bicycle, Maigret does the same, putting himself into the skin of the victim. "*The Chief Inspector muttered to himself, 'He came back this way, upset.... He got off his machine, no doubt about here.... He rounded the house, holding his bike by the handlebars'*" (HOL: 10).

In *Les caves du Majestic*, to interrogate Donge without being disturbed, Maigret took the route Donge bicycled to go back home, and rode part of the way with him. And finally, in *Félicie est là*, the Chief Inspector uses a bicycle for several trips between the *Anneau-d'Or* bistro and Félicie's house. He also uses it to go down to the inn at Poissy to interrogate the *patron* about the Sunday when Félicie slapped her dancing partner, and it's perched on his bike that he'll bring Félicie the famous lobster.

Maigret and the Sea

Maigret maintains a rather special rapport with the sea for a landsman, one of both wonder and apprehension. We'd do better to speak of his rapport with *seas*, for he has a very different relation with the liquid element depending on whether it's a northern sea, nearly always described by Simenon in the cold and windy atmosphere of late autumn, or a southern one, evoking summer heat and laziness.

THE ENGLISH CHANNEL
AND THE NORTH SEA

Maigret's first confrontation with the sea takes place very early in the saga—already in *Pietr le Letton* (LET: 16), when Simenon evokes the dramatic meeting of Pietr and Maigret at Fécamp, a city he will return to in *Au rendez-vous des Terre-Neuvas*. Maigret returns again to the English Channel in *Le port des brumes*, at Ouistreham, where he's literally bewitched by the misty atmosphere of the harbor, then in *Maigret et la vieille dame* (Etretat in autumn), in *Tempête sur la Manche* (where there's a storm, obviously!), and he'll fly over it in *Le revolver de Maigret* to go to London. The North Sea is evoked in *Un crime en Hollande*.

THE ATLANTIC

There's the Atlantic in *Le chien jaune* (Concarneau), and in *La maison du juge* (L'Aiguillon, where Maigret quickly surrenders to the first opportunity to escape to the marshes of the Vendée). He crosses the ocean to visit America, (and clear up a storm, of course!) in *Maigret à New York*; it's present in *Les vacances de Maigret* (Sables-d'Olonne), *Maigret à l'école* (near La Rochelle, where Maigret lets himself be dragged into an investigation, lured by a maritime whiff of oysters—that he won't get to eat, alas!—and of white wine). He'll make another fast trip to La Baule (*Maigret et l'homme tout seul*), just enough time to get a magnificent sunburn!

THE MEDITERRANEAN

Maigret meets the Mediterranean for the first time in *Liberty Bar* (Antibes and Cannes). Immediately, the climate awakens in him a holiday atmosphere, and Maigret, dazzled by the heat and the vibrant colors ("*The sea was red and blue, shading through orange…*"), will have difficulty getting to work. He'll find this same sensation of laziness in Cannes in *L'improbable Monsieur Owen*, and he'll have just enough time to breathe the odor of mimosas there during a brief trip in *Les caves du Majestic*. And then he'll be able to see the "*silver wake*" of a sailboat, before counting the seconds between the ebb and flow of a "*lazy sea*" in Nice (*Maigret voyage*). He'll pass again to Toulon, to discover a "*sea the same blue as postcards*" (*La folle de Maigret*) and to Bandol where the sea is "*the blue of a flag*" (*Maigret et l'indicateur*). But it's especially the memory of his investigation at Antibes (*Liberty Bar*) that haunts Maigret when he decides to go to Porquerolles (*Mon ami Maigret*). And there again, he rediscovers "*with a little dizziness, the bottom of the sea … some ten meters deep, but with water so clear that you could distinguish the least details*"—aquatic plants and rocks, schools of fishes. Maigret sets off to prowl the harbor, irresistibly attracted by the spectacle of the sea, which he prefers to discover from the shore, not being a swimmer and not feeling the desire to paddle in this liquid, in contrast to his English colleague! For Maigret, it's not the tactile "contact" with the water that he looks for, but rather it's a visual contact that he establishes with the sea, with the dazzling "*sea so smooth, so luminous that, when you had fixed on it a long time, for a moment you could no longer distinguish the contours of objects…*" (AMI: 6)

MARITIME ATMOSPHERE

This sea evokes for him memories of holidays, those which he couldn't take when he was young, "*in school, and had seen his comrades returning from their holidays, tanned, filled with stories to tell, and seashells in their pockets…*" (*Maigret et la vieille dame*, DAM: 1), and then, those he'd spent at the seashore with Mme Maigret.

For the Chief Inspector the sea is not only images, *"white cliffs on the two sides of the pebble beach," "the dazzling froth of the waves," "the girls who danced in the waves."* It's also odors of kelp and boarding houses. And there are sounds, *"the rhythmic noise"* of the waves, the *"raucous calls"* of the foghorn. And finally a taste, and a quivering on the skin—the taste of white wine and oysters, the fresh air of the morning, *"with a tasty freshness which you breathed through all your pores."*

11

Investigations

Are the Maigrets Detective Stories?

In the novel *Maigret et le client du samedi,* we find the Chief Inspector battling an unusual case, in the sense that he's been consulted more as a confessor than a policeman, before a crime has been committed. Once more, Simenon deviates from the classic rules of the detective story—and moreover we can ask whether the *Maigrets* actually *are* detective stories in the traditional sense—where we expect the investigator, policeman or detective, to be presented with a corpse whose murderer he must discover. As in *Les scrupules de Maigret,* the Chief Inspector will intrude into a milieu where he is not only not obligated to, at first, but not authorized to, since he hasn't the right to act until a crime has been committed. We can find similar cases in more than one novel in the saga. We can ignore, for the moment, those novels where there has not actually been a murder, as *Maigret, Lognon et les gangsters,* where it is an unsuccessful attempted murder, and *Maigret chez le ministre* where the crime is a theft, and those where the murder was actually a suicide, as *Monsieur Gallet, décédé, Maigret et les vieillards,* and *Maigret se fâche.* And we find a number of novels where the murder becomes, in a way, the background, and the object of the plot is less the search for the guilty person than a search for the victim's past (*Maigret et la jeune morte, Liberty Bar, Maigret au Picratt's*), or an attempt at understanding the motives of the murderer (*Maigret et le tueur, Maigret et le corps sans tête,* and *Maigret et le marchand de vin*).

We also note that often Maigret, led by his innate gift of empathy, tries not only to *understand* the criminal, but sometimes goes to the verge of absolving him (as in *Chez les Flamands,* where the Chief Inspector doesn't have Anna arrested.) And when Maigret must, in spite of everything, deliver the guilty party to justice, he does so almost reluctantly (as in *Maigret voyage, Maigret en meublé, Maigret à Vichy,* or *Maigret et l'homme tout seul*), or he arranges to be in some way relieved of the task. He arranges for *Pietr le Letton* to get a revolver with which he can kill himself, he transforms the attempted murder of his inspector into a bungled burglary (*Maigret en meublé*), or he allows the guilty one to escape (*Un échec de Maigret*). If we calculate the number of arrests of murderers in relation to the number of murders, we find that in about a third of the cases, the murderer was not arrested, either because he escaped justice by death (*Le port des brumes, Le charretier de La Providence, Maigret et les braves gens*) or by flight (*Maigret et l'affaire Saint-Fiacre*), because Maigret decided not to arrest him (*Au rendez-vous des Terre-Neuvas, L'inspecteur Cadavre*) or because he is restricted by an intervention "from higher up" (*Maigret et le clochard, La première enquête de Maigret*).

Maigret's attitudes towards crime and criminals are simply a reflection of the actual attitudes of the author. Simenon, in his novels, tries to show that man is never completely responsible for his actions, and that (nearly) all murders are, if not excusable, at least explainable by an almost unconscious logic which has pushed the perpetrator to the enactment.

Murders in the Saga

MOTIVES

If we analyze the murders described in the texts, we realize that they all have motives which explain, and sometimes almost justify them. We can classify these crimes into various categories: Murders where the perpetrator acts out of revenge or because of humiliation (*Pietr le Letton*: Pietr kills his brother who has humiliated him; *Maigret et l'affaire Nahour*: Ouéni kills his boss to avenge his humiliation and to cast suspicion on the one who has supplanted him; *Maigret et le marchand de vin*: Pigou kills Chabut who has humiliated him and taken away his "human dignity"). Murders committed in the underworld are often connected to robbery (little Albert killed by the Polish gang in *Maigret et son mort*, the fortuneteller killed by Justin in *Signé Picpus*, the Goldbergs in *La nuit du carrefour*). Murders "by accident," where the murderer had not necessarily intended to kill, but was forced into it by circumstances (*La danseuse du Gai-Moulin*: Delfosse surprised by Graphopoulos, *L'ami d'enfance de Maigret*: Lamotte hits Josée while firing at Florentin, *Maigret à Vichy*: Pélardeau squeezes Hélène's neck too tightly when she refuses to talk). Murders committed "out of necessity" that the murderer was driven to commit, as to eliminate a witness to a previous crime (Darchambaux kills Willy Marco in *Le charretier de La Providence*, Bellamy kills little Lucile in *Les vacances de Maigret*). Murder for profit, as to appropriate or keep a fortune

(Valentine kills Rose in *Maigret et la vieille dame*). Murders committed as a form of madness (*Maigret a peur, Maigret et le tueur, Maigret tend un piège*). We note that murders due to revenge or humiliation are significantly more frequent than others in the saga, which is not surprising, considering the frequency with which Simenon treats this theme in his work as a whole. Murders connected to or resulting from theft are also relatively frequent; there too, nothing very surprising, as this category of murder is part of the "everyday fare" of the Chief Inspector's work. Accidental murders or those committed out of a sense of necessity, taken together, also form an important group, which, once again, support Simenon's thesis of the non-responsibility of the guilty.

Murders for profit are a little less frequent, but we must note that in these cases Maigret is less indulgent towards the perpetrators. If there's a tendency to "excuse" those guilty of a murder for revenge or humiliation (*Le charretier de La Providence, Maigret se défend, Maigret et le marchand de vin*) or by accident (*La guinguette à deux sous, Le revolver de Maigret*), it's towards those who murder for sordid self-interest that he has the least understanding, and it's those he remands to justice with the least remorse (*Maigret et la vieille dame, Mon ami Maigret, Maigret et la Grande Perche, Les caves du Majestic, Maigret et le client du samedi, Maigret et l'indicateur*). And it's only in these cases that he permits himself his rare displays of brutality in his career; the slap to the "nasty boys" De Greef and Moricourt (*Mon ami Maigret*), the punch in the face to Ramuel (*Les caves du Majestic*), the breaking of Valentine's carafe (because even so, one doesn't slap an old lady) (*Maigret et la vieille dame*).

Women Who Murder: The Passionate and the Self-Seeking

In examining the texts of the saga, it appears that female murderers are significantly fewer than males. Indeed, we find in the novels, out of sixty murderers, only twenty women. The motives which drive them are more or less twofold; the first, "murder for love," the case of Anna in *Pietr le Letton* (she kills Mortimer to "save" Pietr), Any in *Un crime en Hollande* (a love transformed into hate), Anna in *Chez les Flamands* (an almost incestuous love for her brother), Jaja in *Liberty Bar* (jealousy and disappointed love due to the relationship between William Brown and Sylvie), Yvonne Moncin in *Maigret tend un piège* (she kills to foster a belief in her husband's innocence), Jenny in *Les scrupules de Maigret* (wanting to help Marton kill his wife). We can add to this group the women who kill in complicity with a lover, when it comes to eliminating a cumbersome husband (Renée in *Maigret et le client du samedi,* Aline in *La patience de Maigret,* Line in *Maigret et l'indicateur*).

In the second group, we find "murder for self-interest," those who kill to preserve their fortune, or their social position, which they believe threatened: Mme Martin in *L'ombre chinoise,* Valentine in *Maigret et la vieille dame*; Mme Serre in *Maigret et la Grande Perche,* Mme Gouin in *Maigret se trompe,* Mme Parendon in *Maigret hésite.* The case of Nathalie in *Maigret et Monsieur Charles* is more complex, both a murder out of self-interest to eliminate the husband, and then Fazio's for disappointed love. There are some cases which don't fall into either of these two categories, Cécile in *Cécile est morte* (rebellion) and Paulette in *Maigret et les témoins récalcitrants* (self-defense).

The Methods of Murder

"Now, neither Maigret nor Lucas, in spite of numerous years of service in the police, could remember a single underworld murder committed by strangulation. Each quarter of Paris, each social class, has, you might say, its own way of killing.... There are quarters for stabbing, others where they prefer a bludgeon, and those, like Montmartre, where firearms dominate" (*La colère de Maigret,* COL: 1).

In his career, Maigret has above all investigated murders committed with firearms (more than a third of the murders described were done in this manner). The other types of murders are distributed fairly equally among murders by strangulation, by a "sharp instrument," by a "blunt instrument," and finally by "various methods," for example, suffocation (Mme de Caramé in *La folle de Maigret*), a needle plunged into the heart (Torrence in *Pietr le Letton*), or an accusatory letter (the Countess in *L'affaire Saint-Fiacre*). Murder by poison remains rarer, conforming thus to the theory, mentioned in more than one novel, according to which murders by poison often go unpunished.

Examining the relationship between the motives of the crimes and the methods used to commit them, we find that murders by firearms are most often a result of vengeance or humiliation, probably committed following a "fit of rage." This could also include murders committed by the underworld. We note that murders committed through madness aren't committed (at least in the *Maigret* saga) with the aid of a firearm. Madness prefers more "hand to hand" methods, such as a knife, a blunt instrument, or strangulation. The knife is used either for vengeance, affairs of the underworld, or madness. The motives for strangulation are various: vengeance, necessity, self-interest, or other, no motive dominating this category. It is interesting to note, in contrast, that strangulation is not used in the underworld, confirming well what was said in the opening citation above. For murders committed using a blunt instrument, there are various motives, but we note however that it's not a method utilized in murders committed "out of necessity," which might be explained by the fact that when a murderer feels obliged to eliminate an embarrassing witness, he plans his crime, so he doesn't use the first thing that comes to hand to bludgeon his victim. Murder by blunt instrument is rather a last resort; picking up the first available heavy object to strike the victim, so that it seems "normal" for this method to be fairly frequent in murders "by accident." Poison, if it's less frequently used, is however a method very dominant in murders for self-interest; murders brooded over, plotted, skillfully prepared, often by old ladies in the saga, where the murderer want to escape punishment even more that the others, since the murder is precisely to preserve a fortune or social status, for which they won't hesitate to take a person's life.

Time and Duration of an Investigation

THE DURATION OF THE INVESTIGATION

Simenon often provides sufficient textual elements in the novels of the saga for us to determine how much time Maigret spends on a case. We find that the average duration of an investigation, considering all the novels, is five days, whatever the writing period (Fayard, Gallimard, or Presses de la Cité). Examining the cases taking one to five days in Fayard period, there are 10 of 19; in the Gallimards, 3 of 6, and for the Presses de la Cité, 34 of 49 cases take from one to five days. So the Chief Inspector has rather a tendency to favor short investigations, probably both because results should be obtained in the shortest time, on the principle of efficiency (*"he hated to interrupt an investigation, believing that one of the best chances for success was speed. As days pass it becomes more and more difficult to obtain accurate witnesses.... He himself needed to keep forging ahead, to stick with the little world in which he found himself immersed"* [*La colère de Maigret*, COL: 6]), and because Simenon's method of writing required this "condensation" of the narrative. As for the stories, 10 take but a single day, 7 take two days, 4, three days, and 7 stories take a week or more.

THE DATE THE CASE BEGINS

Another interesting aspect from the "chronological" point of view of the investigations, is that of the temporal markers given by the author. While he always indicates the season of an investigation, and almost always the month as well, he is less often precise about the day of the month the investigation begins on. We've been able to identify the date for 38 novels, which are either mentioned explicitly, or which could be deduced from clues present in the texts. Among these 38, there seems to be a slight indication that giving the date may be more important for the author depending on the month, in particular for March. We recall the importance of the month of March as a symbol of the beginning of spring in the *Maigrets* (see below, *The weather in the investigations*) And it's probably for this reason that the date is often mentioned for this month, for the date indicates the debut of the spring season. That's the case in *Maigret et le corps sans tête*: "*It was March 23. Spring had officially begun the day before yesterday, and … you felt it in the air* "; in *Maigret et le clochard*, "*Although it was already March 25, it was the first true day of spring*"; and in *Maigret hésite*, "*although it was only March 4, you got to thinking of spring.*"

THE DAY THE INVESTIGATION BEGINS

For the day of the week on which an investigation begins, it's sometimes mentioned, and sometimes has to be deduced from clues in the text, which is not always easy. We've succeeded in identifying the day in 58 novels out of 74. The results show that investigations often start at the beginning of the week, most frequently on Tuesday (17 cases), and slightly less often on Monday (12 cases), since Monday is considered a kind of "slack day," a day when, in principle, there shouldn't be a murder (see *Maigret et l'homme du banc* … "*it's generally accepted at the Quai des Orfèvres that people are rarely killed on Monday*"), and on Wednesday (12 cases as well). Thus Maigret often starts his work week with the opening of a new case. Similarly, it's fairly logical that few investigations begin on the weekend.

THE TIME OF DAY

While we may not have a systematic indication of the day of the week, in contrast, Simenon always gives us an indication of the time of day that a novel begins. Given very precisely by clock time in 50 of the 74 novels, this information can be a mention, implicit or explicit, of a moment in the day (i.e. morning, afternoon, evening, night). Maigret starts his investigations by preference in the morning (32 cases out of 74), sometimes in the afternoon (17), or at night (14), and more rarely, in the evening (11 cases). Is Maigret, a "day person"? Perhaps, though we note that if the story begins in the daytime, Maigret often continues his investigation until well into the evening or the night.

THE PLACE THE INVESTIGATION BEGINS

Lastly, we note that 27 novels begin at the Quai des Orfèvres, 14 at the Boulevard Richard-Lenoir, and 33 elsewhere. In the Fayard and Gallimard periods, novels begin much more frequently elsewhere than at Quai des Orfèvres, which is not surprising, given the number of novels of these periods which take place outside of Paris. In contrast, in the Presses de la Cité period, Maigret investigates most often in Paris, and the novels open most often in his office (22 of 49). And we note the increased presence of the Maigrets' home (12 novels), with either the action beginning during Maigret's breakfast, or by a phone call awakening him in the middle of the night, while he's sleeping beside his wife.

The Weather of the Investigations

When we think of Maigret, we often imagine our good Chief Inspector, hands shoved into the pockets of his overcoat, the pipe in his mouth having been extinguished by a fall downpour. But is that really a permanent reality in the *Maigrets*? Examining the texts, we find that the season in which the majority of Maigret's investigations take place is the spring (26 novels in spring, 17 in summer, 18 in autumn, 13 in winter). Spring is often described by Simenon as a gentle and sunny season. So we are reassured our Chief Inspector has not passed his career uniquely under the chill and damp of autumn. But from where do we get this "myth" of a Maigret doomed to eternal autumn?

THE SEASONS OF THE CASES

Perhaps we can find part of the answer by examining more closely the publication chronology of the saga. Of the 19 Fayard novels, 8 take place in autumn, 6 in spring, 3 in summer and 2 in winter; of the 6 Gallimard novels, 3 are set in winter, and one in each of the other seasons; while of the 49 novels of the Presses de la Cité period, 19 are in the spring, 13 in summer, 9 in the fall, and 8 in winter. It seems that the older Simenon grew, the more his relationship with his character deepened, and the more often he offered him the chance to work during the "fine" season, treating him to more of the joys of springtime, more flashes of sunlight than winter cold and autumn drizzle.

SEASONAL SETTINGS

Might the source for the legend of a Maigret living only under autumn rains be found in the fact that when he was first discovered by readers, at the beginning of the Fayard period, the most popular novels took place in the fall (*Le chien jaune* and *L'affaire Saint-Fiacre*, for example), and that the first cinema adaptation presented primarily a landscape of rain and fog (even though, we note, the novel adapted was *La nuit du carrefour*, which actually takes place in the spring)? Or is it because of Simenon's famous atmosphere, the fact that the author describes so perfectly the cold rains that pierce through hats and overcoats? And yet, when we regard the texts more closely, we realize how he also excels at putting on his canvas the impressionistic colors of the fine season. To give a few examples, but sufficiently eloquent... "*A purple sun was setting over Paris, and the view of the Seine straddled by the Pont-Neuf was smeared with red, blue and ochre*" (*L'écluse n° 1*, ECL: 6); "*That morning, a sun bright and light, which had the gaiety of a lily of the valley, shone over Paris and made the pink chimney pots on the rooftops gleam*" (*Maigret à l'école*, ECO: 1); "*the sky was a slightly bluish pink, the leaves of the trees still a tender green*" (*La folle de Maigret*, FOL: 2); "*It had stopped raining. There were only, in the blue sky, some light white clouds that the sun edged with pink*" (*Maigret et l'homme tout seul*, SEU: 4).

CASES IN THE SPRING

Of the 26 novels that take place in springtime, 21 experience essentially sunny weather, the sun and fine weather seemingly the characteristic of spring as Simenon conceives it, and the month representing it best is March (11 of the 26 cases). As Mme Maigret says in *L'amie de Madame Maigret*: "*For me, March is the most beautiful month of Paris, in spite of the sudden showers.... Some prefer May or June, but March has so much more freshness*" (MME: 1).

CASES IN THE SUMMER

The 17 investigations which take place in summer are all marked with the seal of a bright sun reigning unchallenged until a storm breaks. June and August are both described as months dominated by a stifling and oppressive heat, particularly so for the corpulent Maigret. July is less represented, no doubt because Maigret is more often on vacation during this month, and so doesn't lead any investigations with only a few exceptions (for example, *Maigret à Vichy*).

CASES IN THE FALL

Autumn is generally synonymous with rain in the novels, (dominating 12 of the 18), and it's the month of November which is most frequently evoked (9 novels), described as a month of rain, wind, and fog.

CASES IN THE WINTER

Winter sees intemperate weather more often than the sun, but here the rain can be replaced by snow. And it's the month of January which is most present in this season (7 novels out of 13), described as a month dominated by cold and sometimes snow.

SEASONS IN THE STORIES

We note that for the stories, we find 6 investigations in the spring, 6 in summer, 5 in autumn, 6 in winter, and 5 cases in which the indications are not clear enough to exactly determine the season, but which suggest that they're probably in autumn or winter (with weather described as cold, damp, and disagreeable). And so there are a few more stories taking place during the "bad" seasons (those Simenon describes as generally cold and gloomy, either fall or winter) than during the "nice" seasons (spring and summer).

MAIGRET AND THE WEATHER

In the *Maigrets*, the weather is always an important element in the plot. The Chief Inspector uses the elements as a veritable barometer of his moods. Sensitive to atmospheric conditions, Maigret rejoices like a child at the least ray of the sun illuminating some object, at the odor of spring or the first snow. And often, after the first chapters of novels where Maigret is attentive to the weather, in the following chapters, he forgets the elements because he is immersed in his investigation. And then it's in the final chapters that he becomes once more interested in the weather, and the weather itself, as if to match the more dramatic tone the writing has taken, changes, as the Chief Inspector's mood has changed.

12

Characters

Maigret and the World of Medicine

Maigret's presence in a hospital, and his way of comporting himself there, is evoked in numerous novels. Whether for a visit to patients, victims, witnesses, wounded inspectors (Darchambaux in *Le charretier de La Providence*, Le Clinche in *Au rendez-vous des Terre-Neuvas*, Maria in *Maigret et son mort*; Janvier in *Maigret en meublé*, Lognon in *Maigret, Lognon et les gangsters* and *Maigret et le fantôme*, Pétillon in *Félicie est là*, Antoine Batille in *Maigret et le tueur*), or to meet with the personnel of the hospital (*Maigret se trompe, Maigret et le corps sans tête*), or indeed if Maigret is hospitalized himself (*Le fou de Bergerac*), or if his wife is (*Les vacances de Maigret*), it's interesting to note that the Chief Inspector is always ill at ease in this environment, that he feels out of place. Curious, all the same, for someone who once felt himself destined for medicine!

MAIGRET AND DOCTORS

We recognize the special relationship Maigret has with medicine, a discipline he would perhaps have pursued himself if not for the interruption of his studies by the death of his father. Maigret talks about this in *Les mémoires de Maigret*, the role Dr Gadelle's story played in the course of his life. And while Maigret may not practice physical medicine, he has nonetheless become, in a way, a "doctor of the soul."

While Maigret feels uneasy in hospitals, he maintains rather positive relationships with the doctors themselves, at least with certain of whom he shares the same vision of humanity: Dr Pardon, the Chief Inspector's friend, Dr Paul, the forensic doctor, and psychiatrists like Dr. Tissot (*Maigret tend un piège*).

Ignoring the special role of forensic physicians, Maigret encounters doctors in some 52 novels and 8 stories. Which is to say their importance in the saga and in the spirit of Simenon, as Didier Gallot noted in his book, *Simenon ou la comédie humaine.* Some doctors play an important role in the novels, and we note with some astonishment that the role is rarely positive. If not the victim (Dr Janin, in *La maison du juge* or the ex-doctor-become-*clochard*, Keller, in *Maigret et le clochard*), he is often the murderer himself (Dr Michoux in *Le chien jaune*, Dr Rivaud in *Le fou de Bergerac*, Dr Bellamy in *Les vacances de Maigret*, and Dr Jave in *Maigret s'amuse*). Other doctors are depicted either as incompetent (Bouchardon in *L'affaire Saint-Fiacre*), ludicrous (Van De Weert in *Chez les Flamands*, "*a little man with the pink skin of a baby ... across whose chest was a thick watch chain, and who wore an ancient jacket* "; Dr. Mertens of the group at *La guinguette à deux sous*, "*thin, puny, with movements as delicate as an anemic young girl*"), admitting to shady dealings (Bresselles in *Maigret à l'école*), or to morphine addiction (Dr Bloch in *Maigret au Picratt's*). They can sometimes be hostile to Maigret (Steiner in *Les scrupules de Maigret*, and Liorant in *Une confidence de Maigret*), or pathetic, like Dr Vernoux in *Maigret a peur*. Rare are those who escape a negative role—Négrel in *Maigret s'amuse*, and Dr Larue in *Maigret et les braves gens*. More difficult to classify is Prof. Gouin in *Maigret se trompe*, for whom the Chief Inspector feels a certain fascination mixed with repulsion.

Nurses

Nurses, in the texts, can be divided into two categories: they're either rather young and pretty, attractively shapely, or older, and relatively sour, and seem unimpressed with the Chief Inspector's notoriety. Among the first, a nurse at the hospital where Maigret had been admitted (*Le fou de Bergerac*): "*a beautiful girl, large, strong, strikingly blonde*"; a nurse at the hospital where Jacques Pétillon was cared for (*Félicie est là*), "*a young nurse with platinum hair, in an outrageously tight blouse that hugged her shape*"; and a nurse at the hospital where Maria had just given birth (*Maigret et son mort*), "*young and blonde, plump under her blouse.*" Among the second type, we find, in *Maigret et le clochard*, that the head nurse who works at the hospital where Keller had been admitted, doesn't welcome Maigret with much enthusiasm: "*She turned to Maigret. 'It's you who's come to see the clochard?' 'Chief Inspector Maigret...'* he repeated. She searched her memory. The name meant nothing to her.*" And in *Maigret et le fantôme*, when Maigret visits Lognon in the hospital, "*It was the office of the head nurse, whom Créac had called 'the dragon.' Maigret knocked. An unfriendly voice bid him enter. 'What is it?' 'Forgive me for bothering you, Madame. I'm the head of the homicide division of the Police Judiciaire...' The cold regard of the woman seemed to say, 'So...?'*"

Portraits of Some Inspectors

THE MEN OF THE HOMICIDE BRIGADE

Barnacle, an old-timer, already in place when Maigret arrived at the Quai, who never advanced in rank. He's two years older than Maigret. Nicknamed "I've-got-a-cold," he has very big feet and always wears a shapeless black suit, giving him the air of an old bachelor, although he's married. His wife deceives him blithely, and it's he who must take care of the household after work. But his "mangy aspect" gives him an incontestable advantage in his profession, allowing him to pass unobserved in a crowd and to take photographs of suspects without being noticed. We see him at work in *Maigret se défend*.

Dufour, one of the first inspectors to appear in the saga, since we meet him for the first time in *Pietr le Letton*. At the time, he's 35 (Maigret about 45), speaks three languages, but has a mania for "complicating the simplest stories." On the other hand, he has an "uncommon tenacity" for surveillances and tails, in spite of his tendency to put on mysterious airs, which irritates Maigret. He's small ("small and neat"), has a hopping gait and wears a gray suit with a high, stiff, false collar, and he has a pretty young wife. We see him at work in *Le charretier de La Providence* and *La tête d'un homme*.

Dupeu, an excellent inspector, but who has the defect of producing his reports in a monotone while giving masses of useless detail. He has 6 or 7 children. We find him in *Maigret aux assises, Maigret et les vieillards, Maigret et les braves gens, Maigret et le client du samedi, La colère de Maigret* and *Maigret et l'homme tout seul*.

Lagrume, a tall, thin, sad man, he's the eldest and most lugubrious of all the inspectors. Afflicted with a chronic cold, he has large, flat, sensitive feet. (Almost a twin brother of Barnacle!). We find him in *L'ami d'enfance de Maigret*, in *Maigret et le fantôme* and in *La patience de Maigret*. He's one of the rare inspectors, outside of Maigret's team, to earn some pages in *Les mémoires de Maigret*. Like Lognon, he has a sick wife who waits up evenings for him, and for whom he does the housekeeping, in addition to staying up nights taking care of his daughter's baby.

Santoni, a Corsican, small, with heavily oiled hair, highly fragrant. He's also a newcomer, had worked ten years in gambling, then in vice, where he'd picked up some attitudes that will displease Maigret. ("*You could easily tell that Santoni had not been on the team long. Everything that he said—and even the tone in which he said it—didn't jibe with the attitudes of Maigret and his collaborators! It was always the same thing when he took on an inspector from* *another service"* [*Maigret et l'homme du banc*, BAN: 3]). But Santoni will learn the spirit that reigns in Maigret's team, and remain there, since we find him mentioned again in *Maigret s'amuse*.

MAIGRET'S "REAR GUARD"

Baron, appears for the first time in *Les scrupules de Maigret*, then we find him again in *Maigret et le voleur paresseux*, where he's on stake-out in Cuendet's former room. Stake-outs are something of a specialty for him, and Maigret knows that nothing can distract him when he's in position. He speaks English with a bad accent. We see him at work in *Maigret aux assises*, *Maigret et les braves gens*, *La patience de Maigret*, *Maigret et l'affaire Nahour*, *Maigret et l'homme tout seul*, and *Maigret et Monsieur Charles*.

Bonfils comes on stage in *Un échec de Maigret*. We know little about him—he's married, and a good one for not letting someone get away from him on a tail. And yet he's mentioned in numerous novels, *Maigret s'amuse*, *Les scrupules de Maigret*, *Maigret et les témoins récalcitrants*, *Une confidence de Maigret*, *Maigret aux assises*, *Maigret et les vieillards*, *Maigret et le fantôme*, *La patience de Maigret*, *L'ami d'enfance de Maigret* and *Maigret et Monsieur Charles*.

Janin comes on the scene in *Un échec de Maigret*. He's skinny, has an odd gait and the perpetual air of a beaten dog. He's married, with children. We find him also at work in *Les scrupules de Maigret*, *La colère de Maigret*, *La patience de Maigret*, *La folle de Maigret*, and, under the name of Jamin (presumably the same character) in *Maigret et le fantôme* and *Maigret et Monsieur Charles*.

Lourtie we meet for the first time in *Le revolver de Maigret*. There he's described as one of Maigret's old inspectors, who's been named to the Flying Squad of Nice. The investigation is said to take place toward the end of the Maigret's career, which makes this inspector's return in following novels plausible. He's a big, strong, bony man, often called "Fat Lourtie," or even "Fatso," according to Aline Bauche (*Maigret se défend*, DEF: 4). He has a strong and resonant voice, and Maigret likes him. He smokes cigars or cigarettes, or even a pipe! He's a conscientious inspector, who knows his profession, and he's the fastest inspector on a typewriter. He appears again in *Maigret et le voleur paresseux*, *Maigret et le fantôme*, *Maigret se défend*, *Maigret et l'affaire Nahour*, *Le voleur de Maigret*, *L'ami d'enfance de Maigret*, *Maigret et le tueur*, *Maigret et le marchand de vin*, *La folle de Maigret*, *Maigret et l'homme tout seul* and *Maigret et Monsieur Charles*. His manner and appearance are reminiscent of Torrence, of whom he is, in a way, a pale copy.

Neveu first appears in *Un échec de Maigret*. Before joining Maigret's brigade he worked ten years on the streets specializing in pickpockets. His neutral and *petit bourgeois* bearing doesn't stop him from going sailing on the Seine, and he loves to disguise himself when he's on a tail. We'll see him again in *Maigret s'amuse, Maigret aux assises, Maigret et le clochard, Maigret et le fantôme, Maigret et le tueur, La folle de Maigret* and *Maigret et l'homme tout seul.*

Vacher appears for the first time in *Maigret en meublé*, where he's on a stake-out in the house of Mlle Clément, smoking cigarette after cigarette, drinking coffee prepared by the "portly demoiselle *en chemise*," with whom he "*[would have] gladly shared a few words*" (MEU: 7). He has children, that he's had occasion to take to Maisons-Laffitte. Maigret hesitated to drag him into action with him against gangsters, preferring to leave him on duty and to go off with his "team." It's in this sense that we call this type of inspector the "rear guard," because Maigret himself establishes a sort of hierarchy between his four favorites and the others, whom he also calls "my children," but for whom he doesn't have the same deep affection that binds him to his personal group. We will see Vacher again in *Maigret et la Grande Perche, Maigret, Lognon et les gangsters, Maigret et la jeune morte, Un échec de Maigret, Maigret aux assises, Maigret et les braves gens, Maigret et le client du samedi, La colère de Maigret* and *La patience de Maigret*, in his usual detective's role (tailing, researching information, etc.)

Provincial Policemen

THE INSPECTORS

The inspectors, often young, irritate Maigret by their casualness. The Chief Inspector is perhaps also a little jealous of their knowledge of the "territory," that he himself lacks, causing him to feel clumsy, out of place, annoyed … "*[the Inspector] played the old-timer, who knows the places and people.... Maigret was the newcomer, always an unpleasant enough role*" (*Mon ami Maigret*, AMI: 2).

Benoît, a young inspector at the Nice airport (*Maigret voyage*, VOY), who greets Maigret dressed "*light and summery*" (no jacket, straw hat and white shirt), precisely the kind of clothing that irritates the Chief Inspector when he disembarks wearing his dark Paris suit, in a place of vivid sun and heat.

Boutigues, an inspector from Nice, who welcomes Maigret to Antibes (*Liberty Bar*, LIB). He wears a pearl-gray suit, a red carnation in the buttonhole (!), and shoes with cloth ankles. (Which will annoy Maigret, who doesn't much care for inspectors "dressed to the nines"!). He's small, has a hopping gait, speaks quickly and much, with passion. He hovers around Maigret a little like a buzzing fly, whereas the Chief Inspector is overwhelmed by the heat and the sun.

Castaing, has worked with the Le Havre police for six years (*Maigret et la vieille dame, DAM*). He has thick brown hair, a low forehead, ruddy face. Married, he drives a small black Simca, plays cards. He makes his notes in a pretty notebook with a red leather cover (Maigret, jealous with his black notebook like a laundress's?!) He pursues his investigation diligently, likes to reason things out, but is driven to despair at presenting his reasoning to Maigret, who listens to him with only half an ear. He has difficulty understanding Maigret's way of working, his placidity and manner of "impregnating" himself with the atmosphere. Castaing's serious and "busy" air seems comical to Maigret. He ends up calling him "*tu*," however, which was "a sign," and sometimes "*Mon petit*" or "Son."

Grenier, inspector from Nevers, dispatched to Sancerre (*Monsieur Gallet, décédé, GAL*). Married, he was about to leave on vacation when the Gallet business fell to him. He talks for the pleasure of talking, and Maigret hardly listens to his "obstinate" buzz (he doesn't like overly talkative inspectors!). Grenier makes only a brief appearance in the story, happy to concede the investigation to Maigret and be rid of it (at least one who is not jealous of Maigret!).

Lechat, with the Flying Squad of Draguignan, is investigating at Porquerolles (*Mon ami Maigret, AMI*). Maigret knew him from when he worked at Luçon. Born by the sea, he is small ("minuscule," thinks Maigret), blond, and he welcomes Maigret wearing (he too!) summery clothes—a light green suit and an open-collared shirt, no hat (which will earn him a beautiful sunburn!) and sandals on his feet. That's going to annoy Maigret, who endures the heat in his dark suit again! He calls Maigret "*Patron*," because there are "*few policemen in France who can resist the pleasure of calling him "Boss" with an affectionate familiarity.*" Nevertheless, if Maigret is at first a little irritated by the energy displayed by Lechat, exuberant, impatient, excited like a "hunting dog running helter-skelter around his master" he ends up appreciating his efficiency, and calling him "*Mon petit*" and using "*tu*," as he does in Paris with his closest collaborators.

Leroy, of the Rennes Flying Squad, who accompanies Maigret to Concarneau (*Le chien jaune, JAU*). He's 25, with the air of very well-mannered boy. He has just finished his studies and is working for the first time with Maigret, whose behavior will upset him considerably. His head freshly filled with academic knowledge, he can't understand why Maigret doesn't attach more importance to fingerprints and the other scientific means of investigation, nor how the Chief Inspector can operate without concerning himself too much with the strictest legality. Maigret uses "*vous*" with him, calls him "*mon petit*" or "old man," watches him with an affectionate irony, as he seeks, worthy of an emulator of Sherlock Holmes, to extract findings and deductions from his observations, whereas Maigret, himself, "never thinks." It will take some time for the young inspector to begin to "sense" the methods of the Chief Inspector, who warns him specifically "*not to make him a model, nor to try to base theories*" on the methods of Maigret, whose "*method is precisely, not to have one...*"

Machère, an inspector from Nancy sent to Givet (*Chez les Flamands*, FLA). A young man, with a round face, jovial and *very* active. He doesn't smoke, but drinks happily, which makes him talkative. He is delightedly triumphant when he discovers something, an attitude that Maigret doesn't appreciate. Maigret addresses him with "*vous*," calls him "*mon vieux*." He switches to "*tu*" when Machère comes to violently wake him up, but this is more due to Maigret's bad mood on being suddenly awakened, than to any real sympathy on his part. The proof is that Maigret is not troubled by splashing the inspector while he is washing up! Not spiteful, the Chief Inspector leaves the triumph of the investigation to Machère, while warning him however, as he did with Leroy, "*Be careful of conclusions, Machère! It is so dangerous to want to draw conclusions....*"

Méjat, inspector at Luçon when Maigret was "exiled" there. (*La maison du juge*, JUG). Maigret, here, is not overwhelmed by the heat of the south, but rather tries to drown his boredom in the rains of the Vendée, and his mood shows the effects strongly. Meaning that if he little appreciates Méjat, whose presence is intolerable, he being the sole inspector, there is nothing that can be done about it. Méjat has his hair plastered down with brilliantine of a disturbing odor, laughs stupidly at the statements of Adine Hulot, and brags happily about his female conquests. He speaks with a strong Toulouse accent in a strident tone on the telephone, is insensitive to subtlety. Always dressed to the nines (he sometimes sports a ridiculous green scarf), he has a mania for writing his reports in longhand. Portrait of a character most irritating to Maigret, who finds him "totally stupid" and compares him to a "*wet cockerel drying his feathers in the sun*"! Maigret uses "*tu*" with him, calling him familiarly "old man," but he doesn't have the relationship with him that he maintains with his Parisian collaborators, because Méjat doesn't understand how to react to Maigret's "methods" of interrogation.

THE CHIEF INSPECTORS

Now we'll meet Maigret's colleagues from the provinces, whom he knew, for the most part, from when they were in Paris before being posted outside of the capital. From these, we can cite:

Lecoeur, was, 15 years earlier, one of Maigret's inspectors, and has become Chief of the PJ of Clermont-Ferrand (*Maigret à Vichy*, VIC). His first name is Désiré. Five years younger than Maigret, Lecoeur is married with four sons, the eldest 18 and potentially a swimming champion. Maigret addresses him with "*vous*" (Lecoeur has the rank, after all!) and calls him "*mon vieux*." Lecoeur, from his side, continues to call Maigret "*Patron*," as when he was still in his service, but, as Mme Maigret notes, all policemen do so, not so much from habit, but rather as a sign of affection. Over the years, Lecoeur has acquired a paunch, and some white hairs in his red pointed mustache. He smokes cigarettes in a cigarette holder. He has blue eyes, and is slightly naive, but Maigret remembers him as one of his better collaborators, even though they have a different approach (anyway, who could have the same approach as Maigret, his manner of "sensing" and "impregnating himself in the atmosphere" unique to him). Lecoeur has the heart (no pun intended) to lead his investigation well, doing good work, an excellent investigator, according to Maigret (for don't forget that Lecoeur had a good teacher!).

Leduc, an ex-colleague of Maigret's from the PJ, who retired two years earlier and settled in Dordogne (*Le fou de Bergerac*, FOU). Leduc never married, lives with an elderly maid, and drives an old Ford. Since leaving the police, he acquired a pink and rosy complexion, and gained weight. He smokes a pipe, has a small red mustache, and chubby hands. He wears a straw hat and heavy hunting shoes. He must have "lost his hand" a little, become more timorous, more prudent, worrying about what people might say, offended by the direct and enjoyable manner with which Maigret leads his investigation. But he will nevertheless help Maigret, if somewhat reluctantly, to finish his investigation.

Mansuy, Chief Inspector at Sables-d'Olonne (*Les vacances de Maigret*, VAC). A small redhead, with pale blue eyes, a shy and well-mannered air, and a large head. Unmarried. He doesn't seem like a real Chief Inspector, and further, he's somewhat impressed by Maigret, not imagining that a Chief Inspector of the PJ can lead an investigation in the way Maigret does. His reaction to the death of little Lucile shows well that he was "*not born for the profession*," and that he is out of his depth. And it's Maigret, once more, who will lead the investigation to its conclusion.

Marella, head of the PJ at Toulon (*La folle de Maigret*, FOL). He started at the same time as Maigret at the Quai des Orfèvres, and the two men call each other "*tu*." He is dark, not very big, but quick. He has developed a paunch (like Maigret, probably?!). Their understanding is very good on this investigation (they share a small Provence rosé, a pledge of friendship), and there's no trace of rivalry between them. Marella was born in Nice, and he knows all the bad boys and girls of the Coast. He's married to Claudine, and has a son of 15, Alain, who definitely doesn't want to become a policeman!

Justin Cavre, whom the Chief Inspector meets at St-Aubin-les-Marais (*L'inspecteur Cadavre,* CAD), is not, in fact, a provincial inspector, nor even a true inspector, since he's been struck from the police rolls and works as a private detective. We speak of him here, nevertheless, because Maigret meets him in an investigation that takes place in the provinces. Cavre has a pale and sinister face, with red lids, a sad and emaciated profile, and his aspect earned him his nickname, one given to him more than twenty years earlier at the PJ. He's intelligent (probably the most intelligent Maigret had known in the police), and he would possibly have become Chief Inspector before Maigret, were it not for his distrustful character and irregularities that he committed in his service, because of his wife. He suffers, in addition, from a serious liver ailment, which doesn't permit him to drink anything but water.

Maigret finds him on his path throughout the investigation, in a kind of "hide-and-seek," competing as to who will be the first to find the useful information. The actions and gestures of the Chief Inspector at St-Aubin will be conditioned in part by the presence of Cavre, who Maigret tries all along to precede, and, in this sense, the English translation of the title of the novel (*Maigret's Rival*) gives a good idea of their relationship, because it certainly involves a *rivalry*. Maigret finds Cavre ridiculous and irritating, but at the same time he feels a certain pity in his consideration ("*In the end, Maigret held nothing against him. He felt sorry for him. He had fought against him, known himself to be right, but at the same time he felt a certain mercy for this man who was, in the end, a failure*"), probably because Cavre, with his congenital distrust, his hatred and his pessimistic view of the world, is the very opposite of Maigret, who, in spite of (or because of?) his experience, still maintains a fundamental optimism about people, reflecting well his creator's ideas.

Foreign Policemen

THE ENGLISH

Bryan, a Scotland Yard man put at Maigret's disposal in London by Mr. **Pyke** (*Le revolver de Maigret,* REV). Maigret finds him elegant—he wears a white flower in his buttonhole. Maigret, furthermore, has almost a "fixation" about buttonhole flowers (see *above*, the provincial inspectors), a symbol for him of a certain elegance that irritates him but that he also envies a little.

Bryan is intelligent, but Maigret is a little vexed that he prefers to address his reports to his superior, rather than directly to him. Decidedly, Maigret is not at home, and his renown hasn't crossed the Channel! Also in *Le revolver de Maigret*, we find **Fenton**, a colleague of Bryan's, a very good agent, but who is too easily noticeable, because he is small, very redheaded, with a flaming mustache. Maigret understands quickly that he is "unusable"!

Pyke, whom Maigret meets for the first time in France (*Mon ami Maigret*, AMI), at the time of a visit of the inspector from the Yard, sent to learn the "methods" of Maigret. But Maigret is not flattered—on the contrary, he has the impression of being "*put on display,*" a little like a bug under a microscope. Mr. Pyke is 35 or 40, but he seems so young that he appears more like a student. He gives the impression of being very intelligent, so much so that you "*can almost hear him thinking,*" which Maigret ends up finding tiresome. (We understand, he who always maintains that "*he never thinks*"!). Maigret is a little ashamed at being angry at Mr. Pyke's presence, because he is "*the nicest man on earth,*" but he is so discreet, so unobtrusive, but at the same time so present that it becomes exasperating! And in addition, Mr. Pyke has a way of looking at Maigret that obliges him to speak (he who hates explaining himself!).

Pyke speaks French with very precise and terrifying nuances of irony. Nothing astonishes him and his face betrays no feeling (ah, the English imperturbability!!). He doesn't smoke. He is as correctly impeccable in his gray suit as he is "comfortable" in a bathing suit and sandals. He plays chess, likes whisky and champagne. Maigret learns to appreciate his tact however, and his discretion. And if he remembers with displeasure having been awfully ill at ease working in front of "*a witness attentive to his every act and gesture*" (*Maigret et les témoins récalcitrants*, TEM), he all the same feels a slight regret at having received him as he did in Paris, when he himself undergoes the same treatment in America (*Maigret chez le coroner*, CHE). He is even disappointed not to meet him at the time of the Bordeaux convention (*Maigret a peur*, PEU). Maigret meets Mr. Pyke again during a journey to England (*Le revolver de Maigret*, REV), where Pyke lends him a helping hand by sending him two of his men (*above*). Mr. Pyke greets him at the airport, in dark gray suit, somewhat thin, a black felt hat and a carnation in his buttonhole (yes, him too!). His handshake is dry and firm, but he hides his emotions. He is embarrassed by some mistakes in his French (did he forget his excellent French of Porquerolles?). He's cultivating new varieties of hydrangeas. Maigret has several telephone contacts with him after Pyke has become Superintendent (*Un échec de Maigret*, ECH) and Chief Inspector (*Maigret et le fantôme*, FAN).

THE AMERICANS

Cole, Harry Cole, FBI officer (*Maigret chez le coroner,* CHE). He wears gabardine slacks, and has the air of a young sportsman. He smokes cigarettes, is married and the father of three children. Maigret is irritated by his "eternal confidence," and because he sees that Cole, while aware of Maigret's reputation, thinks that Maigret cannot understand Americans. Maigret will prove him wrong by discovering who is guilty, solely by intuition.

Lewis, Lieutenant and colleague of O'Brien (*Maigret à New York,* NEW). He has a very distinct voice, with a pronounced American accent. He smokes cigarettes, but doesn't drink. He's married, of average size and build, has a long nose and thick glasses. He's very serious and a little cold, and his attitude puts Maigret, in contrast, in a good mood.

MacDonald, Jimmy MacDonald, who works for the FBI in Washington (*Maigret, Lognon et les gangsters,* LOG). He knew Maigret at the time of Maigret's visit to the U.S. He's a large man with blue eyes and a happy and friendly voice. Maigret phones him to ask for information about some gangsters, Cinaglia and Cicero.

O'Brien, Captain Michael O'Brien, of the FBI (*Maigret à New York,* NEW), whom Maigret meets again in New York after knowing him some years earlier in France. He's big, a redhead, has a soft and shy smile, 46 years old. He's married, with a son in university and a daughter married two years earlier. He smokes a pipe. His irony puts Maigret off, but O'Brien will earn the Chief Inspector's good graces by taking him for *coq au vin* and an authentic Beaujolais (in the heart of New York City!).

O'Rourke, Mike O'Rourke, Chief Deputy Sheriff of an Arizona county (*Maigret chez le coroner,* CHE). A very strong, redheaded man, with lavender eyes and brush-cut hair, about the same age as Maigret (50-ish), and with about the same build. He's of Irish extraction, seems placid, smokes cigarettes or cigars. Straightaway, Maigret finds him agreeable, because he has the same way with people as the Chief Inspector, and is, basically, an American copy of Maigret: "*This rough-cut man was not without finesse ... on the contrary, and.... Maigret felt he could relate to him.*"

Pills, Harry Pills, Assistant District Attorney from Saint-Louis (*Maigret, Lognon et les gangsters,* LOG). He's big, athletic, blond, fairly young, and wears a soft hat pushed back on his head. He smokes cigarettes and speaks French with a strong accent. He was in France during the Liberation. He met Maigret, whom he admires a lot, at the time of Maigret's visit to the U.S. He comes to France to look for Mascarelli, and Maigret, although irritated by the casualness with which Pills acts, ends up making up with him over a glass of whisky!

BELGIAN AND DUTCH

Delvigne, Chief Inspector of the Sûreté in Liège (*La danseuse du Gai-Moulin*, GAI). A big redhead with a mustache, who smokes a pipe. At first glance we could take him for a Belgian double of Maigret (he smokes a pipe, drinks beer, grumbles, paces back and forth in his office), but he seems like a caricature of a policeman—there's a sort of derision in the description of his relationship with Maigret, who seems to make a big joke of this Belgian Inspector. Delvigne, for his part, feels for his colleague "*the involuntary consideration that they have, in the provinces, and especially in Belgium, for everything that comes from Paris*," but at the same time, he's afraid to appear ridiculous—and to be ridiculed, by his colleague. And he has every reason to feel that way, because Maigret simply goes on "*to take over direction of the investigation, without seeming to*," leaving no chance for the Belgian Chief Inspector to discover the truth (though would he even have been able to?).

Keulemans, Chief of the Crime Squad of Amsterdam (*Maigret et l'affaire Nahour*, NAH). He's hardly 40, but looks ten years younger, because of his lanky student's build, his pink face and his blond hair. His first name is Jef and he always sounds happy. He'd met Maigret in Paris, where he'd come to a practicum at the PJ. The two men became good friends (to the point where Keulemans takes pleasure in calling Maigret "*Patron*"), sometimes meeting again at international conventions. Maigret had even invited him to dine at his home, which gave Keulemans the rare privilege of tasting Mme Maigret's cooking!

Pijpekamp, Groningen Inspector dispatched to Delfzijl (*Un crime en Hollande*, HOL). He's a tall, thin, blond, very gracious (a little too much so?!), who speaks French in a slow and precise way, which irritates Maigret, who hardly listens to him, and who interrupts him continually, making him jump. Pijpekamp loses hope of making Maigret understand his point of view, because they decidedly don't share the same approach to problems. "'*What do you think?' finally murmurs the Groningen policeman.*" "*That's the question! And there is really the difference between the two of us! You, you think something! You think many things! While me, I believe that I still don't think anything….*" As for Maigret's "*heavy irony, hardly noticeable*," it will divert the Dutch policeman, as it has diverted many others.

THE SWISS

We'll look lastly at the Chief of the Sûreté of Lausanne (*Maigret voyage*, VOY). Delighted to finally meet Maigret (whose reputation, decidedly, crosses borders!), he invites him to lunch, *"very simple, close to the lake, in a quiet Vaud inn."*

The Swiss policeman is a big, strong, athletic man, no doubt a skier (logical, in Switzerland!!), with a clear and closely-shaven complexion, strong blue eyes, whose father is a vintner (something that would probably have pleased Maigret, to have a father who produced wine!), and a smile full of humor. And Maigret will long remember this lunch (especially the small white country wine!) with his Swiss colleague, whose name he has already forgotten, but of whom he will preserve a memory full of intimacy and complicity.

Deputies, Lawyers and Solicitors

Deputies: *Substituts* and *Procureurs*

Besides the Examining Magistrates, illustrating the theme of antagonism between the police, as conceived of by Maigret, and the judicial system, we encounter other members of the Prosecutor's Office (the *Parquet)*, like the deputies—the *substituts* and *procureurs*. On the whole, we meet fewer of these than Examining Magistrates in the Maigret saga, or in any case the relationships that the Chief Inspector has with the former are more distant—or less conflictive—than with the latter. *Substituts* and *procureurs* function most often at the beginning of an investigation, at the famous "invasion of the *Parquet"*—which Maigret hardly cares for, and he impatiently waits for them to finish so that he can finally proceed with his investigation in peace— since it's they who must affirm that a murder has been committed. It could be said that they're only there to conform to the legal rules regarding the development of an investigation, and to give the novel a sense of judicial veracity.

Maigret encounters his first *substitut* in *Le charretier de La Providence*. They do no more than exchange a look and a greeting. Later, in *Le port des brumes*, Maigret runs into a *substitut* who enjoys showing off his social status by speaking "man-to-man" with some of the upper crust of Caen. In the novels, the *substituts* are usually satisfied with a "quick look," during the customary visit after the discovery of a corpse, occasionally exchanging a brief handshake with the Chief Inspector. Most of the time they leave Maigret to his work, even if one of them happens to be disagreeable, as in *Maigret et le voleur paresseux*, the *substitut* Kernavel, *"tall and thin, in his thirties, very elegant,"* who affirms peremptorily to Maigret that the Cuendet affair is not the

Chief Inspector's business. In *Maigret et le client du samedi*, Maigret must request, because of *"new laws, never-ending decrees,"* from *Substitut* Méchin, authorization to direct his interrogations, while the Chief Inspector remembers with nostalgia *"a time when you could lead an investigation to the end without referring to anyone."* *Substitut* Méchin is *"tall, blond, his dark suit marvelously cut,"* he has *"beautiful hands, with long, narrow fingers."* Once more, Maigret is confronted with an insolent aristocratic youth of another world. Similarly in *Maigret et le clochard*, where the *substitut*, named Parrain, is also *"tall, blond, thin and distinguished looking, and the Chief Inspector thought once more that it was a specialty of the Parquet."* In contrast, in *Maigret et l'affaire Nahour*, *Substitut* Noiret is a *"middle-aged man, with an old-fashioned gray goatee."* But that's the exception that proves the rule, since in *Maigret hésite*, *Substitut* De Claes is *"tall, blond, very thin, dressed to the nines, always, summer or winter, a pair of white gloves in his hand,"* and, in *Maigret et Monsieur Charles*, substitut Oron *"was not more than thirty, very elegant, very distinguished looking."* Of course.

As for *procureurs*, Maigret deals first, in *Le fou de Bergerac*, with a rather "colorful" character, Duhourceau, *"a tiny little man, with white brush-cut hair," "a little ball of a nose,"* a *"very stiff"* mustache, affecting *"coldness and nastiness,"* wearing a bowler hat, morning coat, gray pants and patent leather shoes, resting on a cane with a sculpted ivory knob, who lived in an opulent-looking house. In short, the symbol—or the caricature—of a certain provincial bourgeoisie. Maigret meets next, in *La vieille dame de Bayeux*, a *procureur* who also symbolizes—in Maigret's and Simenon's eyes—the haughtiness of the upper crust. We encounter other *procureurs*, more or less anonymous and incidental, in the saga, among them Bourdeille-Jaminet (*La maison du juge*), *"so tall that his look seemed not to reach the ground "* or, in *Maigret et le voleur paresseux*, Dupont d'Hastier (whose name already tells us everything!). A *procureur* a little more atypical (perhaps explained by his operating in the provinces) is present in *Maigret a peur*, *"a handsome boy, hardly thirty,"* who doesn't hide his infidelities from his wife. We find next a more "classic" *procureur* in *Maigret voyage*, a *"very dignified magistrate, of the old nobility of the robe."* The one who appears in *Les scrupules de Maigret* already makes life difficult for Maigret, who tries as well as he can to explain his concerns in the Marton affair. It's also in that novel that Simenon makes a long digression on the more or less stormy relationship that Maigret has with magistrates in general, because of the different points of view of their two worlds. *"The men of the Parquet, procureurs, substituts, Examining Magistrates, almost all belong to the middle class, if not higher, of the bourgeoisie. Their kind of life, after purely theoretical studies, hardly puts them in contact, except in their chambers, with those they will pursue in the name of society. From which, for them, an almost congenital incomprehension of certain problems, an irritating attitude with certain cases, that the men of the PJ, living, you might say, in an almost permanent and almost physical intimacy with the world of crime, evaluate instinctively"* (SCR: 4).

LAWYERS

Among other characters in the judicial system, lawyers rarely play a good role in the saga. When Simenon describes them, it's generally in a rather negative fashion—a scrawny lawyer "hunting for a client," or an arrogant lawyer crossing swords with Maigret, it's never a pleasure for the Chief Inspector to meet one. We can classify them into several categories: the "anonymous," who are only there for their presence with a defendant or the condemned, and who only make incidental appearances, like Lenoir's lawyer in *La guinguette à deux sous*, Lecoeur's in *Maigret et l'homme du banc*, or those of Renée and Prou in *Maigret et le client du samedi*; the "extras," that we simply see pass in their wide-sleeved robes in the hallways of the *Palais de Justice*; the "auxiliaries," that have the same status as those in the first category and are there to assist a client, but they furthermore have names, and sometimes merit a short description, their presence more or less important according to the novel. Thus Leloup, Monfils's lawyer in *Cécile est morte*, Radel, Mme Lachaume's lawyer in *Maigret et les témoins récalcitrants*, Lenain, Josset's lawyer in *Une confidence de Maigret*, Duché and Lamblin, the Meurants' lawyers in *Maigret aux assises*, Huet, the thieves' lawyer in *Maigret et le tueur*, and Loiseau, Mahossier's lawyer in *Maigret et l'homme tout seul*; the "utilitarians," Maigret phones them to get information, like Me Chavanon in *La colère de Maigret*, Bouvier in *Maigret hésite*, Demaison in *Maigret et Monsieur Charles*; the "colorful ones," Maigret runs across them for various reasons, but their descriptions, if not much more sympathetic than the others, often include a touch of humor, like Me Tallier, Métayer's lawyer in *L'affaire Saint-Fiacre* or Ramuel in *La colère de Maigret*; the " nice ones," much rarer, we find but two in the saga, Me Chapuis, Martine's father in *Maigret s'amuse* and Me Parendon in *Maigret hésite*.

Lastly, we'll mention four lawyers with characters much more questionable: Me Gaillard in *La colère de Maigret*, a lawyer become murderer; Me Liotard in *L'amie de Madame Maigret*, whose role is somewhat suspect in the Steuvels case; and finally, two characters, one of whom turns out to be a murderer and the other an accomplice, one a lawyer, one becoming one. Is it so surprising, considering the negative description Simenon gives to lawyers throughout the saga, that Any, Popinga's murderer in *Un crime en Hollande*, did her law studies, and that Joseph, in *Chez les Flamands*, was preparing for his law examinations?

SOLICITORS

This type of lawyer (also referred to as a notary) is a character Maigret calls on when there are questions of inheritance in a case. The man of the law is the guardian of the secrets of succession, the secrets of the family. Consider Mᵉ Braquement, Lise Gendreau's solicitor (*La première enquête de Maigret*)... "*He was in his eighties. All the others were afraid of him, because he was the only one who knew.*" The first solicitor we encounter in the saga is Mᵉ Petit, in *Monsieur Gallet, décédé*. Maigret doesn't actually call on his services, but it happens that the Chief Inspector is seeking a doctor, and that he's about to play bridge at the lawyer's. He's "*a very neat old man, with silky hair, skin as smooth as a baby's.*" We will see that this distinguished portrait is often applied, in the saga, to the characters of solicitors. Here's Germain La Pommeraye, in *L'auberge aux noyés*, practicing in Versailles, a "*gray-haired*" man, "*tall and elegant, a dull complexion,*" who remained "*calm and dignified*" in spite of the circumstances. The paragon of solicitors in the saga is doubtless Mᵉ Motte, in *Le notaire de Châteauneuf*, "*a man of fifty or sixty, dressed in black, with a cold propriety, almost excessive,*" with a "*head of thick, white hair.*" He comes seeking the assistance of Maigret, this lawyer, whose coolness and seriousness make the ex-Chief Inspector want to joke with him, but is nevertheless able to convince Maigret to investigate. And Maigret notices that he "*had let himself become spellbound*" by this "*strange man, master of himself, with the careful speech, and impeccable manners.*" We find a somewhat similar situation in *Maigret à New York* with Jean Maura's lawyer, Mᵉ d'Hoquelus, an old man whose seriousness impressed Maigret, who succeeds in convincing our ex-Chief Inspector to embark for distant America.... In *Maigret se fâche*, we find Mᵉ Ballu, who lives on the Quai Voltaire, in Paris. He's Bernadette Amorelle's solicitor, and Maigret goes to question him about the will made by the old lady. Mᵉ Ballu is "*very old.... His lips were all yellowed from nicotine, he spoke in a soft, shaky voice, then pointed his ear trumpet towards the speaker.*"

Parisian lawyers seem to have less class than those of the provinces. We cite as evidence the portrait of Mᵉ Canonge, in *Maigret et le corps sans tête*, "*a fine-looking man of around sixty,*" "*tall and strong, ... dressed almost too fastidiously,*" "*a ruddy complexion below his silver hair, ... neat, clean-shaven, perhaps a discreet hint of eau de Cologne,*" "*he listened to himself talk,*" *holding his cigar in his manicured hands in a well-practiced gesture, which showed off his gold signet ring"*; in short, a sort of dandy lost in the austere world of legal studies, but not averse to adventure, when business brings him to Paris. In *Maigret et les vieillards*, Count de Saint-Hilaire's solicitor is Mᵉ Aubonnet, *"a very old man, who was, further, not in very good condition,"* and who *"retained a certain stoutness, but his body was soft, completely wrinkled. He had a shoe on one foot ... on the other, the ankle swollen, a felt slipper"*; *"his mouth was soft as well, and the syllables which came out formed a kind of porridge"*; far from the almost aristocratic style of Mᵉ Canonge. The last solicitor we will meet in the saga is quite different. Maigret will not meet him in person, and for good reason, but he will have to investigate him, since he is Mᵉ Sabin-Levesque (*Maigret et Monsieur Charles*), disappeared, and then found murdered. This last lawyer is quite different from the distant and senile old men previously encountered by Maigret. "M. Charles" is one of the most important lawyers in Paris, with a high-class clientele, brilliant in his profession. He *"manages the assets entrusted to him with exceptional flair,"* which doesn't hinder him from being *"very gay, playful, enjoying the bright side of life,"* wearing *"light colored suits, sometimes checked tweed vests," "Already somewhat pudgy.... Blond hair starting to thin, and a chubby face...."*

A Gallery of Characters

Obviously, a Maigret novel couldn't exist without the presence of its hero. However, to exercise his talents, the Chief Inspector needs some response, and thus the appearance of the "supporting cast"—victims, witnesses and suspects—that Maigret confronts. Without forgetting, of course, Mᵐᵉ Maigret and his inspectors, who nourish his affections.

But even they're not enough to provide full scope to the setting; we have to add a whole crowd of extras, who will populate the space and make the novels come alive. Sometimes described in just a few words, sometimes in several sentences, the shortness of their appearances does not detract from the power of their presence at the heart of the plot.

CLEANING WOMEN

As typical as the concierges of Parisian buildings, cleaning women are characters the Chief Inspector often meets in the course of his investigations. The first one mentioned in the saga is Cageot's, in *Maigret*; named Marthe, unfriendly, dressed in black, she inaugurates the gallery of these physically unattractive middle aged women, who've had nothing but misery in their lives, and who load the weight of their unhappiness onto everyone they meet. Among those found in the texts, we'll mention the picturesque Désirée Brault, in *Maigret se trompe*, very small and thin, dressed somberly, a former thief and woman of the streets, whose husband is a drunk. In *La patience de Maigret*, Mme Martin, the Palmaris' cleaning women, older, with a sick son, she wears shapeless black dresses, worn-out shoes, and has a habit of "*grumbling vengeful sentences*" while she works. In *Maigret et l'affaire Nahour*, Maigret has to deal with Louise Bodin, thin, with an obstinate look and an aggressive voice, she's the widow of a man who dies in prison. In all these portraits, there's a constant: Maigret has always encountered elderly cleaning women, neither alluring nor friendly, and though Simenon has written, "*There exist in Paris, as elsewhere, numerous types of cleaning women*" (*La patience de Maigret*), Maigret has not had the luck to know any except those "*who have suffered, that life has battered, and who, without hope, await an old age even more painful. Then they get hard and, distrustful, and blame the whole world for their misfortunes*" (*Maigret et l'affaire Nahour*, NAH: 2).

MAIDS AND CHAMBERMAIDS

Happily for Maigret, alongside these shrewish cleaning women, he has known their counterparts—young maids and chambermaids with appetizing, well formed bodies. *Maid, servant, domestic*, the three terms are used by Simenon to designate, as indicated by the definition of *maid* in the dictionary, a "domestic who does the housework, the shopping, often prepares the meals, and who lives in the home of her employer." The *chambermaid* is generally more specifically attached to the service personnel of a lady, but in the novels she plays a role similar enough to that of a maid.

We find two types of maids and servants in the texts; they're either rather old, sour-tempered and physically unattractive, or fairly young, with appetizing bodies. Among the first, we can mention Mélie, in *L'écluse n° 1*, the servant who works in Ducrau's country house, who has "*no age, no spirit, no charm*," "*with no bust, no femininity*"; the old maid, "*dry and mustached*" who works at the judge's house in *Le témoignage de l'enfant de chœur*; Mme Bellamy's chambermaid (*Les vacances de Maigret*) "*a thin girl, with no breasts or hips, an unattractive face with irregular features, and unhealthy-looking teeth*"; in *Maigret et les témoins récalcitrants*, Maigret deals with the Lachaumes' servant, old Catherine, flat-chested, with "*her dirty black skirts hanging down*."

Among the second type we find, in *Signé Picpus*, Emma, the little maid at the creamery, "*a large girl of eighteen, with a well-developed chest, and pink skin.*" In *La première enquête de Maigret*, here our hero comes to grips with another type of character, the hilarious Germaine, the Gendreaus' maid, "*her heavy breasts full of life.*" In *Le revolver de Maigret*, the Chief Inspector encounters an additional full-bodied type, Jeanne Debul's maid, Georgette: "*She was pink, with large breasts.*" In *Maigret et le tueur*, the Batilles' chambermaid is "*young and pretty*" and wears a "*stylish uniform*"; and the Chabuts' (*Maigret et le marchand de vin*) is of the same sort: "*brunette, pretty, her black silk uniform showing off her figure*"; at Mme Marcia's (*Maigret et l'indicateur*), the young chambermaid has "*enormous breasts.*" We note that the more we advance through the chronology of the writing of the saga, the more often Simenon gratifies Maigret with enticing encounters; after several cantankerous old servants, the Chief Inspector more and more frequently meets young maids whose black uniforms and white aprons seem to be mainly for emphasizing their harmonious curves. Under the satin, linen or silk, it takes our Chief Inspector but a brief (professional?) glance to spot a curvaceous bodice or a voluptuous bottom.

VALETS AND BUTLERS

When Maigret investigates in the mansions of the gentility, he encounters various characters typical of their domestic service. Women, as maids, chambermaids, and cooks, and men, as butlers, valets, and chauffeurs. The valets and butlers (terms more or less interchangeable in Simenon's writing) are in charge of greeting visitors, and responsible for the personal belongings of the master of the house. The butler exercises the additional function of serving at the table. These two types of characters act in a way as symbols of the aristocratic world. Their most characteristic features, in the texts, are their outfits—for the valet, either a striped waistcoat, or a white jacket; for the butler, livery and white gloves. Here are some of them we meet in the saga:

The Saint-Marcs' valet (*L'ombre chinoise*), in the aristocratic apartment at the Place des Vosges, in the evening, draws the curtains "*slowly, conscienciously.*" When Maigret questions Victor, the valet at Philippe Deligeard's (*La vieille dame de Bayeux*), the valet "*showed in his responses an almost mathematical precision, and Maigret wasn't surprised to discover that he was a former artillery sergeant.*" At Dr. Bellamy's (*Les vacances de Maigret*), the valet in the white linen jacket, Francis Decoin, was a blond Belgian. Victor Ricou, the valet in the service of Ferdinand Fumal (*Un échec de Maigret*) had very thick hair and eyebrows, a low forehead, and he wore a vest, "*with black and yellow stripes.*" Carl, the valet working at Norris Jonker's (*Maigret et le fantôme*) was "*fairly young, very blond, with a ruddy complexion,*" and he wore a white jacket. The butler at the Parendons' (*Maigret hésite*), Ferdinand Fauchois, also wore a white jacket, and he greeted Maigret "*with calm dignity.*" "*Proper and formal,*" he was no less than a former Legionnaire; when he served at the table, "*he wore white cotton gloves.*"

In *L'affaire Saint-Fiacre*, the general decline of the château is felt in the personnel. The first appearance of the butler, Albert, is symptomatic. When the Countess's body is brought back to the château, the butler appears "*half-dressed in livery.*" Later, when the Count arrives at the château with his guests before dinner, he rings for the butler, who "*makes him wait a long while, arriving with his mouth full, his napkin in his hand.*" In contrast, during the dinner, he finds again a certain dignity, as if he feels that the Count is once more in charge. Albert serves the diners, "*his hands gloved in white,*" and when he "*notices a hand reaching for a bottle, he approaches noiselessly. A white-gloved black arm moves forward. The liquid flows. And it is all done completely silently, with great dexterity….*" Then, when the Count begins to discuss the diners in turn, speculating on their possible guilt, sending Albert to bring the revolver, the butler becomes in a way his second, a kind of duplicate Count, "*turning towards the butler, a kind of demon with hands white as chalk….*"

In *La première enquête de Maigret*, the butler working at the Gendreaus', Louis Viaud, wears a "*black butler's uniform,*" "*starched shirtfront, … collar, black tie*" "*large and broad,*" "*his shaven chin blue, his eyes very dark, his eyebrows abnormally thick.*" Arsène, the Vernoux's butler (*Maigret a peur*), has "*brown hair, coarse skin, between 40 and 50. He gave the impression of a tenant farmer's son who wouldn't want to work the land.*"

CHAUFFEURS

Most of the time, chauffeurs make but brief appearances in the texts, their function being—besides driving their master's car—to provide a typical touch of the milieu in which they operate, the houses of the gentility or aristocracy. The chauffeurs of the mansions wear, of course, livery or a uniform, to distinguish themselves from other professional drivers, taxi drivers or those of leased vehicles. Thus, the mayor of Concarneau's chauffeur (*Le chien jaune*) wears "black livery," like the chauffeur of the Countess de Saint-Fiacre (*L'affaire Saint-Fiacre*); like Arsène, Deligeard's chauffeur (*La vieille dame de Bayeux*), who wears "a very elegant gray uniform," or Vittorio, the Sabin-Levesques' chauffeur (*Maigret et Monsieur Charles*), "*dressed in an austere chauffeur's uniform … so well trained that you always expected to see him standing at attention."*

We often see the chauffeur in a courtyard, washing a fancy car. Thus, in *L'écluse n° 1*, Edgar, the chauffeur, at Ducrau's country house, "*who, at the back of the courtyard, was washing down a gray auto with a hose*." Similar to the image we find at Malik's (*Maigret se fâche*): "*Behind the villa, a chauffeur in shirtsleeves was hosing down a powerful American car with dazzling chrome*" And at the Gendreaus' (*La première enquête de Maigret*), "*in the courtyard, the chauffeur, who'd taken off his jacket, was busy hosing down a car … a black limousine, with large brass headlamps.*" At the Princess de V.'s (*Maigret et les vieillards*), "*the courtyard … with a uniformed chauffeur washing a long black car.*" Again at the Parendons' (*Maigret hésite*), "*a chauffeur in blue overalls, hosing off a Rolls-Royce.*" And lastly, Félix, Fumal's chauffeur (*Un échec de Maigret*) whom we see "*in the courtyard, in blue overalls, directing a stream of water from a rubber hose at the limousine.*"

CURÉS—THE PARISH PRIESTS

In Maigret's childhood memories, an important role is given to his reminiscences of his past as an altar boy, echoing the author's experiences. Puffs of incense, responses to the Mass, and the curé himself occupy a prominent place. The first curé to make an appearance in the saga is the one—not at all surprisingly—Maigret encounters in *L'affaire Saint-Fiacre*. A character contrasted with that of the doctor, the other inescapable figure in the world of Maigret and Simenon. While the curé of Saint-Fiacre is young, most of those Maigret encounters, often on the occasion of a funeral, are rather elderly. Some of them, more detailed in the texts, have as a distinctive feature a mystical allure. The curé of Saint-Fiacre has a "*passionate look,*" and "*regular features, but so severe that they evoked the fierce faith of monks of old.*"

In *Le témoignage de l'enfant de chœur*, the curé of the chapel is a "*very tall and gaunt priest,*" with "*the blue eyes of a stained glass saint.*" In *Maigret et les vieillards*, Abbé Barraud, Jaquette's spiritual leader, is "*very old indeed, skeletal, with wild hair, very long, in a halo around his head. His cassock was shiny with wear, poorly mended…. The priest was sitting on a chair, took from his cassock a wooden box, inhaled a pinch of snuff. This action, and the shreds of tobacco on the gray cassock, brought back old memories to Maigret.*" A memory we find in *Maigret à Vichy*, when Maigret is questioned by the doctor about his drinking habits: "*That brought him back to his childhood, the village confessional which smelled of musty old wood and the curé who took snuff.*"

POSTMISTRESSES

The telephone is a tool often required by Maigret. In a time when there were not yet any of the mobile devices which have made today's communications so banal, the police had to find other ways of getting in contact or finding information. In Paris, when he's working away from his office, the Chief Inspector often goes into a café to telephone—a good excuse to order at the same time a little white wine or a brandy. In the cases he investigates outside of Paris, Maigret also finds the need to phone. When it's not from his hotel room, he naturally goes to the post office, where he meets the postmistress. In the *Maigrets*, it's always a woman who takes care of the postal service and telephone, in the suburbs or the country.

Among the postmistresses encountered by Maigret, we can mention, in *L'inspecteur Cadavre* (CAD: 7), Mlle Rinquet, *"petite, dressed in black, black hair, an ageless face."* Maigret, himself, *"was too broad and too heavy for the little kitchen appropriate to the tiny postmistress, surrounded with china trinkets, spun glass bought at a fairgrounds, embroidered doilies."* The words create an image, and thanks to the novelist's skill, we see the scene as if we were there, the contrast between the heavy silhouette of the Chief Inspector and the frail woman. We encounter another postmistress in *Mon ami Maigret…* *"It wasn't her nickname. The fat girl hadn't created it herself. She'd actually been called Aglaé ["radiant beauty"] since her baptism. She was very fat, especially her lower half, deformed like a woman of fifty or sixty who grew heavy, and, in contrast, her face was completely childlike, for Aglaé was merely twenty-six."* And he discovered that she, like Mlle Rinquet, listened in on the conversation, with a certain naïveté, perhaps less innocent than she seemed: *"When he left the booth, he saw Aglaé who, calmly, without a trace of shame, took off her headphones.*

"You listen to all the conversations?"

"I stay on the line in case you get disconnected. I don't trust the operator at Hyères, who's a vixen.

"You do the same for everyone?"

"In the morning I don't have time, because of the mail, but in the afternoon it's easier."

POSTMEN

The postman is essentially, in the *Maigrets*, a typical character of the rural world. Perched on his bicycle, he traverses the country roads, the suburbs, a link between the inhabitants of the villages. And so it's during his investigations outside of Paris that Maigret encounters postmen. For example, the one he meets in Saint-Fargeau (*Monsieur Gallet, décédé*), a postman on a bicycle, "*with the purple neck of the apoplectic.*" Or the one at Saint-André (*Maigret à l'école*) named Ferdinand Cornu. He'd lost his left arm, probably in the war, and it had been replaced by an iron hook; his face was "*the sanguine reddish-brown face of a man who spends his days in the sun,*" and he drank a lot.

The only postman met in Paris is found in *Maigret*, the one the Chief Inspector sees enter the hotel, rummaging through his leather bag, while Maigret is waiting for a saw to cut off a piece of a broom handle. The appearance of this postman is, however, quite astonishing in this context, so we have to wonder whether the author didn't put him in simply for decoration, to complete the sunny scene of "*joyful craziness,*" such as is described in this novel.

REPORTERS

In the course of his career, Maigret has routinely dealt with journalists, with whom he maintains more or less cordial relationships, using them sometimes, but often annoyed by their persistence, all the while recognizing that they're doing their job. Generally anonymous in the novels, some receive a name, sometimes a physical description. We'll mention the journalist Vasco, in *Le chien jaune*, wearing golf culottes and a red sweater; the reporter Lomel, in *Maigret a peur*, a redhead with plump red cheeks, wearing a tan raincoat; in *Une confidence de Maigret*, the reporter Pecqueur, with a chubby face, large cheeks, blue-eyed with red hair, smoking a too-big pipe to make himself look important; in *Maigret s'amuse*, little Lassagne, thin and redheaded, lively as a monkey. We have to wonder whether redheads are a journalistic specialty, for we also find in *Maigret et l'indicateur* a nameless reporter, but described as a tall redhead, with his hair unkempt! And we also note in *Maigret à l'école*, the reporter Albert Raymond, his raincoat cinched with belt, a too-big pipe in his mouth, not more than 22, thin, with long hair... Doesn't that bring to mind a certain young Sim, newly disembarked in Paris, filled with ambition?

THE POLISH GANG

These characters are mentioned in the saga for the first time in the story *Stan le Tueur*, where they live in the Marais district, between three streets describing a square parallel to Place des Vosges: Rue Saint-Antoine, Rue de

Birague, and Rue des Tournelles. Simenon describes the district for us such as it was in the years 1920–1930, peopled by colonies of immigrants, particularly populations from Eastern Europe, Poles, Czechs, Russians and Jews. Rue Saint-Antoine, which crosses Rue de Birague, also follows the Saint-Paul district, meeting further along the Rue du Roi-de-Sicile, that Maigret visited in *Pietr le Letton* when he was searching for the hotel where Fédor Yourovitch and Anna Gorskine lived.

The Poles of the Rue de Birague will be met again, in a sense, in *Cécile est morte*, where the gang is always led by a young woman. In *Maigret et l'inspecteur Malgracieux*, Maigret mentions a case with the Poles, but this time, the head of the gang is a *man* named Stan. In *Les Mémoires de Maigret*, we find two more allusions to this case, the first at the beginning of the novel, when the head of the PJ asks the Chief Inspector, "*Well, Maigret, haven't you arrested your Pole on Rue de Birague yet?*," and another towards the end of the novel, when Maigret, to "inaugurate" his nomination to the Special Squad, is entrusted with the arrest of a Czech, in a rooming house on Rue du Roi-de-Sicile. It's in *Maigret et son mort* that the affair of the Poles is brought to a conclusion, thanks to the intervention of little Albert. Although, this time too, the gang is Czech and not Polish, it is however the same story: a gang plundering farms in the north, led by a woman, the brunette Maria replacing the blonde Stéphanie of the story *Stan le Tueur*.

Recurring First Names

We find over 400 first names of characters in the saga. Some of them are only used for a single, unique character, as if the name in question was only suitable for such a person, and thus couldn't be used for another. We can mention, among these, for female characters, Beetje (Liewens in *Un crime en Hollande*), Else (Andersen in *La nuit du carrefour*), Mirella (Jonker in *Maigret et le fantôme*), Nathalie (Sabin-Levesque in *Maigret et Monsieur Charles*), Nouchi (Siveschi in *Cécile est morte*), and Yvonne (Moncin in *Maigret tend un piège*). For male characters, Alban (Groult-Cotelle in *L'inspecteur Cadavre*), Dieudonné (Pape in *Maigret et le corps sans tête*), Norris (Jonker in *Maigret et le fantôme*), Omer (Calas in *Maigret et le corps sans tête*), Prosper (Donge in *Les caves du Majestic*), and Tiburce (de Saint-Hilaire in *Monsieur Gallet, décédé*).

Among the names used numerous times, certain of them have a particular connotation that we can find in most of the characters bearing that name.

Adèle and **Sylvie** are names attributed to "easy women" (Adèle Noirhomme in *Au rendez-vous des Terre-Neuvas*, Adèle Bosquet in *La danseuse du Gai-Moulin*, and Adèle the musician's companion in *Félicie est là*; and three Sylvies, in *Liberty Bar, Maigret, Lognon et les gangsters* and *Maigret et le client du samedi*). As for **Arlette** (Sudre in *Maigret et la vieille dame*, the dancer in *Maigret au Picratt's*, a girl in *Maigret et l'homme du banc*, a prostitute victim of Moncin in *Maigret tend un piège*), while two of them are officially registered "streetwalkers," the two others also maintain multiple relationships with men. The same for **Fernande**, attributed equally to women who have or who have had numerous relationships with men (Bosquet in *Maigret*, Steuvels in *L'amie de Madame Maigret*, Fumal's mother in *Un échec de Maigret*, and a girl, a regular at the *Vieux Pressoir* in *Le voleur de Maigret*).

    Dédé, Jo, Fred and **Pepito** are names reserved for members of the underworld, like Bob's friend Dédé in *La première enquête de Maigret*, Jo the boxer in *Maigret et son mort*, Jo the wrestler in *La colère de Maigret*, Fred Alfonsi in *Maigret au Picratt's* and Fred Michaud in *Vente à la bougie*, Pepito Moretto in *Piet le Letton*, Pepito Palestrino in *Maigret*, and Pepito Giovanni in *La folle de Maigret*.

    Anna is a name borne by women of foreign origin, especially Flemish (Peeters in *Chez les Flamands*, Bebelmans in *Mon ami Maigret*, and Keegel in *Maigret et l'affaire Nahour*). It's the same for **Jef**, a name assigned to men originating in northern Europe—Flemish, Belgian, or Dutch—, like Lombard in *Le pendu de Saint-Pholien*, de Greef in *Mon ami Maigret*, Van Meulen in *Maigret voyage*, Claes in *La patience de Maigret*, and Keulemans in *Maigret et l'affaire Nahour*. We often find it on seamen—Van Cauwelaert in *Maigret et les témoins récalcitrants*, Van Houtte in *Maigret et le clochard*, and Van Roeten in *Maigret et Monsieur Charles*.

    We often find, among servants, maids, waitresses and other housekeepers and cooks, **Thérèse** (*La maison du juge, Maigret à l'école, Vente à la bougie*), **Eugénie** (*Monsieur Gallet, décédé, Maigret se fâche, Maigret et le tueur, Maigret et la Grande Perche, Monsieur Lundi*), **Emma** (*Le charretier de La Providence, Le chien jaune, Signé Picpus*), and **Julie** (*Le port des brumes, Vente à la bougie*). As for **Mélanie**, it's the name of three bistro owners (*Cécile est morte, Maigret se trompe, Maigret et le fantôme*). **Rose** is a name for restaurant or nightclub owners (*Maigret au Picratt's, Le voleur de Maigret*), or women "off the streets," or maids (*Maigret et la vieille dame, Maigret et la jeune morte*). **Bob** is a name classically attributed to barmen, while **Félix** is often used for café waiters, and **Fernand** for café owners. **Léon** is the name attributed to bistro and restaurant owners, including that of the Brasserie Dauphine in particular. *Chez Léon* is a sign often encountered in the saga. **Albert** is a name often attributed to personnel in a house, hotel, or café, but it's also the first name of Inspectors Lapointe and Janvier.

If **Monique** is a name reserved for young women (Monique Thouret in *Maigret et l'homme du banc*, Monique Batille in *Maigret et le tueur*), and little girls (like Janvier's daughter in *Maigret chez le ministre*), **Léontine** is a name mostly reserved for middle-aged women, like the Naud's cook (*L'inspecteur Cadavre*), Courçon's housekeeper (*Maigret a peur*), Meurant's aunt (*Maigret aux assises*), or Mme de Caramé (*La folle de Maigret*). **Antoine** and **Pierre** are names of fairly young men (Antoine Cristin in *Maigret et le corps sans tête*, Antoine Batille in *Maigret et le tueur*, Antoine Bizard in *L'amie de Madame Maigret*, Pierre Le Clinche in *Au rendez-vous des Terre-Neuvas*, Pierre Delteil in *Le revolver de Maigret*, Pierre Eyraud in *Maigret se trompe*, and Pierre Mazet in *Maigret tend un piège*). While **Evariste** is reserved for middle-aged men and from a rural environment (Heurtin's father in *La tête d'un homme*, the father of Minister Point in *Maigret chez le ministre*, and Maigret's own father).

Aline is a name given to numerous principal characters who attract Maigret's sympathy (Aline Gassin in *L'écluse n° 1*, Aline Calas in *Maigret et le corps sans tête*, Aline Bauche in *Maigret se défend* and *La patience de Maigret*). We also find three young women named **Louise** (which is also Mme Maigret's name) for whom Maigret is filled with empathy (Sabati in *Maigret a peur*, Filon in *Maigret se trompe*, and Laboine in *Maigret et la jeune morte*), and three **Berthes** who don't leave the Chief Inspector cold (Mlle Berthe in *Mademoiselle Berthe et son amant*, Berthe Pardon in *Cécile est morte*, and Berthe Janiveau in *Signé Picpus*).

Philippe, **Eugène** and **Charles** are names carried by characters to whom Maigret is generally unsympathetic. Among the Philippes, we find de Moricourt in *Mon ami Maigret*, Me Liotard in *L'amie de Madame Maigret*, Mortemart in *Maigret au Picratt's*, and Deligeard in *La vieille dame de Bayeux*. With Charles, Dandurand in *Cécile est morte*, Malik in *Maigret se fâche*, Besson in *Maigret et la vieille dame*, and Cinaglia in *Maigret, Lognon et les gangsters*. And with Eugène, Berniard in *Maigret*, Benoît in *Maigret chez le ministre*, and Labri in *Une erreur de Maigret*.

In conclusion, we can say that certain names are used as points of reference for the reader, who find there a universe in a way "reassuring," giving the illusion of a familiar world, in which maids are called Rose, housekeepers Eugénie, waitresses are Emma, boys of the underworld are called Jo or Fred, and barmen Bob, and where Maigret will take a little white wine or a Calvados at *Chez Fernand* or *Chez Léon*, while, in the cabaret next door, he can spend the evening in the company of an Arlette or a Sylvie.

Maigret's Cats

Apart from a few flies and wasps buzzing and sometimes stinging, some allusions to chickens and rabbits that the Chief Inspector hated to kill in his childhood, several dogs (including a yellow one, above all), one or two horses (often harnessed to a barge or a hearse), the singing of birds in the spring, a shy squirrel and some fish, Maigret's world has relatively few animals. Among them, the one most frequently mentioned is probably the cat.

When Simenon introduces an animal into a description or a plot, it's never without a reason, just as when he mentions a barge passing on the Seine, or a streetlight's glow in the night. All these details serve to emphasize an "atmosphere," to introduce a nuance into the tempo of the action or into the feelings of the Chief Inspector with regard to his case.

The novel *La guinguette à deux sous* opens on an image of dazzling summer, with sunshine and cheerful passers-by. To accentuate the scene, here's what Maigret finds on arriving at the prison where Lenoir will learn that he's to be executed: "*When Maigret reached the gate of the Santé he found the policeman on guard gazing foolishly at a little white cat playing with the dog from the dairy.*" What a contrast between this little cat of innocent white and the observer, whose work consists of guarding a place where men are locked up. We find a similar idea in *Le port des brumes*, when Maigret comes to assist Joris, and while the doctor makes a last attempt to save him, the heavy atmosphere of the scene contrasts with the closing sentence, "*On the garden wall there was a white cat.*"

A cat is often part of the "tableau" of concierge's lodges, as in *Cécile est morte*, "*The concierge didn't want to go to bed before Maigret left, and to give herself the strength to wait, she finished the bottle of red wine, all the while explaining the situation to her cat,*" or in *Le revolver de Maigret*: "*a stove, a very high bed covered with a red eiderdown, a round table covered with waxed cloth, and an armchair with a big orange cat.*" It's also the appointed companion of elderly women living alone, like Mélanie Chochoi in *Félicie est là*, "*she indicated to him the back shop, which served as her kitchen.... In the half-darkness, you could make out a rattan armchair, where an orange cat was rolled into a ball on a red cushion,*" or Jeanne in *Maigret se fâche*, "*The cat was curled up on Mme Jeanne's knees, the pendulum of the clock swinging back and forth in its glass case, and the woman talking...,*" or Valentine Besson in *Maigret et la vieille dame*, a cat of a breed in harmony with the luxury of the room, "*a very stylish room, hung in cream satin. In the center of an immense bed, a blue Persian cat was taking a nap, and he had hardly opened his golden eyes to honor the intruder,*" or Mme Cuendet in *Maigret et le voleur paresseux*, "*a white* cat, *with light brown spots, hardly opened his green eyes,"* which makes part of a tableau: "*You would have said that the least object, the poker, the bowls with large pink flowers, and up to the broom where the cat rubbed his back, had its own life, like in an old Dutch painting.*"

And we also find cats in cafés: "*in the bar, where, including the patron, there were but four people, a black cat curled up on a chair in front of the stove*" (*Maigret et la vieille dame*); "*On the yellow-painted walls, you saw advertisements, like in country cafés and inns, and an odor of stew emanated from the kitchen. To complement the tableau, an orange cat purring on a chair with a straw seat*" (*Maigret s'amuse*). We note the importance of Mme Calas's cat, in *Maigret et le corps sans tête*, a cat which is a little like the soul of the place. When Maigret enters the bar for the first time, there's no one in the room, "*nothing but a fat orange cat, sleeping near the stove,*" symbolizing the apathy-filled ambiance that Aline gives the bar. In the afternoon, on his second visit, Maigret again finds "*the orange cat, still near the stove, from which he seemed not to have budged.*" Immobility of the animal, immutability of things, the lassitude and indifference of Aline.

We note again in passing that Maigret himself had a cat but only once, when he was retired. Besides the chicken, rabbits, and Mme Maigret's goat, we find a cat strolling in the garden at Meung-sur-Loire.

13

Novels

The Proto-Maigrets

At the close of the 1920s, after having written hundreds of "popular" novels and stories, Simenon wanted to move on to what he called "semi-literature," a necessary step before embarking on "true" literature. To accomplish this, he still needed a "playmaker," a character he could rely on to construct his plot, and to sustain and carry it through to the end of a novel. Simenon had tried various characters in this role, including Yves Jarry, an adventurer who appeared in novels of incredible and diverse episodes. But Simenon, all the same, wanted to separate himself from traditional adventurers, and Jarry had going against him the fact that he was too similar to Arsène Lupin to be completely original. Simenon wanted to create a character who *contrasted* with Jarry—instead of a dashing young man, a massive forty-year-old; instead of an aristocratic and multilingual world traveler, a man of plebeian origin, anchored in his French context. In short, a character completely atypical in contemporary popular literature of the time—and so it's easy to understand why his publisher Fayard would have had significant doubts about his future.

Simenon achieved success with the first *Maigret* novels signed with his own name. That explains, at least partially, why he always favored the "official" version of the birth of his hero, according to which Maigret was born, more or less out of the blue, on an old abandoned barge in the Dutch port of Delfzijl. In reality, as shown by Menguy and Deligny in *Les vrais débuts du commissaire Maigret*, an article which appeared in the journal *Traces* nº1, published by the Centre d'Etudes Georges Simenon, the character Maigret had appeared before *Pietr le Letton*, in four novels written by Simenon under pseudonyms, and which are referred to as the "proto-Maigrets," for that's where the first draft of Maigret appeared, before his "official" arrival in the series of 19 novels published by Fayard.

TRAIN DE NUIT

In the first of these four novels, *Train de nuit*, written in 1929 and published in 1930 under the pseudonym Christian Brulls, Maigret's name isn't mentioned until Ch. 6 of Part I, in a newspaper article, as Chief Inspector of the Marseilles Flying Squad. He already has Inspector Torrence under his command. But it's not until Ch. 3 of Part III that we meet him "in the flesh." And then, that's not quite completely accurate, for a physical description of the Chief Inspector—rather summary—won't come until Ch. 6: "*a large silhouette.*" We don't know what he looks like, whether he already wears a bowler hat or an overcoat, or even if he smokes a pipe. His personality is hardly more detailed, "*a quiet man, rough talking, with a violent nature.*" In short, crude and rough. Nonetheless, his intervention in the novel gives an indication of what will later become one of his most essential attributes, his empathy.

LA FIGURANTE

"*That's about all I remember of that meeting. I'd talked with him casually about an affair which had required my attention several months earlier..., in which there was a matter of a young girl and her pearl necklace.... Several weeks passed, months.... One morning, I found on my desk, next to my mail, a little book with a horribly illustrated cover, like you see at newsstands or in the hands of shop girls. It was entitled, "La jeune fille aux perles," and the name of the author was Georges Sim.*"

It's with these lines that Maigret relates, in his *Mémoires*, how, after Simenon's visit to the Quai des Orfèvres, the author published a first novel which used the Chief Inspector's name. Maigret didn't read it, tossed it into the trash, but every morning he found a fresh copy on his desk, placed there through the agency of Janvier. Maigret, on Lucas's recommendation, finally read the novel, halfheartedly. He found himself "*larger, heavier than life,*" using unexpected methods, in short, a kind of caricature of himself, with which he wasn't very pleased.

This novel, written in 1929, under the pseudonym Christian Brulls (and not under Georges Sim, as Maigret recalls in his *Mémoires*) wouldn't appear until 1932, after the debut of the first "official" Maigrets, under the title *La figurante*, a title Simenon didn't like, for he himself had entitled it *La jeune fille aux perles*.

The work straddles two genres. It uses all the clichés of popular literature: the evil villain with the sinister face, who finds redemption at the end of the story, the pure young girl, who remains so despite all the attacks of which she is the object, without forgetting the dramatic scenes where the heroes confess their love. But at the same time, this novel introduces the character of the policeman, and furthermore, a policeman with unorthodox methods. We note that Maigret appears from the first chapter (as Chief Inspector of the Paris Sûreté), and that he's present in 11 chapters out of the 20 which comprise the novel (thus much more often than in *Train de nuit*). And now, certain features are already characteristic: his physical aspect—"*a broad-shouldered man, with a thick face, but bright-eyed, who ate sandwiches,*" "*he slowly filled a pipe, which he lit, planted in front of the window,*" and his character—"*I don't believe anything! I don't think anything!,*" "*He was fatherly and gruff.*" Without a doubt, we are already dealing with the Chief Inspector Maigret we will meet in the official saga.

LA FEMME ROUSSE

This novel, written in 1929, is signed Georges Sim, and no longer Christian Brulls, as the two preceding. And that's a sign—the author is getting closer to the literature he wants to write, and after the popular novels, he's on the route of detective stories. With the use of this pseudonym, he's not very far from the official production. Certainly, it's used to "keep food on the table," but this is the same route the novelist chose for the novels featuring Maigret's two "rivals," Sancette and Jarry. The novel appeared in 1933, not from Fayard, but from Tallandier, in the collection "Criminals and Policemen." And so it's clearly marked as a "detective story," and no longer a "popular," even though we note that the story is still lived through the eyes of a character other than the more or less official "investigator." The hero of the story in a way plays "amateur detective," with all the blunders that entails, and which the author enjoys emphasizing, contrasting it with the calm presence of Maigret, opposing the hero's frantic actions with good-natured serenity, and his wanderings across Paris with the technical workings of a police investigation. We note in this novel as well, the presence of a pure young girl overwhelmed by incredible circumstances, which will permit Maigret to exercise once more his magnanimity and his role as a "mender of destinies," since he offers happiness to the girl by allowing her to marry the man she loves.

LA MAISON DE L'INQUIÉTUDE

This fourth "proto-Maigret" is unique in that it was the first Maigret investigation to be published. Not as a book, but as a serial, in the daily *L'Œuvre*, between March and April 1930. Its publication as a book was not until February 1932, when the novel appeared from Tallandier, in the collection "Criminals and Policemen," the same collection which would host, a year later,

La femme rousse. Readers had thus discovered this new atypical character almost a year before his official launching at the famous "Anthropometric Ball" at the *Boule Blanche.* And yet there was nothing to indicate that the Chief Inspector would achieve his well-known success, and the serial was probably not distinguished from the innumerable texts of the same sort that anyone could read in any newspaper of the period between the two wars.

Why didn't this novel, considered by Simenon scholars as the best of the "proto-Maigrets," receive the honors of the official saga? It combined (nearly) all the ingredients of a "true Maigret." The plot opens on a characteristic setting, an office at the Quai des Orfèvres, bathed in the fog of a November night. Maigret is present from the beginning of the text, and his description already resembles the Maigret we know. He had "large hands," he's "willingly grouchy," "without a jacket, without a false collar," and he's writing a report on a desk lined with empty beer glasses. While listening to the young woman whose visit will trigger the investigation, he fills a pipe "with slow movements." The Chief Inspector, unlike the three other "proto-Maigrets," will be present throughout the entire story, will follow his way of leading an investigation, a way already recognizable, "hands in his pockets, hat pushed back on his head," he interrogates the concierge, rummages through the victim's house, mulls over the information he gathers little by little, has a certain degree of empathy for the characters he encounters, and seeks the truth while depending less on logic than his feelings.

So why did this novel remain a trial, still not quite ready? In fact, looking more closely, while it's almost a true Maigret investigation, there are still some "little flaws" that the author will learn to eliminate in future texts. The novel, though a detective story, still conserves the "little tricks and devices" of the popular novel—fairly sketchy characters, traditional in the genre, a theatrical finale, Maigret's after-the-fact explanations of events to justify, in a way, inconsistencies of the plot.

But above all, what makes it different from the novels of the saga, is that while Maigret is at the front of the stage, it's still described by a narrator— and therefore seen by the reader—"from outside." Simenon "tells" how the Chief Inspector feels things, how he imagines them, how he tries to understand. That's the difference in the novels which follow, where Maigret's impressions are described "from inside," as if the world of the story were seen through the eyes of its main character. In the official saga, the reader "sees and thinks" through Maigret, he experiences things as Maigret experiences them, and its Simenon's talent that he succeeds at moving from a neutral and "objective" narration of a detective story, into a "subjective" view of an investigation, where the reader finds himself taking the part of the hero.

Publication Chronology

THE FAYARD PERIOD

A Productive Debut

There's still no certainty regarding the date and place of the writing of *Pietr le Letton*, the first "official" novel of the saga. Specialists remain still undecided as to whether, as in Simenon's own version of the legend, it was written in September 1929 at Delfzijl, or (at least partially) during the winter of 1929–1930 at Stavoren, or in April or May of 1930, aboard the *Ostrogoth* moored at Morsang.

Whichever it may be, in the summer of 1930 followed the writing of two more novels, *Le charretier de La Providence* and *Monsieur Gallet, décédé*, and that winter, *Le pendu de Saint-Pholien*. This last title was chosen, along with *Monsieur Gallet, décédé*, to inaugurate Fayard's new collection, launched at the "Anthropometric Ball" on February 20, 1931.

In exchange for his agreement, Fayard had required a reserve of novels already written, so that they could publish one a month once the collection was launched. And thus the year 1931 was dedicated to the writing of nine more novels, between March and December, *Le chien jaune, La nuit du carrefour, La tête d'un homme, Un crime en Hollande, Au rendez-Vous des Terre-Neuvas, La danseuse du Gai-Moulin, La guinguette à deux sous, Le port des brumes,* and *L'ombre chinoise*. And in 1932, four more were written between January and May, *L'affaire Saint-Fiacre, Chez les Flamands, Le fou de Bergerac,* and *Liberty Bar*.

A Temporary Retirement

Until May of 1932, Simenon had produced the *Maigret* novels one after another, first in response to Fayard's "order," and after that, since he'd met with success, there was no reason not to continue his momentum, especially since along with his literary success, financial success was also assured, with sales of film rights, and the first translation contracts. But in 1932, Simenon decided to "take a break," and he departed, first to discover Africa, and then to begin reporting in Europe at the beginning of 1933. In April 1933, he wrote *L'écluse n° 1*. Simenon had decided to move on to a new stage, and he dreamed of henceforth writing "true" literature, and no longer "semi-literature," for which he had to rely on the playmaker, his detective. He'd already gotten Fayard to publish several novels without Maigret. He wanted to do without his Chief Inspector, and therefore intended *L'écluse n° 1* to be the last of the series. Which is why, in this novel, Maigret is getting ready to retire professionally, as his author was getting ready to retire him literarily. And as Simenon has decided to leave Fayard, too dedicated to "popular novels and detective stories," in October 1933 he signs a contract with a new publisher, Gallimard.

But Simenon received numerous appeals in letters from readers disappointed by the scrapping of the Chief Inspector with the pipe, and from Fayard himself, and from the editor of the daily *Le Jour*, asking him for one more *Maigret*. And so he agreed to revive his hero. Readers of the daily would find a notice of the upcoming release (February 20, 1934) of a new Maigret investigation. A notice accompanied by a text from Simenon, in which he explained the resumption of his character, but in which he also vowed that this would be the Chief Inspector's last hurrah. This "final" novel, entitled soberly and symbolically *Maigret*, was probably written in February 1934.

THE GALLIMARD PERIOD

The Maigret Short Stories

At the insistence of Gallimard, contemplating the substantial revenue the Maigret texts could generate, Simenon yielded in October 1936, and wrote a first series of nine stories featuring the Chief Inspector. These began as a newspaper appearance, followed by a promised publication as a collection from his new publisher. They show us the Chief Inspector once more fully active, in a sort of "return to the past" in relation to the last novel of the Fayard period. But this appears to be simply an interlude, a kind of game the author is playing with readers of the paper. Yet it's a game he'll take up again in 1938, writing another series of ten stories in which Maigret is the hero, and which will also be first published in a newspaper. Eight of these ten stories will form, along with the nine of 1936, the collection published in 1944 by Gallimard under the title *Les nouvelles enquêtes de Maigret*. The first four stories written in 1938 show us Maigret in action, while the next six present us again the Chief Inspector in retirement. The fifth story (*L'Etoile du Nord*) shows the Chief Inspector two days before his retirement, as *L'écluse n⁰ 1* showed him with six days left.

Maigret Returns

In 1939, Simenon apparently decided, since he was continuing to relate the exploits of his Chief Inspector, to bring him back for good. And so between 1939 and 1943 he wrote, first, two stories, with Maigret again on active duty, then six novels published in two collections by Gallimard—*Maigret revient* published in 1942, containing the novels *Les caves du Majestic*, (December 1939), *La maison du juge* (January 1940), *Cécile est morte* (December 1940); and the collection *Signé Picpus*, published in 1944, containing the novels *Signé Picpus* (1941), *Félicie est là* (May 1942) and *L'inspecteur Cadavre* (March 1943).

THE PRESSES DE LA CITÉ PERIOD

New World and New Editor

In 1945, Simenon prepared for his trans-Atlantic departure, and as a farewell, he wrote a lovely story in June about his hero, whose title, too, is symbolic: *La pipe de Maigret*. Then, in August, at the request of Pierre Lazareff, who had just started a new paper, *France-Soir*, he wrote another short novel to appear in it, *Maigret se fâche*, where his hero is, once more, retired. Simenon was probably thinking of relieving himself of his character, at the same time as he left "old Europe" to discover the New World. A new life, a renewal of his writing, and the abandonment of Maigret, who had become, perhaps, a little too important. But that was without counting on the power the character held over his author, whether he liked it or not. And then his new editor, Sven Nielsen, who had just started his new publishing house, Les Presses de la Cité, was also counting on Simenon to bring him renown, and a few novels on the investigations of Maigret would be very welcome. Nielsen would see, outside of publishing Simenon's "hard novels," the benefits of the large print runs relating the adventures of the Chief Inspector.

And so Simenon wrote a new Maigret in 1946, in which the Chief Inspector is once more retired, *Maigret à New York*. But this would be the last time he portrayed him as retired. Henceforth, and until the last novel of the saga, Maigret will be on active duty at the Quai des Orfèvres. Retirement will not be mentioned again, except as a future possibility during an investigation, a possibility more and more likely as the novels advance in the chronology of their writing.

Maigret Returns to Service

From then on, Simenon will alternate more or less regularly between *Maigrets* and "non–Maigrets." It's first in four stories, written in 1946, that Simenon will put his Chief Inspector back into service (these are the four texts which appeared in the collection *Maigret et l'inspecteur Malgracieux*), then, in November 1947, Simenon will have him lead an investigation while the Chief Inspector is on holiday (*Les vacances de Maigret*). The novelist will realize that not only can't he escape from his hero, but also that he has to put him back on active duty. No more investigations while he's retired or on vacation, it's time to bring Maigret back to the Quai des Orfèvres. Simenon wrote, in December 1947, *Maigret et son mort*, where he found once more all the ingredients of an authentic investigation: the stove in Maigret's office, a *choucroute* in a brasserie, and strolls through Paris, from the Bastille to the Concorde, Marais to Charenton, and a visit to Moers's lab.

In 1948, Simenon amused himself by telling of Maigret's beginnings, in *La première enquête de Maigret*, giving him a past and an intimate life (as he'd already done in *L'affaire Saint-Fiacre*, and as he would do later in *Les mémoires de Maigret* and *Un Noël de Maigret*), endowing his character with additional weight. Then, in 1949, he sends Maigret around, first to Porquerolles (*Mon ami Maigret*), then again to the USA (*Maigret chez le coroner*), and lastly to Etretat (*Maigret et la vieille dame*), before having him lead a series of truly Parisian investigations—*L'amie de M*^me *Maigret* (again in 1949), *Maigret au Picratt's* (1950), in 1951, *Maigret en meublé*, *Maigret et la Grande Perche*, *Maigret Lognon et les gangsters*, and in 1952, *Le revolver de Maigret* (with a visit to London) and *Maigret et l'homme du banc*.

The Deepening of a Character

1929 and 1972 are the two dates which enclose the publishing history of the Maigret saga. We note the interesting fact that *Un Noël de Maigret* and *Les mémoires de Maigret* are situated exactly in the center of this chronology (May and September 1950). It's a little as if Simenon, after the two first periods (Fayard and Gallimard), wanted to do an update on his hero, before launching him on a lengthy series of new investigations. *Les mémoires de Maigret* is Simenon's attempt to anchor his Chief Inspector in police reality, to give a certain "authenticity" to his character by giving him a past, origins, memories, and also providing him the opportunity for some reflection on his métier. *Un Noël de Maigret* puts the Chief Inspector into an emotional and intimate context, giving him still greater depth.

In 1953, with *Maigret a peur*, and another voyage outside of Paris, into the Vendée, constituting a sort of pilgrimage to places previously visited (*La maison du juge*, *L'inspecteur Cadavre*), there appears a first hint of what will become a constant in the rest of the saga, Maigret's reflections on aging and the approach of retirement. The "natural" aging of the character contrasts him with a number of heroes of series novels who remain the same age throughout their adventures. Thus we will watch our hero age alongside his creator, if not with the same rhythm, at least with the same anguish and the same questions, in a play of mirrors more or less desired by the novelist. And we will see more and more often in the novels to come, Maigret evoking the end of his career and his approaching retirement. While in the Fayard period, it was in a somewhat brutal manner that the author sent his Chief Inspector off to finish his days at Meung-sur-Loire, in the Presses de la Cité period, it's little by little that Maigret will detach himself from his career.

When the Detective Stories Join the "Psychological" Novels

Maigret se trompe, Maigret à l'école (both in 1953), *Maigret et la jeune morte, Maigret chez le ministre* (both in 1954), and *Maigret et le corps sans tête* (1955) are the last Maigret novels written on American soil. *Maigret tend un piège* (1955) is the first written by Simenon after his definitive return to Europe, and it inaugurates in a way a "turning point" in his character's career, in the sense that the Chief Inspector's investigations will tend more and more to approach the author's questions with regard to Man, his responsibility and fate, and the legitimacy of the judiciary and the police machine. The titles of the upcoming novels reflect well this evolution: *Un échec de Maigret* (1956), *Les scrupules de Maigret* and *Maigret hésite*. After two novels with a little "lighter" tone (a lightness also felt in the titles *Maigret s'amuse* [1956] and then *Maigret voyage* [1957], the first written on Swiss soil, at Echandens, and in which the author "amuses himself" by leading his character from one corner of France to another, and to Switzerland, as he himself had just done), *Les scrupules de Maigret* (1957) is not only a novel where the Chief Inspector asks himself questions about the responsibility of criminals, and of Man in general, but it's also atypical in the sense that the investigation the Chief Inspector leads is made before the crime rather than after. The following novels will reflect anew all these questions: the effects of aging (*Maigret et les témoins récalcitrants*, 1958), the position of Man in the face of the judiciary (*Une confidence de Maigret* and *Maigret aux assises*, both 1959). Themes we will see taken up again, supplemented by others, in the novels of the last part of the saga, like the deepening relationship between Maigret and his wife, the refined culinary tastes of the Chief Inspector, and the reminiscences of his childhood. And sometimes Simenon, wanting to treat a theme in a "psychological novel," doesn't do so, and uses his Chief Inspector to accomplish his project (as is the case of *Maigret et les vieillards*, written in 1960). More and more, *Maigret* novels and "non–Maigret" novels get closer to each other in their themes and approaches.

The Last Part of the Saga

The six last novels written in Simenon's first Swiss residence are, in 1961, *Maigret et le voleur paresseux* and *Maigret et les braves gens*, in 1962, *Maigret et le client du samedi, Maigret et le clochard* and *La colère de Maigret*, and in 1963, *Maigret et le fantôme*.

In December 1963 Simenon relocated to Epalinges, and it wasn't until July of 1964 that the author once more took up his pen, and began with *Maigret se défend*. In 1965, he wrote *La patience de Maigret*, which forms, in a way, a diptych with the preceding novel, since he incorporates some of the same characters, a unique occurrence in the saga. Then in 1966, *Maigret et l'affaire Nahour* and *Le voleur de Maigret*, in 1967, *Maigret à Vichy*, in 1968, *Maigret hésite* and *L'ami d'enfance de Maigret*, in 1969, *Maigret et le tueur* and *Maigret et le marchand de vin*, in 1970, *La folle de Maigret*, and in 1971, *Maigret et l'homme tout seul* and *Maigret et l'indicateur*.

In February 1972, Simenon wrote *Maigret et Monsieur Charles*. He didn't yet know it, but that was the final novel in the Maigret saga, and his last novel of all. A stage in the life of the novelist had ended. Henceforth, he would only occupy himself with his memoirs. His final novel was a *Maigret*, as was the one which inaugurated his works under his own name. Chance or irony of fate—or perhaps a premonition?—in *Maigret et Monsieur Charles*, he tells how Maigret, in the evening of a fine career, was offered the position of Director of the PJ, and how the Chief Inspector refused, because he wanted to remain a man of the earth, to continue his infinite quest in search of the human. Forever, and for all his readers, Maigret will remain "the man of the Quai," trailing the wreaths of his pipe from his office to the Brasserie Dauphine, from the Saint-Martin canal to the streets of Pigalle, from his apartment on the Boulevard Richard-Lenoir to the little district bistros.

Appendix 1

Maigret Novels and Stories

The entire Maigret saga is currently being republished in translation by Penguin.

The novels, listed in the order of writing, with the date of original publication in parentheses:

Fayard

Pietr le Letton, September 1929 / winter 1929–1930 / May 1930 (see Publication chronology) (May 1931)
Le charretier de La Providence, summer 1930 (March 1931)
Monsieur Gallet, décédé, summer 1930 (February 1931)
Le pendu de Saint-Pholien, winter 1930 (February 1931)
Le chien jaune, March 1931 (April 1931)
La nuit du carrefour, April 1931 (June 1931)
La tête d'un homme, May 1931 (September 1931)
Un crime en Hollande, May 1931 (July 1931)
Au rendez-vous des Terre-Neuvas, July 1931 (August 1931)
La danseuse du Gai-Moulin, September 1931 (November 1931)
La guinguette à deux sous, October 1931 (December 1931)
Le port des brumes, October 1931 (May 1932)
L'ombre chinoise, December 1931 (January 1932)
L'affaire Saint-Fiacre, January 1932 (February 1932)
Chez les Flamands, January 1932 (March 1932)
Le fou de Bergerac, March 1932 (April 1932)
Liberty Bar, May 1932 (June 1932)
L'écluse n° 1, April 1933 (June 1933)
Maigret, February 1934 (March 1934)

Gallimard

Les caves du Majestic, December 1939 (October 1942)
La maison du juge, January 1940 (October 1942)
Cécile est morte, December 1940 (October 1942)
Signé Picpus, 1941 (January 1944)

Félicie est là, May 1942 (January 1944)
L'inspecteur Cadavre, March 1943 (January 1944)

Les Presses de la Cité

Maigret se fâche, August 1945 (July 1947)
Maigret à New York, 27 February—7 March 1946 (July 1947)
Les vacances de Maigret, 11–20 November 1947 (June 1948)
Maigret et son mort, 8–17 December 1947 (May 1948)
La première enquête de Maigret, 22–30 September 1948 (February 1949)
Mon ami Maigret, 24 January–2 February 1949 (June 1949)
Maigret chez le coroner, 21–30 July 1949 (October 1949)
Maigret et la vieille dame, 29 November–8 December 1949 (February 1950)
L'amie de Madame Maigret, 13–22 December 1949 (May 1950)
Les mémoires de Maigret, 19–26 September 1950 (January 1951)
Maigret au Picratt's, 30 November–8 December 1950 (April 1951)
Maigret en meublé, 14–21 February 1951 (July 1951)
Maigret et la Grande Perche, 1–8 May 1951 (October 1951)
Maigret, Lognon et les gangsters, 1–8 October 1951 (February 1952)
Le revolver de Maigret, 12–20 June 1952 (September 1952)
Maigret et l'homme du banc, 11–19 September 1952 (January 1953)
Maigret a peur, 20–27 March 1953 (July 1953)
Maigret se trompe, 24–31 August 1953 (November 1953)
Maigret à l'école, 01–08 December 1953 (March 1954)
Maigret et la jeune morte, 11–18 January 1954 (June 1954)
Maigret chez le ministre, 16–23 August 1954 (January 1955)
Maigret et le corps sans tête, 15/16–25 January 1955 (June 1955)
Maigret tend un piège, 05–12 July 1955 (October 1955)
Un échec de Maigret, 26 February–4 March 1956 (September 1956)
Maigret s'amuse, 6–13 September 1956 (March 1957)
Maigret voyage, 10–17 August 1957 (March 1958)
Les scrupules de Maigret, 9–16 December 1957 (June 1958)
Maigret et les témoins récalcitrants, 16–23 October 1958 (March 1959)
Une confidence de Maigret, 26 April–3 May 1959 (September 1959)
Maigret aux assises, 17–23 November 1959 (May 1960)
Maigret et les vieillards, 15–21 June 1960 (November 1960)
Maigret et le voleur paresseux, 17–23 January 1961 (November 1961)
Maigret et les braves gens, 05–11 September 1961 (April 1962)
Maigret et le client du samedi, 21–27 February 1962 (November 1962)
Maigret et le clochard, 26 April–2 May 1962 (1st trimester 1963)
La colère de Maigret, 13–19 June 1962 (4th trimester 1963)
Maigret et le fantôme, 17–23 June 1963 (July 1964)
Maigret se défend, 21–28 July 1964 (November 1964)
La patience de Maigret, 25 February–9 March 1965 (November 1965)
Maigret et l'affaire Nahour, 02–08 February 1966 (December 1966)
Le voleur de Maigret, 05–11 November 1966 (April 1967)
Maigret à Vichy, 05–11 September 1967 (January 1968)

Maigret hésite, 24–30 January 1968 (1968)
L'ami d'enfance de Maigret, 18–24 June 1968 (November 1968)
Maigret et le tueur, 15–21 April 1969 (October 1969)
Maigret et le marchand de vin, 23–29 September 1969) (February 1970)
La folle de Maigret, 01–07 May 1970 (November 1970)
Maigret et l'homme tout seul, 01–07 February 1971 (May 1971)
Maigret et l'indicateur, 05–11 June 1971 (October 1971)
Maigret et Monsieur Charles, 05–11 February 1972 (July 1972)

The Stories

First series (written in October 1936)
La péniche aux deux pendus
L'affaire du boulevard Beaumarchais
La fenêtre ouverte
Monsieur Lundi
Jeumont, 51 minutes d'arrêt !
Peine de mort
Les larmes de bougie
Rue Pigalle
Une erreur de Maigret

Second series (written in winter 1937–38)
L'amoureux de Madame Maigret
La vieille dame de Bayeux
L'auberge aux noyés
Stan le Tueur
L'Etoile du Nord
Tempête sur la Manche
Mademoiselle Berthe et son amant
Le notaire de Châteauneuf
L'improbable Monsieur Owen
Ceux du Grand Café

Appeared as serials in newspapers, 1936–1937 for the first series, and 1938–1939 for the second. Published in collection (except for the two last ones) for the first time by Gallimard, under the title *Les nouvelles enquêtes de Maigret*, in March 1944.

L'homme dans la rue and *Vente à la bougie*, both written in 1939, first appeared in newspapers, 1940 and 1941, then published in the collection, *Maigret et les petits cochons sans queue*, which also contained "non–Maigret" stories, in August 1950 by Presses de la Cité.

Menaces de mort, written in winter 1941–42, first appeared in a newspaper in 1942, before being rediscovered in 1980 by Deligny and Menguy, and collected for the first time in Volume 25 of *Tout Simenon*, published in August 1992 by Presses de la Cité.

La pipe de Maigret, written in June 1945, appeared in the collection to which it gave its name, with the novel, *Maigret se fâche*, from Presses de la Cité in July 1947.

The following four stories appeared in collection for the first time in *Maigret et l'inspecteur Malchanceux (Malgracieux)*, in October 1947 from Presses de la Cité.
Le témoignage de l'enfant de chœur, 28 April 1946
Le client le plus obstiné du monde, 2 May 1946
Maigret et l'inspecteur Malgracieux, 5 May 1946
On ne tue pas les pauvres types, 15 August 1946

Un Noël de Maigret, **written 17–20 May 1950, appeared in the collection to which it gave its name, along with "non–Maigret" stories, from Presses de la Cité in March 1951.**

Appendix 2

Non-Maigret Works by Simenon

(Titles in brackets are approximate translations
of works not published in English)

Novels:

Cour d'assises, Gallimard, 1941. *Justice*

L'enterrement de Monsieur Bouvet, Presses de la Cité, 1950. *Inquest on Bouvet, The burial of Monsieur Bouvet*

L'homme qui regardait passer les trains, Gallimard, 1938. *The man who watched the trains go by*

Lettre à mon juge, Presses de la Cité, 1947. *Act of passion*

Monsieur La Souris, Gallimard, 1938. *The Mouse*

L'outlaw, Gallimard, 1941. *The outlaw*

Les suicidés, Gallimard, 1934. *One way out*

Le testament Donadieu, Gallimard, 1937. *The shadow falls, Donadieu's Will*

La vérité sur Bébé Donge, Gallimard, 1942. *The Trial of Bébé Donge, I take this woman, The truth about Bébé Donge*

(additional information about these translations can be found at http://www.enquetes-de-maigret.com/semimaig.htm)

Stories:

In *Les 13 coupables*, Fayard, 1932
Philippe

In *Les sept minutes*, Gallimard, 1938
L'énigme de la Marie Galante. [The mystery of the *Marie Galante*]

In *Le petit docteur*, Gallimard, 1943
L'amiral a disparu, The Disappearance of the Admiral

L'amoureux aux pantoufles, Death in a Department Store

La bonne fortune du Hollandais, The Dutchman's Luck

Le château de l'arsenic, Arsenic Hall

La piste de l'homme roux, The Trail of the Red-haired Man

La sonnette d'alarme, The Communication Cord

In *Les dossiers de l'agence O*, Gallimard, 1943
L'arrestation du musician [*The arrest of the musician*]
Le chantage de l'agence O [*The blackmail of Agency O*]
Le club des vieilles dames [*The old ladies' club*]
Le docteur Tant-Pis [*Dr. Too-bad*]
Le prisonnier de Lagny [*Prisoner of Lagny*]
Le ticket de métro [*The subway ticket*]
Le vieillard au porte-mine [*The old man with the mechanical pencil*]

In *Un Noël de Maigret*, Presses de la Cité, 1951.
Maigret's Christmas
Le petit restaurant des Ternes [*The little restaurant on the Place des Ternes*]
Sept petites croix dans un carnet [*Seven little crosses in a notebook*]

In *Trois nouvelles inédites*, supplément au tome 12 de *Tout Simenon*, Presses de la Cité, 1990. [*Three unpublished stories*], supplement to volume 12 of Complete Simenon
La chanteuse de Pigalle [*The songstress of Pigalle*]
L'invalide à la tête de bois [*The invalid with the wooden head*]

Autobiographical writing:

Un homme comme un autre (Dictées), Presses de la Cité, 1975. [*A man like any other*]

Other writing

La naissance de Maigret, avant-propos des Œuvres Complètes, tome I, Rencontre, 1967. [*The birth of Maigret*, preface to the Complete Works, volume I.]

Appendix 3

Works by Simenon
Published Under a Pseudonym

(Titles in brackets are approximate translations
of books and stories not published in English)

As *Christian Brulls*

L'évasion, Fayard, 1934 [*The escape*]
Fièvre, Fayard, 1932 [*Fever*]
La figurante, Fayard, 1932 [*The extra*]
Les forçats de Paris, Fayard, 1932 [*The convicts of Paris*]
L'inconnue, Fayard, 1930 [*The unknown*]
Mademoiselle X, Fayard, 1928 [*Mademoiselle X*]
La maison des disparus (serialized in 1931–1932, private publication [in 2001 under the auspices of the Amis de Georges Simenon]) [*The house of the disappeared*]
Train de nuit, Fayard, 1930 [*Night Train*]

As *Jean du Perry*

Les amants du malheur, Ferenczi, 1930 [*The lovers of misfortune*]

As *Georges Sim*

En robe de mariée, Tallandier, 1929 [*In a wedding dress*]
L'épave, Fayard, 1932 [*The wreck*]
Les errants, Fayard, 1931 [*The wanderers*]
La femme qui tue, Fayard, 1929 [*The woman who kills*]
La femme rousse, Tallandier, 1933 [*The redhead*]
La fiancée du diable, Fayard, 1933 [*The fiancée of the devil*]
L'homme qui tremble, Fayard, 1930. [*The man who trembles*]
La maison de l'inquiétude, Tallandier, 1932 (translated as *The house of anxiety*, at http://www.trussel.com/maig/maison.htm)
Matricule 12, Tallandier, 1932 [*Regiment 12*]

Bibliography

Alavoine, Bernard. *Les enquêtes de Maigret de Georges Simenon.* Amiens: Encrage, 1999.

Alder, Bill. *Maigret, Simenon and France.* Jefferson, NC: McFarland, 2013.

Les Amis de Georges Simenon. *Cahiers Simenon.* Bruxelles: Les amis de Georges Simenon, since 1987.

Baudou, Jacques. *Les nombreuses vies de Maigret.* Lyon: Les moutons électriques, 2007.

Bertrand, Alain. *Maigret.* Bruxelles: Labor, 1994.

Carly, Michel. *Maigret, traversées de Paris.* Paris: Omnibus, 2003.

Courtine, Robert J. *Madame Maigret's Recipes.* New York: Harcourt Brace Jovanovich, 1975.

_____. *Simenon et Maigret passent à table.* Paris: Robert Laffont, 1992.

Dumas, Alexandre, and Auguste Maquet. *Les trois mousquetaires.* Paris: Michel Lévy frères, 1896.

Forest, Jean. *Les archives Maigret. Répertoire analytique complet de ses cent sept enquêtes.* Montréal: Presses de l'Université de Montréal, 1994.

Gallot, Didier. *Simenon ou la comédie humaine.* Paris: Editions France-Empire, 1999.

Henry, Gilles. *La véritable histoire du commissaire Maigret.* Condé-sur-Noireau, Corlet, 1989.

Lacassin, Francis. *La vraie naissance de Maigret.* Monaco: Editions du Rocher, 1992.

Lemoine, Michel. *L'autre univers de Simenon.* Liège: C.L.P.C.F., 1991.

_____. *Index des personnages de Georges Simenon.* Bruxelles: Labor, 1985.

_____. *Paris chez Simenon.* Amiens : Encrage, 2000.

Mercier, Paul. *La botte secrète de Maigret: le verre de cognac.* [S.l.]: Le Cercle Noir, 2009.

_____. *Maigret: mode d'emploi?* Liège (Belgique): Editions du Céfal, 2008.

Meyer-Bolzinger, Dominique. *Une méthode clinique dans l'enquête policière. Holmes, Poirot, Maigret.* Liège: Céfal, 2003.

Sacré, Jacques. *Bon appétit commissaire Maigret,* Liège, Céfal, 2004.

Simenon, Georges, and Michel Carly. *Tout Maigret.* Paris: Omnibus, 2007.

Télérama hors-série no 41: *Maigret, ce phénoméne!,* Paris, janvier 1993.

Traces (Travaux du Centre d'Études Georges Simenon), Université de Liége, Centre d'Études Georges Simenon, since 1989.

Wouters, Els. *Maigret: "je ne déduis jamais": La méthode abductive chez Simenon.* Liège: Céfal, 1998.

Websites

http://www.association-jacques-riviere-alain-fournier.com/reperage/simenon/bibliographie.shtml

http://www.enquetes-de-maigret.com/index.htm

http://simenon.com

http://www.simenon-simenon.com

http://www.toutsimenon.com/

http://www.trussel.com/f_maig.htm

http://www2.libnet.ulg.ac.be/simenon/

Index